Baseball's Creation Myth

# Baseball's Creation Myth

*Adam Ford, Abner Graves and the Cooperstown Story*

BRIAN MARTIN

To STEVE:
Hope you enjoy my little effort.
All the best
Brian Martin

McFarland & Company, Inc., Publishers
*Jefferson, North Carolina, and London*

LIBRARY OF CONGRESS CATALOGUING-IN-PUBLICATION DATA

Martin, Brian, 1950–
    Baseball's creation myth : Adam Ford, Abner Graves and
the Cooperstown Story / Brian Martin.
        p.    cm.
    Includes bibliographical references and index.

    ISBN 978-0-7864-7199-7
    softcover : acid free paper ∞

    1.  Baseball—New York (State)—Cooperstown—History.
    2.  Baseball players—New York (State)—Cooperstown—History.
    I. Title.
    GV863.N72bM37  2013
    796.35709747'67—dc23                         2013009397

BRITISH LIBRARY CATALOGUING DATA ARE AVAILABLE

Front cover baseball image (iStockphoto/Thinkstock)

Manufactured in the United States of America

*McFarland & Company, Inc., Publishers
  Box 611, Jefferson, North Carolina 28640
  www.mcfarlandpub.com*

To my wife, Kay,
and our sport-loving kids,
Lindsey and Scott

# Table of Contents

# *Acknowledgments*

Acknowledging the help provided to an author in the course of his or her research comes with the risk of overlooking someone. But research invariably leads to people who share what they know and the information for which they are responsible. This author has found the most helpful people everywhere he has looked and they must be acknowledged for their time and trouble. So upfront, my sincere apologies to anyone who may have been forgotten in the list that follows.

Special thanks are owed to David Arcidiacono, a baseball researcher from East Hampton, Connecticut, and a fellow member of the Society for American Baseball Research. For years, he and I have swapped information on a little-known but intriguing aspect of baseball. When I told him about this project, David suggested I contact Gary Mitchem, senior acquisitions editor at McFarland.

At the National Baseball Hall of Fame and Museum in Cooperstown, I am indebted to the always helpful reference librarian Freddy Berowski, whose knowledge and skill I tapped on countless occasions. Also at the Hall, photo archivist Pat Kelly and library Steele intern Cassidy Lent were wonderful and patient. In Cooperstown, the village's official historian Hugh MacDougall was most generous, sharing his research into the life and times of Abner Graves. Hugh's efforts as a researcher and his writing ability are truly impressive.

Claire Graves Strashun and her daughters Barb and Edy in the Seattle area were generous and sharing with their memories, photographs and documents. Claire, the granddaughter of Abner Graves, passed away January 21, 2013 while this book was in production. This was just eight days before she would have turned 92, the age at which her grandfather died. Margalyn Hemphill, the wife of one of Claire's grandsons (Luke), who produced a book about Graves for the family, was also extremely kind, supportive and helpful.

I am indebted to many people in Denver. Baseball researcher Jay Sanford, with whom I have swapped baseball research for years, has been a great supporter, adviser and friend. If it happened in baseball in the Denver area, Jay knows it. He also has a vast amount of material about the Negro Leagues. Ken

Burns, the documentary filmmaker, consulted Jay while making his epic series *Baseball*, for good reason. Diana Copsey Adams, with her amazing genealogical and research abilities, her kindness and her friendship, proved to be a real gem in unearthing information and navigating the reference sources in her mile-high city. Christie Wright, another historical researcher who went out of her way to help, deserves a special shout-out. Also in Denver, the amazing staff at the Western History and Genealogy Collection at the Denver Public Library bent over backwards to help find information. At History Colorado, Sarah Gilmor was extremely helpful. The Masons in Denver, particularly historian Claud Dutro and James Brown couldn't have been more kind, giving me rare access to the fine Masonic Building in which Adam Ford once practiced and shared membership information about Abner Graves. Wonderfully eccentric social historian Phil Goodstein provided assistance with invaluable information about his city. It is nice to have such friends in "high" places.

In Canada, sport historian and academic Robert Knight Barney was supportive and helpful throughout, despite his busy and active schedule at an age when others would have slowed down long ago. He drips with New England charm and he is never far from some symbol of his beloved Boston Red Sox. At St. Marys Museum in the lovely town of St. Marys I am indebted to manager Trisha McKibbin and curators Emily Cartlidge and Amy Cubberley. Their cheerful willingness to dig into the thick files of town history and the papers chronicling the life of Adam Ford and his family was impressive. Also at the museum, former curator Mary Smith proved to be a great help and valuable resource over many years. Thank you, ladies. Larry Pfaff, historian and researcher, also provided insight that was most appreciated.

Others deserving thanks include Susan Greer, writing consultant, editor and friend, London, Ontario; Carl MacDonald, curator, Beachville Museum, Beachville, Ontario; Paul Leatherdale, archivist, Upper Canada Law Society, Osgoode Hall, Toronto; Kathryn Clark, senior communications coordinator, College of Physicians and Surgeons of Ontario, Toronto; Andrea Gunn, Christina Archibald and Deirdre Bryden, communications and archives, Queen's University, Kingston, Ontario; Donna Bame, licensing supervisor, Colorado Department of Regulatory Agencies, Division of Registrations, Licensing and Support Section, State of Colorado, Denver; Vicki Thornton, reference librarian, St. Joseph Public Library, St. Joseph, Missouri; editor Bruce Winges, managing editor Doug Oplinger and executive assistant Mary Lou Woodcock, *Akron Beacon Journal*, Akron, Ohio.

Summit Akron (Ohio) Public Library, Akron; Cynthia Osteroff, manager public services, manuscripts and archives, and Judith Ann Schiff, chief research archivist, Yale University, New Haven, Connecticut; Lara Medley, registrar, and Lisa Dunn, head of reference, Colorado School of Mines, Golden; and the Society for American Baseball Research.

# *Preface*

This book may make some ball fans a bit uncomfortable.

It looks at an old story with new eyes, a new perspective, and it draws a conclusion that may upset baseball traditionalists.

Baseball is a game that is near and dear to many of us. We are possessive about it, having spent so much time playing it, reading about it and watching it. Baseball is like an old friend. So anyone who introduces new evidence about its fundamental underpinnings is bound to meet resistance. The game has a long history in North America, research clearly shows. Some Americans may be surprised at the reference to *North* America. The game is known as America's national pastime, not North America's, after all. But the fact is, simple ball-and-bat games were brought to the new republic and to the British colonies north of it in the eighteenth and nineteenth centuries by settlers from England. Those games were refined, developed regional differences and ultimately morphed into the game of baseball we know today.

A parallel pastime has evolved with baseball over the years: the unending search for its origins. Like anthropologists seeking the roots of civilization, the baseball community has been fixated on determining who invented the modern game, when, and where. Accepting it as an evolution of bat-and-ball games played by English children has been difficult, if not impossible, for some Americans to accept.

A bit more than one hundred years ago, Albert Goodwill Spalding settled the issue, in his own words, "for all time," in his book *America's National Game.* The former star pitcher, owner of the Chicago White Stockings, president of the National League and head of the Spalding Sporting Goods empire wrote that baseball captured and reflected all the best qualities of America and Americans. He noted that a special commission (which he himself established) had traced the origins of the game to a small village in New York state where a military man invented it. Spalding asserted that it couldn't have been the product of the English, whose preferred game was cricket, he wrote, because cricket "is easy and does not overtax their energy or their thought."

1

Spalding was not the first, nor the last, to wrap baseball in Old Glory. The result has been that most Americans accept the game as American property. To this day, a surprising number still believe the myth promoted by Spalding that it was invented in Cooperstown by Civil War hero Abner Doubleday. Baseball's "creation myth" is powerful and durable and it has believers in unexpected places. For these true believers, contrary evidence amounts to sacrilege, so they choose to ignore it. They may not realize the National Baseball Hall of Fame and Museum in Cooperstown no longer makes the claim that the game was invented there in back in 1839. More than enough evidence has emerged since the shrine to baseball opened (and even before that) to prove beyond a reasonable doubt the game did not begin there.

Baseball is a game that grew in popularity in the latter decades of the nineteenth century, especially in the United States, which was undergoing a fundamental and profound change. An agrarian society was being transformed into an industrial one with the migrations of millions from the farm to the city. Baseball, with its pastoral connotations, harkened back to simpler days and gave urban dwellers something to cheer for, especially when for so many of them there was so little cheer in their circumstances. A day at the ball park— a term that was coined later—came as a welcome relief from six days in a factory.

It is not all that well known that the game also had a long history north of the border in the British colonies of Upper Canada and Lower Canada, renamed Ontario and Quebec when those colonies federated with Nova Scotia and New Brunswick in 1867 under the name Canada. The same immigrants who brought the game to America brought it to the British colonies. Some of them were literally the same immigrants, having settled first in the new republic before moving to the colonies in pursuit of cheaper land or a different political climate. Upper Canada, particularly, adjacent to the states of New York and Pennsylvania, owed much of its early growth and development to newcomers from the republic. Given the much smaller population of the Canadian colonies/provinces and their cities, the professional game was somewhat slower to develop there, although by the 1870s two Ontario cities fielded successful professional teams that competed against professional nines from Boston, Chicago, Pittsburgh and elsewhere. In the mid–1880s, Spalding tried to persuade Toronto to join the National League.

The story of baseball being invented in Cooperstown was told in 1905 by a man then living in Denver, Colorado, a mining engineer named Abner Graves. No one else had ever made that claim, coming as it did so many years after the alleged event in 1839 that all supposed participants would have been dead or senile. Spalding tried to corroborate it, but failed to do so. Despite that, he embraced the tale and so, ultimately, did America. Somewhat belatedly, Cooperstown did as well. Historians have had a field day for decades debunking the story once taught to American school kids. Aside from using solid research and real facts to puncture the myth, some have attacked Graves and his character. Yet no comprehensive effort has been made to look into the man and try to determine why he told the story that so totally captured a country's imagination. Until now. Research for this book took the author to Denver, to Cooperstown and on a path that led to the discovery of the grand-daughter of Graves, living in Washington state and in her nineties.

The findings and conclusions shared in these pages may surprise, perhaps irritate America–first readers. So be it. But when it comes to the origins of baseball, closed minds have wrought considerable mischief in the past.

This work presents a compelling case that Abner Graves borrowed his story about Cooperstown, or parts of it, changing people and places in order to help Spalding prove an American birth for baseball.

# One

## *A Simple Letter*

The two-page typewritten letter was a modest effort. Rife with typo-graphical errors, inappropriate spacing, odd punctuation and inconsistent spelling, it landed on the desk of William B. Baldwin, editor of the daily *Akron Beacon Journal,* in an envelope bearing the imprint of Akron, Ohio's Thuma Hotel.

Dated April 3, 1905, on letterhead from the Bank Block office of mining engineer Abner Graves, Denver, Colorado, it appeared to be a carbon copy. Graves, who had signed it, went right to the point:

> Dear Sir:—I notice in saturdays [sic] "Beacon Journal" a question as to "origin of "base ball" [sic] from pen of A. G. Spalding, and requesting data on the sub-ject be sent to Mr. J. E. Sullivan, 15 Warren Street, New York. The American game of "Base Ball" was invented by Abner Doubleday of Cooperstown, New York, either the spring prior, or following the "Log Cabin & Hard Cider" cam-paign of General Harrison for President, said Abner Doubleday being then a boy pupil of "Green's Select School" in Cooperstown, and the same, who as General Doubleday won honor at the Battle of Gettysburg in the Civil war.[1]

The letter went on to describe how Doubleday improved upon the child's game of town ball, limiting the game to eleven players on each of two teams, and calling it "base ball" because of its four bases. It recounted how a pitcher tossed the ball to a batsman from within a six-foot ring. Arrayed around and behind the pitcher were four outfielders, three basemen, a catcher and two infielders, the latter taking positions between first and second base and between second and third base, respectively. "Anyone getting the ball was entitled to throw it at a runner and put him out if he could hit him," Graves wrote.

The writer named players in the game he said he witnessed as a young boy sixty years earlier at Otsego Academy Campus and on the Phinney farm along the west shore of Otsego Lake (north of Cooperstown).

"Baseball," Graves's letter concluded, "is undoubtedly a pure American game, and its birthplace Cooperstown, New York, and Abner Doubleday enti-tled to first honor of its invention."

*Above and opposite page:* The article in the *Akron Beacon Journal* that caught the eye of Denver mining engineer Abner Graves when he was visiting that Ohio city in 1905 on business. Albert Goodwill Spalding was seeking stories about the origins of the game of baseball certain that it was American. Reprinted with permission of the *Akron Beacon Journal* and Ohio.com

Only 640 words in all. But those words penned in the Ohio city of 50,000 would go on to make baseball history. Literally.

At the time, a concerted effort was underway to find the origins of the sport America had embraced in the closing decades of the nineteenth century. The game became openly professional in 1869 and took hold across the country on its way to becoming the national pastime. Baseball's first professional league, the National Association, was founded in 1871 and was succeeded five years later by the National League. By 1905, nearly six million fans per season were flocking to games played by the National League and new American League.[2] Baseball was becoming big business and major stakeholders in the game felt it vital to prove the game was an American invention.

Graves was responding to a lengthy article in the April 1 edition of the *Beacon Journal*, under the byline of Albert Goodwill Spalding, a major force in professional baseball as a former star pitcher, then manager and subsequently owner of the Chicago White Stockings. Along the way, he had become a successful sporting goods retailer and manufacturer. But Spalding had a bee in his bonnet. He steadfastly refused to accept that the game had been derived

## OF SPORTS

FOOT BALL
CYCLING
PUGILISM
WRESTLING
RACING

### ABNER DOUBLEDAY INVENTED BASE BALL

#### Abner Graves of Denver, Colorado, Tells How the Present National Game Had Its Origin.

Abner C. Graves, mining engineer of Denver, Col., claims to know all about the origin of the game of base ball. He is stopping at the Thuma hotel, and reading the article in Saturday's Beacon Journal from the pen of A. C. Spalding prepared the following article and submitted it to the Beacon Journal for publication:

"I notice in Saturday's Beacon Journal a question as to origin of base ball from the pen of A. G. Spalding, and requesting that data on the subject be sent to J. E. Sullivan, 15 Warren street, New York.

"The American game of base ball was invented by Abner Doubleday of Cooperstown, N. Y., either the spring prior or following the 'Log Cabin and Hard Cider' campaign of General Harrison for president, the said Abner Doubleday being then a boy pupil of Green's Select school in Cooperstown, and the same, who as General Doubleday won honor at the battle of Gettysburg in the Civil war. The pupils of Otsego academy and Green's Select school were then playing the old game of 'town ball' in the following manner:

"A 'tosser' stood beside the home 'goal' and tossed the ball straight upward about six feet for the batsman to strike at on its fall, the batter using a four-inch flat board bat, and all others who wanted to play being scattered all over the near and far field to catch the ball, the lucky catcher then taking his innings at the bat while the losing batsman retired to the field. Should the batsman miss the ball on its fall and the tosser catch it on its first bounce he would take the bat and the losing batsman toss the ball.

"When the batsman struck the ball into the field he would run for an out goal about 50 feet and return, and if the ball was not caught on the fly, and he could return to home goal without getting 'plunked' with the ball thrown by any one, he retained

his innings the same as in "old cat." There being generally from 20 to 50 boys in the field, collisions often occurred in the attempt of several to catch the ball. Abner Doubleday then figured out and made a plan of improvement on town ball to limit the number of players and have equal sides, calling it 'base ball' because it had four bases, three being where the runner could rest free of being put out by keeping his foot on the flat stone base, while next one on this side took the bat, the first runner being entitled to run whenever he chose, and if he could make the home base without being hit by the ball he tallied.

"There was a six-foot ring within which the pitcher had to stand and toss the ball to the batsman by swinging his hand below his hip. There were 11 players on a side, four outfielders, three basemen, pitcher, catcher, and two infielders the two infielders being placed respectively a little back from the pitcher and between first and second base and second and third base and a short distance inside the base lines. The ball used had a rubber center overwound with yarn to a size somewhat larger than the present regulation ball, then covered with leather or buckskin, and having plenty of bouncing qualities, wonderful high flys often resulted. Any one getting the ball was entitled to throw it at a runner and put him out if he could hit him.

"This 'base ball' was crude compared with present day ball, but it was undoubtedly the first starter of base ball with the older boys, although we younger boys stuck to town ball and the 'old cats.' I well remember several of the best players of 50 years ago, such as Abner Doubleday, Elihu Phinney, John C. Graves, Nels. C. Brewer, Joseph Chaffee, John Stark,

weather, John Doubleday, Tom Bingham and others who used to play on the Otsego academy campus, although a favorite place was on the Phinney farm on the west shore of Otsego lake.

"Base ball is undoubtedly a pure American game, and its birthplace Cooperstown, New York, and Abner Doubleday entitled to the first honor of its invention.

"ABNER GRAVES,
"32 Blank Block, Denver, Col."

### STATE TOURNEY

...nson of the Akron ...iation has been noti... ...entral Passenger asso... ...xcursion rates of one ...fares will be granted ...s in Ohio to the an... ...and tournament of the ...cling association. The ... will be used, and a ...of the association will ...il 19 and 20 to vies the ...those who attend.

#### NOT SHOW UP WELL

April 4—Young Cor... ...r and "Young Erne" of ...red six rounds at the ...porting club last night. ...at and fought wildly, ...udging his distance, and ...ows landed on the back ...nt's head. Erne, while ...mild and much of the ...ted in clinching and ... round Erne was cut ... eye and in the sixth ...h was bleeding. In the ...Corbett rushed Erne ...opes, Erne landed the ...r of blows. He sub... ...sequently and ran away ...s of his opponent, Cor... ...top Erne repeatedly and ...ountered on Erne's jaw, ...lacked decision. Under ...cision can be given in ...he spectators appeared ...opinion that the fight

#### WRESTLER HACKENSCHMIDT

April 4.—All Aptoulu, a ...who hails from Turkey, ...etly yesterday to chal... ...chmidt to a match. Ap... ...at resembles the great ...stands more than six ...weighs 220 pounds. He ...lent record and claims ...hmidt refused to meet ...se. Sam Fitzpatrick is ...of the new arrival and ...,000 that the Turk can ...that comes before him. ...ew to the wrestling fol... ...r country, and would he ...word abroad he has not ...eat wrestlers that have ...Hackenschmidt.

...n Journal Want Ads.

### Hinkley's Bone Liniment

For internal and external use.

Take it in, rub it on. It will quickly relieve the awful pains of rheumatism, make the stiff, aching joints limber and painless. Goes right to the spot every time. Kills the pain. Why suffer when relief is so near and easy to you, and likewise at so little expense. The druggist has Hinkley's Bone Liniment at 50c and $1 a bottle. Remember that for 50 years this medicine has been curing rheumatism and it will cure you.

Gentlemen: I was a fearful sufferer from rheumatism and had given up hope that there was any remedy on earth to relieve the pain or cure the disease, but after trying a small bottle of Hinkley's Bone Liniment I knew it to be a positive cure for rheumatism.—David Pomeroy, Timber Estimator, Duluth, Minn.

Hinkley's Bone Liniment is not one of the oldest, but the one best known to round family medicine there should be a bottle in every home.

Hinkley's Bone Liniment Co., Saginaw, Mich.

For Sale by J. C. Day & Co.

#### THE NORTH-WESTERN LINE.

—One of the most interesting series of articles on the subject of the great railways of the country that has appeared recently is that from the pen of Frank H. Spearman recently published in the Saturday Evening Post, and which has since been printed in book form by Scribners. The chapter descriptive of the Chicago & North-Western railway has been published by the passenger department of that line in pamphlet form for general distribution and will be sent to any address on receipt of 3c for postage. W. B. Knickern, P. T. M., Chicago.

Miss Geraldine Mitchell, who has been the guest of Miss Leona Pettingell for the past ten days, has returned to Wooster, where she is teaching in the university.

from English children's games, including one known as "rounders," and was determined to prove that baseball's pedigree was strictly American.

In his article, headlined "The Origin of the Game of Base Ball," Spalding complained about being "fed on this kind of rounder pap for upward of 40 years and I refuse to swallow any more of it without some substantial proof sauce with it." He took note of a claim that the game may have originated with the old Knickerbocker club of New York in the 1840s, adding "If such an ancestry can be established for base ball, every American friend of the game will be delighted." Spalding appealed for anyone with information about the early days of baseball to share it with James Sullivan, president of the American

Sports Publishing Company, one of Spalding's firms. Sullivan had been assigned the task of assembling and presenting all such information to a special "board of base ball commissioners" established by Spalding to deliberate and decide the origins of the game.[3] At the time, Sullivan was also president of the Amateur Athletic Union.

In his public appeal, Spalding concluded:

> I would strongly urge that everyone interested tranmit [sic] as soon as possible to Mr. Sullivan, 19 Warren Street, New York, any proof, data, or information he may possess or can secure bearing on this matter with the hope that before another year rolls around this vexed question as to the actual origin and early history of the great American national game of base ball may be settled for all time.[4]

The 71-year-old mining engineer born on a farm near Cooperstown had delivered a story Spalding and his hand-picked commissioners had never heard—and wouldn't again despite their three-year quest. There, in 640 words, was Spalding's coveted "evidence" that the game had roots in American soil. And the clincher for him was that the inventor was a hero of the Civil War. For Spalding, this gave the story an unassailable American pedigree.

Newspaper editor Baldwin knew a scoop when he saw it and printed Graves's letter in the next edition of the *Beacon Journal*, on Tuesday, April 4. It appeared in the sports section under the headline: "Abner Doubleday Invented Base Ball: Abner Graves of Denver, Colorado, Tells How the Present National Game Had Its Origin." Aside from an introductory paragraph noting that Graves claimed he had been present for the first game of baseball and that his letter had just arrived from the Thuma Hotel in town, Baldwin provided no further editorial comment.[5]

It marked the first-ever telling of the story about the game's birth in Cooperstown and that its inventor was the late General Doubleday. Despite the revelation that Baldwin had pounced on, few other newspapers of the day picked up the story. Graves's tale would not die, however, because of Spalding's drive to prove something that couldn't be proven. And in the fullness of time, millions more words would be penned about Cooperstown and Abner Doubleday.

Albert Goodwill Spalding was a very successful man by the turn of the twentieth century. Born in Byron, Illinois, in 1850, he became proficient in baseball at an early age and pitched for the successful Forest Citys in nearby Rockford. In 1871, he joined the Boston Red Stockings of the National Association and led them to league championships from 1872 to 1875. Acclaimed as one of the best pitchers of his day, he moved to the White Stockings in Chicago for the 1876 season as player and manager, ending his play after the 1877 campaign when he assumed presidency of the club.[6] Spalding became an ongoing force in the National League in its battle with upstart rival leagues and he spoke often about how the manly sport of baseball reflected the American character.

In 1876, he opened a sporting goods store in Chicago and by 1880 had persuaded the National League to adopt a ball produced by his A. G. Spalding and Brothers (although only one brother, Walter, joined the business) as its official ball. He also published the "official league book," soon renamed *Spalding's Official Base Ball Guide*. The annual publication contained the rules and constitution for the National League as well as descriptions of league play during the previous season, individual and team records, and stories about developments in the game. The guide was also a promotional device for his growing sporting goods empire and was chock-full of advertising for its growing line of equipment for baseball and other sports. Spalding claimed national circulation of 50,000 by 1884. Three years later, A. G. Spalding and Brothers was producing more than one million baseball bats annually.[7]

In many ways, Spalding personified baseball, as a star player, owner, promoter and entrepreneur. His success in sports and business showcased the American Dream and he was proud of that heritage. "As A. G. saw it, if baseball truly had a special contribution to make to shaping the American character, its pedigree had to be impeccably American," wrote his biographer Peter Levine. "He did not doubt that the attempt to prove the point, if carefully managed, might provide good publicity for himself and his business."[8]

But this obsession to claim baseball as America's own was in stark contrast to an earlier assertion from Spalding himself. Following a tour of England by American ballplayers in 1874, in which he participated, Spalding wrote in his 1878 baseball guide that the American game was clearly linked to the English game of rounders. "The Englishmen who watched the American Clubs in England, and accused them of playing rounders were not so far out of the way," he wrote. "The game unquestionably thus originated."[9]

Pioneer baseball writer Henry Chadwick, a Brit by birth, held the same view. In 1881, he became the editor of Spalding's baseball guide. Chadwick was regarded as the authority on the game and because of his knowledge, writings and promotion of it, gained the title "Father of Baseball." As Spalding grew older, however, he began to dissociate himself from Chadwick's view and instead sought American roots for the game that had made him wealthy and had captured the national imagination. "Over time," as Spalding's biographer Levine put it, "he became convinced that a game so fundamentally representative of American values had to be American in origin."[10]

Spalding's views hardened after a world tour he organized in 1889 that included games played in England. Upon his return, in an article for the new family magazine, *The Cosmopolitan*, he dismissed any connection to rounders and went on to suggest there might, instead, be some connection to the old French game of tecque.[11] His hunt for an American sire of the game became an obsession. A constant burr under his saddle remained Chadwick and his rounders theory. Chadwick, at age 79, then took it upon himself to set the record straight in his simmering feud with Spalding, his long-time boss. In the 1903 edition of the *Official Base Ball Guide*, which Chadwick still edited, the preface alerted the reader that "one of the most readable features of the guide of 1903 will be the introductory chapters giving the history of base ball from the time of the earliest known records of the game up to the present period...."[12]

Beginning on page three and continuing for 42 more pages, Chadwick, under the headline "History of Base Ball" and the byline of Henry Chadwick "The Father of Base Ball," discussed the roots of game. At the outset, he noted that the game is "now the permanently established field game of ball for the American people, and it occupies a position in public estimation that which no other sport in vogue equals." He found the first "reliable record" of baseball came from 1833 in Philadelphia, where the Olympic Town Ball Club began play. "The game of town ball of that early period was an American modification of the old English game of rounders," he asserted. Chadwick then reviewed the variations in the "Massachusetts" and "New York" games, before concluding: "There is no doubt whatever as to base ball having originated from the two-centuries-old English game of rounders. But that fact," he added, to lessen the pain for his audience, "does not deprive our present game of its legitimate title to the name American."[13]

One can only imagine Spalding's reaction. A baseball guide with his name on it was telling readers the game he insisted was American had actually been derived from rounders. And the proponent of that tale was a native-born Brit still promoting a British connection. Chadwick's assertion was a blow to his sizable ego and motivated him more than ever to prove that baseball was unquestionably American.

By 1903, Spalding had retired from baseball and the direct oversight of his sporting goods empire. He had moved to California where he had taken up with the Theosophists, having married a woman in 1900 who was heavily involved in the society that studied and disseminated Eastern spiritual teachings. Spalding's new wife was Elizabeth Mayer Churchill, a friend from his childhood in Illinois who had later become his mistress. She was a member of the inner circle of Katherine Tingley, leader of the Point Loma community of the Theosophical Society at San Diego. The Spaldings built a grand Victorian home near the headquarters of the sect, whose members followed a regimen of self-improvement and believed in reincarnation. Coincidentally, a gentleman named Abner Doubleday, a native of Cooperstown, New York, had been president of the American Theosophical Society, but that was many years before Spalding joined. Doubleday, who died in 1893, was more widely known as the artillery captain who had ordered the firing of the first shot of the Civil War at Fort Sumter and who later, as a major-general at Gettysburg, led troops who helped repel Pickett's charge.[14] The appearance of Doubleday, a fellow

Theosophist, in the later account by Graves, must have caught the attention of the sports mogul.

Despite a new wife and home in California, Spalding was sufficiently agitated by Chadwick's assertion that he decided to fight back. In 1904, he began writing a series of articles and delivering public speeches in which he dismissed Chadwick's claim, drawing widespread newspaper attention to the spat between the two titans of the game.

In early November, Spalding sent a letter to John Lowell, who had played a key role in baseball in Boston during the 1860s. Spalding explained that he was seeking information about the Massachusetts and New York games of ball and how they had merged along the way. He also elicited Lowell's thoughts about the beginnings of the current game. Spalding made no effort to conceal his motivations:

> I have become weary of my friend Chadwick's talk about base ball having been handed down from the old English game of "Rounders," and am trying to convince myself and others that the American game of Base Ball is purely of American origin, and I want to get all the facts I can to support that theory. My patriotism naturally makes me desirous of establishing it as of American origin, and as the same spirit will probably prompt you, I would like your ideas about it.[15]

Eleven days later, in Springfield, Massachusetts, Spalding told a YMCA audience about his dim view of rounders, suggested that other games may have been the antecedents of baseball and explained his hunt for evidence of an American genesis of the national game. His speech later appeared in written form in *Spalding's Official Base Ball Guide* for 1905 and was subsequently published in newspapers like the *Akron Beacon Journal*, where it caught the attention of visiting mining engineer Abner Graves.[16]

Spalding came up with the idea of creating a group of like-minded men to help legitimize his quest. He found a handful of cronies from baseball and business willing to act as a commission to review any evidence that his beating of the bushes might turn up and he asked Sullivan of his American Sports Publishing Company to collect the data. However, the information that materialized proved unhelpful to his mission. Many respondents reminisced about the Massachusetts and New York versions of games and versions of a child's game called "old cat." The response underwhelmed Spalding and didn't produce the evidence he'd been hoping to unearth. He was no doubt disappointed.

Enter Abner Graves and his story about Cooperstown and Doubleday. When the letter was forwarded to him from Sullivan, Spalding finally had his "eureka!" moment. In the ensuing months, he and Graves exchanged letters as Spalding sought additional evidence and witnesses that Graves was ultimately unable to provide. In one of those letters, Graves provided a drawing of the ball field he said was laid out by Doubleday. Spalding embraced Graves's story and commended it to the commission he had appointed, which dutifully adopted it in its final report, despite a lack of supporting evidence. The Cooperstown story wasn't a hard one to sell, despite the lack of corroboration. And it didn't hurt Graves's case that 63-year-old Abraham G. Mills, chairperson of the Special Base Ball Commission, had been part of the honor guard for Doubleday when the late general lay in state at New York City Hall. Mills and Doubleday had been members of the same veterans' association and were friends. Mills, as commander of the association, took charge of arrangements that led to Doubleday's interment at Arlington National Cemetery.[17]

Major General Abner Doubleday, the Civil War hero who did not invent baseball, despite the widely accepted story told by Abner Graves after his death. National Baseball Hall of Fame Library, Cooperstown, New York.

In his report for the baseball commission, Mills eliminated Graves's reference to the practice of hitting players with the ball to get an out and arbitrarily chose 1839 as the date of the game described. (By Graves's account it could just as easily have taken place in 1841.[18]) And by eliminating the description of the old practice known as "soaking" base runners with the ball to get them out, Mills was likely trying to make the game described more closely resemble the modern game, helping to distinguish it from other games played in the early 1800s.[19]

Timing was everything. Graves, by responding to Spalding's plea when and how he did, fell into a jackpot beyond anything he could have imagined. Later in life, he grew to enjoy the notoriety of his association with baseball and exploited it for all it was worth. With his simple letter, Graves had provided a very determined man with a proposition to pitch to the American public that would be accepted as fact, even after it was found to be bogus. The famed old pitcher Spalding in turn delivered to fans of the game a story of its birth that would prove potent and durable.

Except for some mentions in a few Sunday newspapers and an account in *Sporting Life* in mid–1905, the general public was largely unaware of the Cooperstown tale until the Mills Commission report was published in the

*Spalding Guide*, released in March of 1908.[20] So appealing was the tale that it received ready acceptance.[21]

Pleased with his cherished "evidence," Spalding asked his old friendly foe and employee Chadwick to write a full book about the origins and the state of the modern game and provided him an outline for it. Chadwick, 83, agreed. The good-natured editor was unwilling to hold a grudge and in a note to Mills wrote: "Your decision in the case of Chadwick vs. Spalding ... is a masterly piece of special pleading which lets my dear old friend Albert escape a bad defeat." He concluded "the whole matter was a joke between Albert and myself."[22] But Chadwick died a month later, so Spalding took it upon himself to write *America's National Game*, which was dedicated to his old friend. The book was printed by Spalding's own American Sports Publishing Company and it promoted the Doubleday story, but like the Mills report from which it quoted extensively, it did not mention Abner Graves by name as the source. The reader could easily judge this book by its cover: it featured a drawing of Uncle Sam holding a baseball bat.

In *America's National Game*, Spalding held nothing back. He boasted that he could "prove that Base Ball is our National Game; that it has all the attributes of American origin, the American character and unbounded public favor in America ... I claim that Base Ball owes its prestige as our National Game to the fact that as no other form of sport it is the exponent of American Courage, Confidence, Combativeness; American Dash, Discipline, Determination; American Energy, Eagerness, Enthusiasm; American Pluck, Persistency, Performance; American Spirit, Sagacity, Success; American Vim, Vigor, Virility."[23]

In his thick volume, the super-patriot then compared baseball to cricket, dismissing the latter as "a splendid game, for Britons.... They play Cricket because it accords with the traditions of their country to do so; because it is easy and does not overtax their energy or their thought." Besides, he argued, cricket matches can last for days, while a ball game can be wrapped up in two hours, a more suitable length for Americans. "Cricket is a gentle pastime," he continued. "Base Ball is War!" At this point, he reminded readers: "The founder of our National Game became a Major-General in the United States Army!"[24]

Not content with restricting himself to national chauvinism, Spalding also argued that baseball was not a sport for women. They could play the gentle games of cricket, or lawn tennis, or basketball or golf—and even win trophies— but: "Base Ball is too strenuous for womankind, except as she may take part in grandstand, with applause for brilliant play, with waving kerchief to the hero of the three-bagger, and, since she is ever a loyal partisan of the home team, with smiles of derision for the Umpire when he gives us the worst of it...." Given the writer's age and his era, in which women were still a decade away from attaining the right to vote, Spalding could perhaps be forgiven his views. But it indicates that the old pitcher was willing to use every trick in his arsenal to show that the game was manly and American.

Spalding then referred to baseball's American invention by citing the Mills Commission report and the "righteousness of its verdict."[25] He repeated its findings and provided the baseball background of its members. He quoted the closing words penned by Mills about "a circumstantial statement by a reputable gentleman" as the basis of the Doubleday story and the commission's conclusion. "I have nothing to add to their report," Spalding said, but then appended a large likeness of Doubleday in dress uniform and a detailed biographical sketch of the major-general from *Appleton's Encyclopedia of American Biography.*[26]

Spalding's 600-page opus, which sold for two dollars, also included accounts of early baseball in New York City and other early teams and the rise of the National League as he stressed the importance of strong organizations and profession-

Formal portrait of Abner Graves in Denver, Colorado. He moved to the Colorado capital in 1894 and it became the base for his mine consulting and engineering work. During his time in Denver he operated out of an office in the Bank Block building. Courtesy History Colorado (Scan #10041219).

alism. His sporting goods and sales staff promoted it heavily and thousands of copies found their way into public libraries and YMCAs as the story of baseball—and its origin in Cooperstown—spread.

Praise for Spalding's effort came from the editor of *Sporting Life*, who, in a note to Spalding, wrote that the old star had ensured that his connection to the game was well understood in its pages. Francis Richter called it "an honest effort to crown a life devoted to Baseball ... a supreme tribute which will outlast all of your work ... you have chosen the very best way to immortalize yourself in connection with the National Game."[27] Aside from immortalizing himself, Spalding had also enshrined a story about the origins of the game, without independent corroboration, that supported his prejudice against English parentage and backed an American inventor. He likely hoped that he had penned the last word on the subject and that the long-contentious issue had been settled once and for all.

Even before *America's National Game* was released in 1911, questions had been raised about the Doubleday story after it was published three years earlier in *Spalding's Guide*. The first to challenge it was Will Irwin, a sportswriter, in a series of articles in *Collier's* magazine in May of 1909. He wrote about the history of the game, arguing that it predated Cooperstown and Doubleday and even the invention of rounders. Irwin pointed out that Doubleday couldn't have been at Cooperstown in 1839 because at the time he was enrolled at West Point, about 150 miles to the south. Another writer, veteran baseball scribe William M. Rankin, dismissed the Cooperstown story on the same grounds and attributed the modern game to the Knickerbocker Base Ball Club of New York City in 1845.[28] Theirs would not be the last voices to discredit the tale.

But for the most part, Americans seemed willing to embrace the story told by Abner Graves, even if they didn't see his name attached to it. Irwin and Rankin remained voices in the wilderness. As historian David Block aptly put it:

> These critics carried little weight compared to the towering influence of Spalding and his commission, and the American public was quick to welcome Abner Doubleday as the nation's newest icon. The Cooperstown tale rapidly found its way into children's schoolbooks, taking its place alongside other historical anecdotes like Ben Franklin and his kite, and George Washington and the cherry tree. The debate over baseball's origins quietly slid into the shadows. In part this peace was due to the passing of those two old warriors, Chadwick and Spalding [who died in 1915], whose personalities and friendly rivalry had so long fueled the controversy. More to the point, in the minds of most observers, there was nothing left to debate.[29]

America was becoming a dominant world power, setting a course free from the shackles of the old world. It was a time for a self-confident nation to flex its muscles, promote itself and its values. Expansionism was the prevailing mood. The U.S. had spanked Spain militarily, relieving her of Puerto Rico, the Philippines and Cuba during the brief Spanish-American War of 1898. Those conquests were duly noted by Spalding in *America's National Game* as part of his unabashed flag-waving.[30]

Spalding had appealed to the need for an American origin for a game so popular among Americans. The notion of schoolboys playing the first game in an idyllic little town in upstate New York, organized by a young man who went on to become a hero of the Civil War, was just too irresistible. And so the story sat, mostly unchallenged. Among those choosing to believe it and ignore the growing evidence against Doubleday were residents of Cooperstown. They seized an economic opportunity and persuaded major league baseball to erect the National Baseball Hall of Fame museum there. The building opened in 1939, on the centennial of an event that didn't happen.

Baseball, and America, had settled on a story and that was that. Harold

Peterson, biographer of Alexander Cartwright, a member of the Knickerbockers, wrote in *The Man Who Invented Baseball*: "The Myth that Abner Doubleday invented baseball is one of the most amusingly fraudulent pieces of manufactured history, extant. Yet what it lacks in authenticity it amply makes up in obstinate durability."[31] Peterson coined the best phrase to capture the handiwork of Albert Goodwill Spalding and his commission, aided by the hapless accomplice, Abner Graves: "Abner Doubleday didn't invent baseball. Baseball invented Abner Doubleday."[32]

In recent decades, so much has been unearthed and written to debunk the Cooperstown tale that it moved Spalding's biographer, Levine, to conclude in 1985: "No one today, not even baseball's officialdom, recognizes Abner Doubleday as the inventor of baseball. Yet baseball's continual hold on the American public as more than a game owes much to Spalding."

Even more recently, in 2010, Lawrence McCray, chairman of the Origins Committee at the Society for American Baseball Research, expressed wonderment that the Cooperstown story retains any adherents. A professor at the Massachusetts Institute of Technology, McCray told the *New York Times*: "The thing that amazes me is the durability of this idea. You just don't run into people now who think of this as historically accurate."[33]

McCray apparently had never met Bud Selig, commissioner of Major League Baseball. Or his friend, Ron Keurajian.

In October 2010, Selig sent a note to autograph collector Keurajian, a commercial banker and attorney, who was working on a book about baseball autographs. The commissioner was replying to a letter from Keurajian, who sought Selig's views on the Mills Commission. Selig's reply, which found its way onto the Internet, was: "From all the historians which I have spoken with, I really believe that Abner Doubleday is the 'Father of Baseball.' I know there are some historians who would dispute this, though."[34]

Serious baseball historians marveled at Selig's admission and could be forgiven for wondering upon which historians he was relying. Certainly none from the modern era. It was clear that the commissioner was woefully ill-informed. The baseball community was atwitter and Selig was ridiculed by bloggers and others. It wasn't the first time Selig had made a suggestive reference to Doubleday. In 2000, while laying a wreath at Arlington National Cemetery, Selig had taken note that Doubleday was buried there. "It is a profound honor to be at this hallowed resting place to so many American heroes, including baseball's own Abner Doubleday," he was quoted as saying.[35]

Keurajian's views coincided with the commissioner's and when he saw Selig take heat for them, he contacted the media to support Selig and offer his own take-no-prisoners opinion:

For years Union General Doubleday was the uncontested "Father" of the game, having first organized the game back in 1839 on farmer Phinney's cow pasture

...For many years this was accepted as fact, a fact backed by concrete evidence unearth [sic] by the Mills Commission. Fast forward a few decades and suddenly a few, mind you just a few, baseball buffs, who called themselves "historians" challenged the long accepted fact of Doubleday and birth of baseball. You know the type, those who try to make a name for themselves by trying to "upset the apple cart" merely to see what reaction they get. These are the people with too much time on their hands and like to cause trouble.... They really have no evidence to the contrary but what the hell, never let facts get in the way of a good story ... who did they interview? Really what was their evidence that could trump the Mills Commission, maybe they were reading tea leaves or more properly ... smoking them. I think it's pretty clear which determination is based on fact and which is based on folly ... I get so tired of those who have this uncontrollable need to distort facts in a weak attempt to change history ... most real students of the game hold that belief [in Doubleday]. Yet Selig is basically lynched by those who hold a different view ... Doubleday is the Father of the National pastime and will remain so for centuries to come. Sorry, that's just the way it is. To this small handful of baseball experts I suggest they concentrate of [sic] some other interest and stop trying to distort baseball history to satisfy some personal shortcomings.[36]

Keurajian's strongly worded view shows how deeply and passionately some Americans continue to cling to the Doubleday myth. It's almost a point of faith for them.

A few months after discovering that his notion was at odds with "true" history, an apparently embarrassed Selig created a twelve-member task force, chaired by John Thorn, the newly appointed historian for Major League Baseball. The mandate of the task force was "to determine the facts of baseball's beginnings and its evolution." Selig agreed to serve on the panel along with luminaries who included filmmaker/historian Ken Burns, historian Doris Kearns Goodwin, authors Jane Leavy and George F. Will, and the aforementioned Lawrence McCray of the Society for American Baseball Research.[37] Interestingly, the Thorn task force was established exactly one hundred years after publication of *America's National Game,* which was subtitled *Historic Facts Concerning the Beginning, Evolution, Development and Popularity of Base Ball.*

For baseball, in America, some quests just never seem to die. The obsession with baseball's birth continues long after Spalding thought he had put the issue to rest. And what about Graves, the man who started it all?

For some time now, Graves has remained a mystery man to most baseball historians, some of whom simply opted to dismiss him as a crank, a mental case, senile, a conspirator with Spalding or a practical joker. Not believing his story, they saw no need to investigate him further.

"What could possibly have motivated the Denver businessman to fabricate a yarn that would fall apart under minimal scrutiny?" historian David Block asked, without finding a plausible answer.[38]

Millions of words have been penned by historians and others since Graves pecked out his original 640 words that day on a typewriter in his hotel room. But a fundamental question remains. Where did he come up with that story?

Delving into the life of Graves suggests an answer that may surprise. And it certainly would not sit well with Spalding.

# Two

## *A Son of Cooperstown*

Over the years since he shared his story about Cooperstown, Abner Graves has been largely forgotten. His story certainly hasn't.

When historians have written about Graves, it generally has been with derision and even the slightest piece of information was used to further discredit him. John Thorn described the mining engineer as a "mysterious traveler" who wrote his letter from a hotel in Akron, "a city not noted for its mineralogical opportunities."[1] But Graves traveled widely, often looking for capital to fund mining ventures such as his operation in Mexico, and oftentimes went east to see friends and family still in Cooperstown. He may have been seeking potential investors in Akron.

Historian David Block used an unsubstantiated assertion from yet another historian, Phil Goodstein, that Graves spent time in mental asylums in Iowa before moving west to Denver. There is no record of that and his descendants deny it vehemently.[2] It is known, however, that he spent the final three years (1924–26) of his long life in the state mental hospital. The same writer and others have suggested that Graves lied when he claimed he rode with the Pony Express in 1852, noting that the short-lived cross-country Pony Express didn't begin until 1860. But Graves, in fact, did ride for two California-based regional pony express firms in the early 1850s. It has been further suggested Graves may have told his story as a "practical joke" or as a "deliberate deception," cynically knowing what Spalding was seeking and then slyly playing into his hands. The writers responsible for these claims then concluded Graves could not have concocted such a "whopper," and the old man may simply have been off the mark in memories of a game played when he was at a tender age.[3]

Abner Graves was, in truth, a complex individual. Notwithstanding the bashing he has taken at the hands of some baseball historians, Graves was a hard-working man who had a long and successful life. It ended in tragedy in his nineties, but that was two decades after he had written about Cooperstown and Abner Doubleday. His descendants are proud of his accomplishments as a pioneer in business, in the cattle industry and in mining. He is remembered as a devoted father, a respected Shriner and a man who bounced back from economic setbacks. His family privately published a book about him in recent years, recounting his life, warts and all. They provided a copy to the library at the National Baseball Hall of Fame. His descendants frankly acknowledge problems with Graves's Cooperstown story, gently noting that experts "have found Abner's claim to have been largely false, based on several dates not adding up right."[4]

Hugh MacDougall, official historian for the village of Cooperstown, set about the task of documenting the life of the man whose story transformed the sleepy little community into a shrine for baseball that attracts visitors from around the world. With access to early local newspaper accounts, genealogical records and local history, MacDougall chronicled the life of the man who put his hometown on the map, particularly in his early years. MacDougall acknowledged that very little is known about Graves, observing: "When he is spoken of, or written about, it is usually with scorn."[5] MacDougall tracked down the modest history assembled by the descendants of Graves and, after reflecting on what he found, is of the opinion that the Cooperstown tale was not based exclusively on Graves's own childhood memories. He said it was more likely shaped by his contact and ongoing conversations with relatives who stayed in the village he left in 1849.[6]

Abner Graves was born on a farm just south of Cooperstown on February 27, 1834, the third of eight children of Horatio Nelson Graves and Sabra Green. He attended Frog Hollow School in Cooperstown, where he later said he watched as older students from two private schools, Green's Select School and Otsego Academy for Boys, played the first game of baseball.[7] Graves would have been five years of age in 1839. Among his schoolmates was Abner Demas Doubleday, a cousin of the Abner Doubleday who went on to fame in the Civil War.[8] Some suggestion has been made that Graves merely confused the two Doubledays, despite his specific reference in his famous letter to Doubleday as the Civil War hero. The cousin, Abner Demas Doubleday, also enlisted as a Union soldier in the war, but reached only the rank of lieutenant and was discharged with sunstroke in early 1865.[9]

Gold fever gripped America as word spread of the discovery of the precious metal in California in 1848. Cooperstown and Otsego County were not immune and newspaper accounts of the riches being found on the West Coast captured the imagination of young and old alike. Early in 1849, a group called the Otsego Mining Company was formed by eighteen men in the area. Among them were Horatio Graves, 42, and his 15-year-old son, Abner, the youngest member of the group.[10] The Otsego group was among several that booked passage on the sailing ship *Samoset* bound for San Francisco by way of the southern tip of South America. The *Samoset* left New York on March 22, 1849, for the trip south and around Cape Horn and up the west coast. The ship took 171 days to reach San Francisco in early September, tying up in the crude port city that had just been renamed from Yerba Buena. The New Yorkers promptly made their way inland to the Auburn gold fields along the north fork of the American River. They panned for gold there, but failed to find the riches they sought and members of the group began to scatter. The most easily discouraged began trickling home. But as late as 1854, some members of the group were still panning for gold along the American River.[11]

Abner Graves, presumably disappointed in his success as a prospector, tried his hand at a new business springing up to serve the new mines. In 1852 and 1853, now in his late teens, he delivered mail and packages on horseback for Adams and Company and then for the Wells Fargo pony express firms. Back east, Abner's grandfather, also named Abner, had been a "post rider" before the U.S. Post Office was established, so the young man was following in his namesake's hoofprints.[12] Adams and Company, a Boston-based firm, opened its San Francisco office in 1849. Most of the company's business involved shipping gold from the mining areas to the bustling port city, guaranteeing delivery to its customers. The firm grew rapidly, despite the arrival of Wells Fargo in 1852, but began to suffer from robberies and a run on its assets organized by its competitors. In 1854, when its parent company back east reorganized as Adams Express, the California service ceased.[13]

Both pony express firms in California sought strong young men as riders and Graves later boasted that he was the second best in his outfit, although he didn't specify which outfit.[14] In subsequent years, he spoke about his experiences as a rider with the California express services and newspaper writers (and, even later, historians) often mistook his accounts as relating to the more famous Pony Express service. Despite its fame, that service operated for only 19 months from April 1860 to October 1861, connecting the railhead at St. Joseph, Missouri, to Sacramento, California. The need for that arduous, 2,000-mile, money-losing mail service ended with the completion of the Pacific Telegraph service.[15]

Horatio and Abner Graves never made a big strike in gold country, but it wasn't for lack of trying. Their whereabouts in the next few years are difficult to determine, independent of the biographical material Abner provided for his entry in *The Semi-Centennial History of the State of Colorado*, published in 1913, which documented people in the state to which he eventually moved. The biographical sketch noted that by September 7, 1849, Graves had arrived in Auburn, Placer County, California.

> [He] remained there until 1856, when he went to the hydraulic mines at Forest City, Sierra County, afterward mining in Shasta and Trinity counties. At the outbreak of the Nevada excitement, he located at Virginia City, working there for a number of years. He participated in the Shoshone [Indian] wars near Battle Mountain, and was wounded while serving with the Home Guards of Unionville, Humboldt County. In 1865, Mr. Graves returned to California, his mining operations being conducted in Shasta County and in other sections of the state.[16]

The reference to the Shoshone wars denotes the many conflicts in the 1850s and 60s between the tribe whose homeland was at Battle Mountain, Nevada, and the white men who were moving into their lands.

The "excitement" in Nevada was yet another gold rush that attracted Abner Graves, now 25 and on his own. His father had returned to Cooperstown and in the mid–1850s relocated to Iowa. In 1859, the richest silver deposit in American history was discovered at Virginia City, just east of the California state line. Prospectors were initially looking for gold and some was found. But to get to the gold, prospectors were faced with a bluish clay that they ignored and pushed out of the way. However, it soon became clear that the clay contained silver of exceptional quality and a rush was on. Virginia City became a boomtown, growing from 2,345 in 1860 to 4,000 in 1862 and rising to 25,000 by 1874. Silver from the mines at Virginia City helped finance the Union side in the Civil War. For a time, Virginia City was the most important city between Chicago and San Francisco, but its decline began in 1877.[17]

Always quick to spot an opportunity, Abner Graves was among the early arrivals and dreamed of the same sort of riches that built fine mansions and generated untold wealth for local prospectors and for the investors in California who transformed San Francisco. Another early arrival was a young man named Samuel Langhorne Clemens, a year younger than Graves. There is no proof the two men met in wild and woolly Virginia City in the two years both lived there; however, in a town that small at the time—even with a fluctuating population of transients—Graves would have to have been familiar with Clemens, a reporter for the local newspaper and master raconteur who would become renowned as Mark Twain. Clemens, a Missourian who had been a steamboat captain, arrived in Carson City, Nevada, in 1861. The outbreak of the Civil War brought a halt to shipping on the Mississippi and he was out of work. After a brief stint in the militia, Clemens went west to assist his older brother, Orion, who had been appointed secretary of the Nevada Territory by President Abraham Lincoln. The younger Clemens, a clerk for the new territorial secretary, was soon investing in timber, silver and gold claims, but found little success. He quit the clerical job (for which he was not paid) and worked for a time in a quartz mill in California near the Nevada border, but found manual labor was tedious and not to his liking. During this time, he had written several letters to the *Territorial Enterprise* in Virginia City under the pen name "Josh" that caught the attention of the editor. In mid–1862, the newspaper offered him a job at twenty-five dollars a week and the 26-year-old Clemens jumped at it.[18]

Clemens found a perfect fit in the boisterous, vibrant publication owned by two proprietors even younger than himself. His penchant for exaggeration, ridicule and his irreverent outlook quickly became known as he chased news stories in the streets of the booming wild west community. By his own choice, he was one of the few reporters in town who opted not to pack a pistol. Clemens didn't restrain himself by the facts when he spun his stories, amusing and sometimes outraging readers and his competitors.

He readily admitted inventing facts to make his accounts more compelling. Early in his career at the *Territorial Enterprise*, he perpetrated a hoax on readers when he wrote about the discovery of a petrified man in the mountains nearby: "The body was in a sitting posture, and leaning against a huge mass of croppings; the attitude was pensive, the right thumb resting against the side of the nose; the left thumb partially supporting the chin...." A local justice, he reported, held an immediate inquest after the discovery and the verdict of the jury was that "the deceased came to his death from protracted exposure."[19]

Exaggeration came easily to Clemens, as was again evidenced when he described a nasty windstorm that ripped into Virginia City late in 1862. According to his account, "The wind commenced blowing after a fashion to which a typhoon is mere nonsense, and in a short time the face of heaven was obscured by vast clouds of dust all spangled over with lumber, and shingles, and dogs and things. There was no particular harm in that, but the breeze soon began to work damage of a serious nature."[20]

A few years later, in his book *Roughing It*, Twain recalled seeing a wagon of immigrants arrive in Virginia City that had suffered a rough crossing through Indian territory. He explained the sort of intrepid—and resourceful—reporter he became:

> I made the best of the item that the circumstances permitted, and felt that if I were not confined within rigid limits by the presence of the reporters for the other papers, I could add particulars that would make the article much more interesting. However, I found one wagon that was going on to California, and made some judicious inquiries of the proprietor. When I learned through the short and surly answers to my cross-questioning that he was certainly going on and would not be in the city the next day to make trouble, I got ahead of the other papers, for I took down his list of names and added his party to the killed and wounded. Having more scope here, I put this wagon through an Indian fight that to this day has no parallel in history.[21]

The young reporter's way with words could not be ignored, even though his facts might be suspect. By early 1863, he was in full stride. A January column, written on a slow day a month before he adopted the pen name of Mark Twain, was a classic example of the writing talents of a man who would go on to become a national treasure as a tale-spinner and humorist: "A beautiful and ably constructed free fight came off in C Street yesterday afternoon, but as nobody was killed or mortally wounded in a manner sufficiently fatal to cause death, no particular interest attaches to the matter, and we shall not publish the details. We pine for murder—these fist fights are of no consequence to anybody."[22]

His efforts and ethics rubbed some of his competitors the wrong way. In August of 1863, the rival *Evening Bulletin* described him as "that beef-eating, bleary-eyed, hollow headed, slab-sided ignoramus—that pilfering reporter, Mark Twain."[23] When Twain, somewhat the worse for drink, wrote disparagingly about the Sanitary Commission, a national agency of women that tended to the sick and wounded of the Civil War, he went too far. Controversy raged and he was challenged to a duel. At the end of May 1864, he left Virginia City, a town that had witnessed the first steps in a career that would make him an internationally acclaimed author.[24] Twain relocated to Calaveras County in California, where he would write a popular story about its jumping frogs, then on to San Francisco and Sacramento to continue plying his trade as a reporter.

Graves, who would become a storyteller in his own right, left Virginia City about the same time. He sought more mining adventure in California, still seeking his El Dorado, but he would not remain long in the west.

While Graves had been chasing his fortune in California and Nevada, enough of the residents of his hometown of Cooperstown had moved westward that Cedar Rapids, Iowa, could be described as "Cooperstown West."[25] The migration to the new frontier for farming began not long after a leading citizen of Cedar Rapids married Frances Rebecca Graves in Cooperstown in 1855. The groom was George Greene, an English-born adventurer who had moved to the newly established territory of Iowa in 1838, after an upbringing in Buffalo, New York. In Iowa, Greene became a lawyer, territorial legislator and judge.[26] It's not known how Greene met the Cooperstown woman thirteen years his junior, but the union proved successful and he and Frances had eight children to add to the four Greene had fathered during a previous marriage.

The bride's father was Calvin Graves, an uncle of Abner who was a successful banker, merchant and land speculator in Cooperstown.[27] After his daughter married Greene, Calvin Graves apparently liked what he learned about Iowa from his daughter. He moved to Cedar Rapids where he bought more than one thousand acres and went into business with his new son-in-law. Calvin Graves eventually moved back to Cooperstown, where he died a wealthy man, but his reports about his experience and the opportunities in Iowa triggered great interest among others in the New York village along Lake Otsego. In 1855, his son, John Carlisle Graves, moved to Cedar Rapids with his young family, as did John Carlisle's sister, Harriet, with her husband George Wilson.

By 1856, Abner Graves's parents, Horatio and Sabra, were also living in Cedar Rapids with their four youngest children.[28] Horatio Graves farmed for a time until he retired, then he and Sabra operated a boarding house. One of Abner's older brothers, Joseph G. Graves, opened a bookstore in Cedar Rapids and years later sold it to Abner.[29] Home for most of Abner's family was now Iowa. It's unclear when he arrived there, but in 1924, on his 90th birthday,

Graves told a Denver newspaper that he arrived in Cedar Rapids "shortly after the Civil War ended."[30] It was most likely 1865, when his mother died.

Graves found employment in a furniture company operated by two of his cousins, but the business foundered in 1870 when one of them, John Boyce, died.[31] In the meantime, Graves found love while representing the company in western Iowa. On March 28, 1868, the 34-year-old married 20-year-old Chloe Alma Dow, a daughter of Simeon Elbridge Dow from Crawford County, Iowa.[32] Simeon Dow had come west from Michigan in 1855. He owned a large property about ten miles southwest of Denison, in an area that became known as Dowville in 1869.[33] Dow had a large family, in which Alma was the oldest. He raised shorthorn cattle and owned a lumber mill.

There were no structures in Dowville, but there was a railway line and the always resourceful Abner Graves spotted a business opportunity. In June of 1870, even before a rail depot had been established, Graves, who now had joined his father-in-law's lumber business, unloaded ten rail cars full of lumber.[34] The firm became known as Dow, Graves & Co., with a farm machinery business and a grain elevator on the Boyer River. The enterprising partners prospered as the community grew around them and soon Dow, Graves & Co. became the leading business firm in the western part of Crawford County.[35]

Abner Graves as a young entrepreneur in Dow City, Iowa. After seeking gold in California and Nevada, the Cooperstown native settled in Iowa. He married well, partnered with his father-in-law, the town founder, and ran several businesses and a bank. Used by permission of Claire Strashun.

Despite the demands of the firm, Graves had enough spare time to devote some of it to baseball. In an interview with a *Denver Post* reporter in 1912, Graves reminisced about having organized the Dowville ball team in 1872 and managed it for "a number of years."[36]

The one-time prospector also found success in farming. In 1877, Graves put pen to paper to write the editor of the *Cedar Rapids Times* to describe severe weather that ripped into his farm. The avid newspaper reader had good facility with the English language, despite a lack of formal education, and on occasion decided to write to newspapers. His account of the storm is somewhat reminiscent of Twain's account of that windstorm a few years earlier in the *Territorial Enterprise*, complete with flying animals:

> At 7:30 P.M. Saturday, a cyclone came in from the northwest and a tornado from the southwest and locked horns and had a pitched battle in my barnyard. When they separated, the tornado took the roof of my hog palace a hundred feet higher than and over the top of my house, and dropped part of it near the schoolhouse, while the cyclone took the rest of the building clean, not a sill or a stick left in the lot; and it rained dead Berkshires for half an hour. One sow, weighing over 300 pounds, was dropped half way to Denison, and footed it back to her pigs next morning, as well as ever ... three churches and many dwellings in Denison were badly wrecked.[37]

Some storm. Some story.

In 1878, Dowville was renamed Dow City and incorporated with Simeon E. Dow as mayor and Abner Graves as treasurer and trustee.[38] The pair not only controlled the business life of their community, but now its municipal life as well. Graves must have done a credible job because twelve years later it was jokingly reported in the *Denison Review* that he had been re-elected yet again, and was "still treasurer, frisky with funds."[39]

Frisky or not, Graves likely had a talent with money, because in March of 1879 he opened Dow City Bank, in a building he erected specially for the new enterprise.[40] His venture into banking soon provided more "adventure" than Graves could have imagined. A year after he opened it, he had a harrowing experience. The *Carroll City* (Iowa) *Herald* of March 30, 1880, carried an account of the incident.

"Near To Death," the breathless headline read, followed by the sub-headline "The Peculiar Adventure of the President of the Dow City Bank." The report reads as follows in its entirety:

> The *Denison Bulletin* of last week says: One of the most peculiar incidents which illustrates the hand of Providence in the affairs of men occurred in Dow City Monday evening of last week, involving the narrow escape from death of one of our most respected citizens, Mr. Abner Graves. The presence of suspicious characters in the town during the day induced Mr. Graves to arrange a bed upon the floor of the bank in order to watch over the interests of the insti-

tution during the dead hours of night, when the incursion of burglars would be most likely to take place. Curiously enough, Mr. Graves neglected to inform his book-keeper, Mr. Platt, of his intention. The latter gentleman is in the habit of entering the bank before retiring for the night, to replenish the fire, that the rooms may be comfortably warm in the morning. The evening in question, while attending to this duty, he was startled by what he supposed to be one or more burglars behind the counter, but which in reality was Mr. Graves moving about on his bed. He was aware of Mr. Platt's presence but did not think it necessary to accost him. Being unarmed Mr. Platt sought to convey the impression to the supposed burglars that their presence was unknown to him, by performing his duties expeditiously and retiring in good order. Seeking Mr. Wm. Sullivan, he informed him that burglars were operating in the bank, and the twain, accoutered with a large Colt's revolver and a lantern, proceeded to investigate the state of affairs. Mr. Graves, in turn, supposed that burglars were entering the building, and prepared himself for hostilities. Mr. Platt raised the lantern to guide the aim; Mr. Sullivan pointed his weapon at a man's head as it appeared above the counter, and with the death-dealing instrument within three feet of its target, his finger was pressing the trigger when to his horror he recognized Mr. Graves. A man with less nerve than Mr. Sullivan could not have averted a disaster—it would have been too late to have eased the strain upon the trigger, and a horrible tragedy would have been the result. No blame whatever can be attached to the gentlemen who so fearlessly attempted to save the bank from loss, at the risk of their own lives, as they had every reason to suppose. All heartily unite in congratulating Mr. Graves upon his almost miraculous escape from sudden death.[41]

Had death been his fate then and there, Graves could never have spun the tale of Cooperstown. Baseball history—and the controversy surrounding it—would have been decidedly different.

In the early 1880s, Graves and his father-in-law opened the Dow City Flouring Mill and Graves dabbled in Republican politics, running unsuccessfully for state senator in 1881.[42] The same year, his father Horatio passed away at age 75. The widower had remarried a woman named Nettie Buck and the couple lived next door to Abner and Alma. The following year, Graves and his wife decided they weren't going to let her inability to conceive stand in the way of starting a family. In late 1882, as Abner approached his forty-ninth birthday, the couple adopted a baby boy born earlier that year and named him Nelson Dow Graves.[43] The dark-haired boy and his father bonded instantly and Abner adored him, eventually taking him on vacations to Hot Springs, South Dakota, Catalina Island, California, and elsewhere to broaden his horizons.[44]

Graves was continuing to experience success as a farmer and a report in an area newspaper during the spring of 1883 reveals that he was no stranger to hard work:

On Tuesday of last week, Mr. Graves drove twelve miles from Dow City to his farm, and commenced sowing wheat at 10 before 9 o'clock, using a machine Frank Hildenbrandt brought from California. Mr. Graves handled the wheat and attended the machine, and Mr. Hildenbrandt drove the team of four horses used to draw it and the wheat to be sown. One hundred and one acres of fall plowing were sown from 10 minutes before 9 until 15 minutes after 6 in the evening, 9 hours and 25 minutes, which included a stoppage for dinner and walking three-fourths of a mile and back for water.[45]

Meanwhile, Graves's interest in beef cattle, likely inspired by his father-in-law's shorthorns, prompted him to begin breeding Aberdeen Angus, also known as "Polled Angus." He was among the first cattlemen to do so in Iowa and he became quite successful with the breed. In 1883, he attended the founding meeting of the American Aberdeen Angus Breeders Association in Chicago.[46] Graves was named a director of that body and his subsequent transactions were duly recorded in the association's herd books. The following year, he became president of the state association and sold a prized bull for $600. In 1886, he attracted praise as "one of the principal breeders of Polled Angus cattle" in Iowa.[47]

By 1883, Graves also was a member of the Freemasons, the secretive fraternal organization that derives its symbols from geometry and architecture and has as its basic tenets brotherly love, relief (concern for others) and truth. "Freemasonry," one source notes, "believes in building a Mason's character and the cornerstone of good character is honesty and truth in all its forms."[48] Masonic records show that in a "return" sent to the Grand Lodge of Iowa, Graves was listed as one of 42 members of Hospitable Lodge, Number 244, in Dunlap, a community just southwest of Dow City.[49] Joining the Masons proved a positive experience and he quickly rose through the Masonic hierarchy. He became a Shriner in 1889, joining the Mystic Lodge in Cedar Rapids.[50] As a Shriner, he remained a member of the Freemasons. His involvement with these fraternal organizations was one of the few positive things to happen to Graves at a time when his business ventures began to go sour.

Despite his many and varied business and farming interests, Graves chose to describe himself as a "banker" in the 1885 Census of Dow City.[51] As the decade wore on, however, tough times beset Abner Graves and his many businesses. By early 1886, there were reports that he and another Dow City man had "disposed" of some fine Angus cattle to "parties in Nebraska."[52] A history of Dow City, culled from the pages of the *Denison Review*, took note of the downturn:

The firm of Dow & Graves was the all-important one during the first decades of Dow City's history and the financial embarrassment of this firm brought with it distress to many others and was a blow to the prosperity of the entire western portion of the county. The deterioration of the firm's holdings came on

Abner Graves and beef cattle, Dow City, Iowa. He was a leading breeder and founder of the American Aberdeen Angus Breeders Association. Graves also had a variety of business interests in the western Iowa area. Used by permission of Claire Strashun.

gradually, and we find no record of the exact date the firm ceased to function, but deduce this occurred about 1890.[53]

Another history put it this way: "The year 1890 closed with disquieting rumors as to the solvency of the firm of Dow and Graves, a firm which had been the predominating influence in the western part of the county."[54]

Things were becoming bleak in Dow City for Graves and his father-in-law. Trouble apparently arose in a transaction that attracted unfavorable attention from the credit rating agency Bradstreet (later Dun and Bradstreet). Simeon Dow transferred property he owned to S.E. Dow & Co. (recently renamed from Dow & Graves), which had significant real estate holdings. Dow personally received $19,000 worth of stock in exchange.[55] According to later court pleadings, H.S. Green, a Bradstreet agent in Dow City, filed a report with his office in Des Moines saying that Dow had "transferred large blocks of real estate in such a way as to affect the mercantile credit and financial standing, and to cast suspicion on his honesty and integrity."[56] The agent, it was further claimed, filed another report with his Des Moines office stating that Dow's business had failed.

Longtime partners Dow and Graves were stung at the reports of bad credit and business failure, which they claimed were false and libelous. Jointly they filed a lawsuit against Bradstreet seeking $100,000 in damages. Their interests were still so closely linked that aspersions against one of them were seen as being against both. Their business continued to falter, however, and several years later, after finding little relief in the protracted litigation, Graves voluntarily declared bankruptcy to extricate himself from the mess.[57]

Concerned about his future, Graves pursued other interests. Yet again he showed a high degree of resiliency and willingness to tackle new challenges as he reached an age at which other men might have retired. He became first vice-president of the Mill Owners Mutual Fire Insurance Company of Iowa, based in the Masonic Temple in Des Moines.[58] Graves remained in Dow City as he helped run the company that offered insurance that was needed by mill owners, but who, because of the fire hazards they faced, could not obtain policies from mainstream carriers. Soon he moved to Des Moines where he worked for a firm that sold barbershop furniture, while staying in a boarding house. Not long afterward, he found a position with a company that distributed the recently invented rechargeable fire extinguisher.[59]

Simeon Dow and Abner Graves were not alone in their struggles as the 1890s dawned. In Dow City, a fire in June of 1891 destroyed the flour house at Dow City Mills and caused extensive property losses. Coupled with the collapse of Dow and Graves, things were looking grim locally and across Iowa as the economy was going sour. Improved farming methods combined with the vast new tracts of land now under cultivation led to overproduction and low prices that hit particularly hard in farm-belt areas like Iowa. At the same time, railroads had expanded beyond good business sense and those that weren't failing were forced to retrench. A collapse of the American economy in 1893 produced one of the country's worst recessions.

At the outset of the same year, Civil War General Abner Doubleday passed away at his home in New Jersey and was buried with honors in Arlington National Cemetery. The next year, as the depression deepened, Mark Twain, author of such popular books as *The Adventures of Tom Sawyer* and *The Adventures of Huckleberry Finn*, published his eighth and last novel, *The Tragedy of Pudd'n'head Wilson*. It had modest success. But his publishing house went broke and Twain, living in England to save money, was forced into bankruptcy.[60]

Graves turned sixty early in 1894 and decided yet again that his fortune lay in the west. His well-honed ability to adjust, recalibrate and reinvent himself would be put to the test in coming years as he left behind family and the bucolic expanses of Iowa where he had spent nearly 30 years. For reasons known only to him, Abner Graves picked Denver, Colorado, as his next stop.

# Three

## *A Letter from Denver*

When they first set eyes on Denver, Adam Enoch Ford and his sons, Arthur, 20, and Leon, 17, found a raw western city barely two decades old. The year was 1880 and the Canadian physician and his boys were anxious for a fresh start in a new city ten times the size of the conservative farm town they left nearly 1,500 miles behind. Most other arrivals were lured by the gold and silver that was being found in the nearby Rocky Mountains, making some of them rich. Others came for the good of their health, attracted by the clean, fresh air with which they hoped to fill their ravaged lungs. The Fords relocated to Denver, simply because it was a world away from the world they knew.

The discovery of gold had put Denver on the map that delineated the western reaches of what was then known as the Kansas Territory. During the summer of 1858, prospectors found flecks of the precious metal along the banks of the South Platte River, twelve miles east of the Rocky Mountains. Just nine years after the beginning of the California Gold Rush, this find triggered what became known as the "Pikes Peak or Bust" gold rush, named after the towering 14,000-foot landmark about seventy miles to the south.[1] As in California, a stampede of prospectors, adventurers and fortune-seekers swarmed into the region. Log cabins, tents, lean-tos and other shelters rose along the South Platte and Cherry Creek in the crude community named Denver City after just-resigned territorial governor James Denver.

Newcomers had barely settled in when gold was discovered in significant quantity near Central City in the mountains fifty miles to the west. A sudden exodus of humanity left the new settlement along the South Platte nearly deserted. The timing proved fortuitous, as prospectors were seeing the placer deposits at Denver begin to peter out.

It wasn't long, however, before many of the adventurers lured to Central City found the harsh weather and high elevations in the mountains too much to bear, and they returned to Denver. At 5,200 feet above sea level, Denver was anything but low country, but it enjoyed a relatively mild climate. The city at the edge of the plains grew into a bustling trade center for prospectors and it offered them plenty of diversions in its gambling dens, saloons and houses of ill-repute. Many of the adventurers opted to abandon a rugged life in the mountains for urban life.[2]

In its formative years, Denver struggled. During the Civil War, a Confederate regiment from Texas marched into Denver with its eye on gold, but a hastily assembled volunteer army fended off the rebels and kept the new Colorado Territory in the Union fold. Much of the small community's business district burned to the ground in 1863; the following year, a springtime flood of Cherry Creek killed eight residents and swept away many buildings. Then came an Indian war that cut off the struggling community's supply lines from the east, at one point leaving it with only a six-week supply of food. In 1865, however, good news came when the hard-luck town became capital of the new Colorado Territory. The early setbacks only served to stiffen the character of the residents of Denver, so much so that when the Union Pacific Railroad opted against crossing Colorado on its transcontinental route, residents fought back. They raised $300,000, which was combined with a $500,000 bond issue, to create the Denver Pacific Railroad to link with the Union Pacific line one hundred miles north in Cheyenne, Wyoming. The Denver Pacific opened in 1870, by which time Denver was approaching 5,000 inhabitants.[3]

Much of the 1860s saw economic stagnation for Denver, but by the 1870s, when three railroads were serving it, the community was transformed almost immediately. That decade saw the population soar by more than seven hundred percent to 35,629. As Denver historians Stephen J. Leonard and Thomas J. Noel put it: "Within a single generation, railroads transformed a pokey frontier crossroads into an industrialized regional metropolis. Without railroads, Denver would have withered, as did many other frontier towns. With their spiderweb of steel, Denverites began bragging that they had built the Queen City of the Plains."[4] The city had developed into an important hub for the mining and agricultural industries, for wholesale trade, food processing and manufacturing.

Denver's fortunes were also tied to a rich mining area two miles high and just over the continental divide to the west of the city. In 1859, gold was discovered in California Gulch, about sixty miles west of Denver. Within two years, more than 5,000 prospectors converged on the area and the settlement of Oro City came into being. After about $4 million worth of gold had been found, using the sluice-and-pan method, most of the placer deposits were exhausted. One mine opened in 1868, but by then most fortune-hunters had moved on to "golder" pastures. The settlement was largely deserted by the mid–1870s. Its fortunes changed in 1875, when a metallurgist discovered that the heavy clay that had jammed sluice boxes and infuriated gold prospectors was incredibly rich in silver content. When word leaked out, another rush was on, this time for silver. Thousands returned to the gulch and the town of Leadville came into being. The city was incorporated in 1878 and a year later it boasted a population of 18,000, half that of Denver.[5]

By 1880, silver production reached $11 million, hovering around $10 million annually for several more years. Early arrival Horace Tabor prospered by grubstaking prospectors and used his newfound riches to build the Tabor Opera House and Tabor Grand Hotel. Other fine buildings for business and solid Victorian homes quickly rose in the wealthy community. The surrounding mountains were dotted with mines and 24 smelters and reduction plants were in operation.[6]

Denver had developed a reputation as a rough-and-tumble frontier community, but Leadville was decidedly more Wild West. In Leadville, violence and prosperity had an uneasy co-existence. Gunplay was not unknown in the saloons of the community also known as Cloud City (because of the fluffy white neighbors scudding by the highest incorporated municipality in the United States).[7]

In 1878, gunslinger and gambler Doc Holliday came to town and found that the thin mountain air of the mining town provided some relief for his "consumption," a disease known today as tuberculosis. He made Leadville his headquarters for most of the rest of his life. Another notable gunman attracted to the area was outlaw Jesse James, who robbed stagecoaches. Unlike Holliday, James didn't stay around.

Holliday was called away to Tombstone, Arizona, in 1881 by his friend, lawman Wyatt Earp. While there, he took part in a fatal gunfight at the OK Corral, but a judge found insufficient evidence to try Holliday on murder charges. He returned to Leadville where he enjoyed acceptance and friends among community leaders, provided he abided by the law. But trouble again found him in 1884, when Holliday learned that a former policeman was pursuing him for an unpaid gambling debt and the two had a confrontation at the Monarch Saloon. The ailing gunfighter shot the debt collector as he strode in the front door, making the unarmed man the last of several victims of Holliday's deadly marksmanship. The shooting led to a charge of assault with intent to kill, but a Leadville jury acquitted the well-liked gunslinger, accepting his lawyer's argument that he feared for his life and was entitled to defend himself. As his health deteriorated, Holliday travelled to a spa at Glenwood Springs in 1887, where the altitude and natural springs were touted as particularly good cures for consumptives. Holliday died there in his bed at age 36, bringing to an unexpectedly peaceful end the life of a dentist who had traded in his tools for playing cards and a handgun.[8]

Leadville continued to boom and by the time of the devastating Silver Panic of 1893, it was approaching a population of 60,000 while Denver had grown to about 110,000 inhabitants. Doc Holliday was among many thousands attracted to Colorado in the years after the Civil War because of the state's growing reputation for healthy living conditions as a result of its clean, semi-arid air, abundant sunshine and mineral hot springs. Tuberculosis was the leading cause of death in the world during most of the nineteenth century and at the time was little understood. Many believed it to be genetic, or simply an ailment, not the contagious disease it was discovered to be early in the next century. The treatment of choice was to rebuild the patient's strength through fresh air, sunshine, rest and good food. Medical intervention was minimal.[9]

Colorado was promoted as a healthy place to live for anyone with lung disease or respiratory problems by railroad companies anxious to promote business, as well as by chambers of commerce, doctors and journalists. Even Governor Frank Pitkin got into the act, declaring: "We can almost bring a dead man to life." The pitches worked terrifically well and a large influx of immigrants poured into Colorado, seeking a cure in its sunshine. Sanitariums sprang up in Denver and in many towns that had rail service or hot springs, among them Colorado Springs, Manitou Springs, Clark Mineral Springs and Glenwood Springs (where Doc Holliday breathed his last). A sizable proportion of the early population of Colorado came to the state because of tuberculosis. In 1880, Dr. Samuel Edwin Solly of Colorado Springs, himself a sufferer, estimated that fully one-third of the state's population had been attracted by the promise of better health for them and their families. Already, by 1876, the state was described and promoted as "The World's Sanitarium."[10]

Adam Ford and his sons, Arthur and Leon, were seeking a new climate and a fresh start for personal reasons unconnected to the breathing problems plaguing other newcomers. Ford, 49, left behind his wife, Jane, and daughter, Julia, 22, in Canada. Ford had come from the Southern Ontario town of St. Marys, where he had established his practice and raised a family. Residents of the town weren't the least bit surprised he had left for greener pastures given the notoriety he had achieved there. Ford selected Denver to begin anew, picking that city for reasons unknown, but once there, he decided to stay. Many years later, shortly before he died, Ford described arriving in Denver and "my conclusion to stay here on account of the climate."[11]

Adam Ford had no family in the city other than the young men who accompanied him. Ford was a fan of baseball, having witnessed his first game as a boy in his hometown of Beachville, a few miles from St. Marys. He still played the game when he could. A raconteur, lover of sport, and public speaker, he was a man whose taste for liquor was easily satisfied in the saloon-town of Denver, where prospectors, speculators and others were never far from a watering hole. Ford and his sons found Denver to be a new world, far removed from the traditional farm and mill town of St. Marys, where the temperance movement was strong and lay at the root of his troubles there. When Ford and his sons left St. Marys, a town where he had once been mayor, it had a population of 3,400. The bustling, wide-open city of Denver, ten times the size of St. Marys, presented the Fords with all kinds of exciting new opportunities. Ford senior decided to continue his career in medicine and in July 1881, he was issued Colorado physician license number 261.[12]

Late that same year, Ford contacted his old minister back in St. Marys, asking him for a letter of recommendation that he hoped would open doors for him. The Rev. John Wakefield, now living in the Ontario city of Hamilton, complied. A minister in the Methodist Church of Canada, Wakefield provided these words for his congregant on church letterhead, dated October 11, 1881:

> Hearing that A. E. Ford M.D., is about to settle and practice medicine in the City of Denver Colorado, I have great pleasure in saying that I have known him as a physician for more than 25 years; that during my pastorate in the Town of St. Marys he was my family physician and a constant hearer of the word of God in the church of which I had charge. As a skillful and trusty physician I believe Dr. Ford has few equals, while as a man and a friend I have always found him reliable and trustworthy. I trust he may be as useful in the far west, as he has been for so many years in this land.[13]

Wakefield was obviously aware of the circumstances that led to Ford leaving St. Marys, which the minister described in an accompanying note intended for the doctor's eyes only, as "deep waters," and extended his sympathy to his old friend. In that same side note, Wakefield wrote that he couldn't close without "one or two plain words. I think that had you been more pronounced and constant in your religious life much pain and suffering might have been spared you." He suggested Ford would do well to rediscover his faith in the remaining years of his life.

Within months, Ford was attracting press attention for his medical skill. An account in the January 27, 1882, edition of the *Rocky Mountain News* of Denver related the story of a man named F. J. Lyster, whom Ford had attended. Lyster had been hurt when struck by the collapsing rear wall of a downtown building during a fire. His injury, the story said, "was looked upon at the time as certain to prove fatal, [but] has been followed by one of the most extraordinary cures on record." It continued:

> The wounds which Mr. Lyster received consisted in having a cut in his scalp eight inches in length, the scalp itself forced down over his right ear and a ten-penny nail driven over an inch deep into his forehead, besides being generally badly crushed, and bruised almost beyond recognition. The strangest part of it is that Mr. Lyster was walking the streets of Denver yesterday and feeling quite well. Dr. A.E. Ford, who attended the case, and who has wide experience, declares the case to be one of the most remarkable ever coming within his knowledge and other doctors who examined the injuries of Mr. Lyster fully agree with him. The doctor with characteristic modesty ascribes a large share of the credit of the cure as owing to the air of Colorado.[14]

Ford's medical career in Denver was off to a fine start. Less than two weeks later, Ford was again in the newspaper as part of a medical team that tended to a young man accidentally shot by his younger brother. William Warwick, aged 18, had been in an indoor shooting gallery downtown on Larimer Street practicing his shot with a rifle. Without warning, his older brother,

George, 21, entered by a side door near the target area and was promptly felled by a bullet to his forehead. A doctor named Newman appeared first on the scene and called upon doctors Ford, Cranston, and Clark to assist. Despite their ministrations, the victim passed away. The newspaper account extended sympathies to the dead man's family and noted that while a coroner's inquest was deemed unnecessary, the incident "should teach the authorities to see that every shooting gallery is so arranged as to offer as little danger as possible from similar accidents in the future."[15] Indeed.

That same year, 1882, Ford sat for a formal portrait by local photographer Harold S. Bellsmith. He also made his first appearance in the Denver city directory, listed as a surgeon at 450 Larimer Street, mere doors from the shooting gallery where young Warwick met his end. The following year, Ford had relocated to two rooms in the Steele Block building at the downtown corner of 16th and Stout streets. Son Arthur, now 23, was listed at the same address as a student.[16]

Ford's practice was proving successful and his abilities were attracting attention within the Denver medical community. Evidence of that was contained in yet another press account, this from the April 1, 1883, edition of the *Rocky Mountain News*, about a man killed in a street accident the previous day. A gentleman named John Murray had been in his carriage heading home from downtown about 11:30 A.M. when a runaway horse with a boy clinging to its back ran into Murray's horse, causing Murray's buggy to overturn and throwing him to the ground. A doctor named Bancroft was sent for, who in turn called in doctors Blickensdorfer, Ford, Edson and others, but the patient succumbed to a fractured skull.[17] Bancroft was Frederick J. Bancroft, the pre-eminent physician in Denver, if not all of Colorado. A giant of a man at six-foot-four-inches tall and weighing about three hundred and fifty pounds, Bancroft had arrived in Denver in 1866 after serving as a Union Army surgeon during the Civil War. In the Mile High City, he quickly established a private practice and became Denver's most prominent physician. Bancroft was hired by the new railroads that arrived in town and was named Denver city physician. Elected president of the Denver and Colorado medical societies, Bancroft also became active in public health and was a member of the faculty of Colorado's first medical school when it opened in 1881.[18] Bancroft, like many of his colleagues of the day, also touted the health benefits of the Colorado climate. For Ford to be called upon by a medical man of Bancroft's stature in a tough case was a sign of the respect earned by the newly arrived Canadian doctor.

Leon Nelson Ford and Arthur Beecher Ford, his sons, had different interests and personalities. Leon, three years younger than Arthur, was more independent-minded and liked the outdoors. He immediately took to prospecting and was forever trying to make a big strike at camps in Colorado, Nevada, California and Mexico. While Arthur seldom strayed far from his father, Leon was often on the road, living in his father's household for only part of the

1880s.[19] Like many others who picked up their knowledge about mining in the field, he began calling himself a mining engineer. In later years, Leon claimed to have been a graduate of the Colorado School of Mines, as well as of McGill and Queen's universities in Canada, but those claims were all bogus.[20] He wasn't unlike many self-promoters at a time when it wasn't easy to check into backgrounds and qualifications. In later life, Leon claimed to have worked at mines as far afield as Korea and Japan. Some proof of the latter assertion came from a newspaper account from 1897 describing his arrival by ship in Tacoma from Yokohama, Japan, bound for the Klondike.[21] In May of that year, he sent a letter to his sister Julia from Kagoshima, at the southern tip of Japan, in

which he discussed mining operations there.[22] Over the years, Leon kept Julia and his mother back home in St. Marys posted about his various mining exploits in California. At one point he was in New Orleans and he also joined the hunt for oil in Texas. His letters to Canada were sometimes on letterhead of L.N. Ford and Company, Engineers and Contractors and he always expressed optimism that success lay just around the corner.[23]

Arthur Ford took a different path. More bookish than his younger brother, Arthur studied law for a few months in 1878 in Ontario and years later described himself as a lawyer.[24] He also claimed to be a graduate of Yale University, although he never even attended Yale.[25] Arthur stayed close to his father and, like Leon,

Formal portrait of Dr. Adam Ford in 1881, shortly after he moved to Denver, Colorado. A baseball fan, he was also active in curling and cricket. Courtesy St. Marys Museum, St. Marys, Ontario.

never married. Arthur and his father shared a strong interest in sports and was quite an athlete. He played the Scottish sport of curling in which Adam had excelled in Canada. In 1881, father and son curled on a sheet of ice they found along Cherry Creek at the outskirts of the city, thereby laying claim to the first match played west of the Missouri River.[26] Arthur was an accomplished runner and he enjoyed baseball as much as his father. Like his brother and other young men in Denver, Arthur was attracted to the excitement of the booming frontier town of Leadville and moved there for a brief time, although he had little interest in the dirty job of prospecting. His thin good looks and sharp mind stood out in Leadville and in 1882 he sat for a formal portrait by photographer Alfred Brisbois, another newcomer to town. Most likely Arthur held clerical jobs, based on the sorts of positions he held later in Denver. At one point in 1882, he appeared in a Denver social column, which reported: "Mr. Arthur Ford, a pleasant and very intelligent young gentleman of Leadville, is in the city."[27]

Arthur moved back and forth between Leadville and Denver, taking on a student-of-law position with a Denver law firm for a brief time. All the while, he participated in footraces, a popular diversion of the day upon which spectators wagered. His successes began to draw newspaper attention as early as 1883, as revealed in this account:

Arthur Ford portrait photo in Leadville, Colorado, circa 1882. The eldest son of Adam Ford was an accomplished sprinter who also played baseball. He worked for a time in Leadville, the booming mining town west of Denver, but for most of the time he lived with his father in Denver. Courtesy St. Marys Museum, St. Marys, Ontario.

> A 100 yards race took place at the fair grounds yesterday afternoon between Arthur B. Ford, a Canadian runner, now studying law in the office of Browne and Putnam, and W.J. Hawksworth, of Denver. There were nearly two hundred people present as spectators. The race was won by Hawksworth; time 10½ seconds. Ford was beaten by four feet. Hawksworth now wants to run him at a distance of 300 yards for from $100 to $500 a side.[28]

One has to wonder about the accuracy of the measuring stick for the distance—or the accuracy of the timepiece. That is a very good time for a sprint of one hundred yards. A month later, the same newspaper reported that Ford and Hawksworth were planning to race at a distance of about seven hundred feet in early August.[29] But no account of that race can be found.

Participating in footraces was an interesting endeavor, and as proud as Adam Ford was of his son, he hoped Arthur would land a good job with some sort of future. Late in 1885, the concerned father wrote directly to Sir John A. Macdonald, the prime minister of Canada, seeking a job for Arthur, or perhaps Leon, in the civil service. It is not known how the doctor now living in Denver came to write the leader of Canada. They shared an interest in strong drink, but beyond that, any connection between the two men is only guesswork. Perhaps there was no connection at all, and Ford, demonstrating considerable nerve, contacted Macdonald out of the blue. Regardless, the reply from Joseph Pope, Macdonald's private secretary, dated December 5, 1885, was cordial and encouraging. Pope said he was replying to Ford at the request of Macdonald, who was "glad to employ one of your sons in the Public Service at Ottawa as you ask." But Pope noted Parliament had recently enacted a requirement that those seeking federal government employment must pass a special examination and obtain a certificate before being considered:

> By Sir John's directions, papers explanatory of the examination will be sent to you. One of your sons can then prepare himself for the next examinations which I think are not till next May. After having done this, he might come to Ottawa, say a month before the examination comes on, during which period Sir John would endeavor to find him temporary employment to pay his expenses. Of course it is understood he must commence at the foot of the ladder.[30]

It is doubtful that either Arthur or Leon made the long trip to Ottawa to take the civil service examination. Given the fact that the examination would have coincided with the beginning of the baseball season, Arthur, in particular, might have been inclined not to leave town for fear of missing any opportunity a game might provide.

Interest in baseball in the Denver area was growing in the 1880s and in April 1886, the Western League was created, consisting of teams from Denver; Leadville; Lincoln, Nebraska; Topeka and Leavenworth in Kansas; and St. Joseph, Missouri. The inaugural season was to run from May 5 to September 19.[31] Given their interest in the sport, it is more than likely that Adam Ford and his son Leon, who was back in town, were in the stands rooting for the Denvers on opening day. Arthur, however, was even more committed than any fan because he was playing professional baseball. An intriguing but brief item in the *St. Joseph* (Missouri) *Daily Gazette* on June 8 stated: "It is said that Arthur Ford, son of Dr. Ford of Denver, who has been playing as substitute in the Cincinnati nine, and a promising young catcher named Lancier, have been signed by the Denvers and are to join the club in Denver on Monday. The question is, who is to go?"[32]

The snippet, part of a roundup of baseball happenings in the National and Western leagues and the American Association, revealed that Arthur Ford, the man of blazing foot speed, was a backup player for the Cincinnati Reds. The Reds had finished second in the American Association pennant race the previous year, but a rash of injuries early in the 1886 season left them struggling in seventh spot in the eight-team league by early June. The *Cincinnati Enquirer* ripped the team for its poor performance. When an *Enquirer* reporter was barred from the ballpark in retaliation, the paper fought back. It claimed to have obtained affidavits from two private detectives stating that Tony Mullane, one of the pitchers, had counseled them to bet against the Reds in a game played in Brooklyn and that five Cincinnati players had "thrown" the game. The allegation was widely reported, including in *Sporting Life* under the headline, "A Sensation. Ball Players Charged With Selling Out."[33] On June 30, however, Mullane was exonerated of any wrongdoing when the paper failed to produce its "evidence."[34] It was a good thing for Arthur Ford that he left Cincinnati when he did.

After joining Denver, the younger Ford continued to draw news coverage. However, with his new team leading the Western League most of the attention concerned his footspeed. The *Denver News* had three accounts that mentioned the ballplayer/sprinter. On July 3, it reported:

Leon Ford in mining country in the American west, 1880s. Leon, Adam Ford's younger son, was often on the road and his letters home invariably spoke about his hunt for riches and how his next big strike was around the corner. His involvement in the mining industry may have seen him cross paths with mining engineer Abner Graves. Courtesy St. Marys Museum, St. Marys, Ontario.

Monday it is expected an exhibition game will be played between Denver and Leavenworth. As both clubs intend going in the grand [Fourth of July] parade at 4 o'clock, game will be called at 1:30. Before the game, commencing at 1 o'clock, a series of races will take place. The first race will be between Hall of Leavenworth and Ford of Denver, for a purse of $100, distance 100 yards. After that race O'Brien will run any man, Hall and Ford barred, in either of the teams, for love or money, the latter preferred.[35]

On July 18, another item related Ford's on-field encounter with Cap Anson, the captain and manager of the Chicago White Stockings, one of the superstars of the game:

Ford, who will run the bases against time this afternoon, is greatly underestimated in regard to his speed. While in Cincinnati recently, he and his backer went to Captain Anson, of the Chicagos, and offered to run [Billy] Sunday or any other player he desired to put up against him but Anson refused to back any member of his club against Ford. Ford is ready at any time to run any base ball player in the country.[36]

The very next day, came a report of Ford running the bases:

Between the fifth and sixth innings, Arthur Ford, of this city, ran the bases, against the record of 15 seconds, which is told to be the best and to have been made by [George] Gore, of Chicago. Captain J.T. Smith and Ed Gaylord acted as timers and credited Ford with 14¼ seconds.[37]

Again, given the timing recorded, one is left wondering about the accuracy of whatever timepiece was used. That sort of speed would be good in a straight line but if achieved while rounding the bases, it was nothing short of amazing.

Ford may have abandoned racing around the diamonds after the 1886 season, because the following August he was a key member of a firefighting team from Leadville that participated in a series of races among hook-and-ladder teams from across Colorado and beyond. Friendly competitions among all-volunteer hose teams were common events during Fourth of July and other celebrations at the time. Oftentimes, humans replaced horses to pull water wagons and hose carts. The Fireman's Tournament, held in Leadville that year, drew as many as 30,000 spectators and heavy betting. The team led by Ford did well and a Leadville alderman was reported to have won every bet he placed on the local crew.[38]

Avid sportsman Adam Ford would have been present for many of his son's exploits, but he had to rely on newspapers when Arthur travelled east to places far away like Cincinnati. For fans of baseball, reading about the game had become much easier with the arrival of *Sporting Life*. In 1883, journalist Francis Richter established the publication in Philadelphia. The weekly magazine was focused on stories from the world of sport, with a strong emphasis on baseball. Under Richter's leadership, it soon became the mouthpiece of the national game. *Sporting Life* found a niche at a time when newspapers generally lumped the coverage of sports, including baseball, into its news pages. By the end of 1886, circulation had climbed to 40,000.[39] The same year, a competitor, *Sporting News*, was launched, but *Sporting Life* ruled the roost. As an amateur player in his youth, Richter wanted to promote and elevate baseball, something he had done as an editor and writer for daily newspapers in Philadelphia.

Ford, an avid newspaper reader, would have enjoyed *Sporting Life's* accounts of games, records, and league decisions. Of particular interest for him were stories about the formation of the Western League and about prospects for the Denver entry. As a Canadian, he might have noted a report from the February 3, 1886, issue in which it was reported that Al Spalding, owner of the Chicago White Stockings, had urged directors of the Toronto Base Ball

Club, poised to join the new International League, to apply for admission to the National League. Spalding, it noted, during his visit to Toronto, was "promising to give the application his earnest support."[40]

*Sporting Life* also included stories about the early days of baseball. Among the reminiscences of games from years ago were those of Tim Murnane, a former player and manager in Boston who was beginning a new career as a sportswriter. In the issue of March 24, 1886, Murnane penned a lengthy article in which he compared the game as played in the 1885 season to the game played ten years earlier. He noted that he did so because "the youngsters now growing up have a poor opinion of their predecessors of ten years ago." Murnane named players still making a contribution to the game after a decade, beginning with Cap Anson of Chicago, "the greatest captain who ever led a club through a base ball campaign.... Anson has held his own amongst the new comers, and as a batsman has no equal." A big change, he conceded, was in pitching, which "is much harder to hit [in 1885] than old style pitching." Murnane explained that improvements had come in the use of gloves for the catcher and first baseman, introduction of the catcher's mask, the use of signs, and improved discipline and team management. The increased dominance of the pitcher, he concluded, left "two men doing all the work," and had reduced the chance of "brilliant" fielding and lively base running. "Looking the case all over," he summed up, "we are of the opinion that the boys played just as good ball in 1875 as they did in 1885."[41]

That spring, as Arthur Ford was having talks with the Cincinnati baseball club about a potential role, it is not unreasonable to think his father was scanning the pages of *Sporting Life* very closely. Soon after the appearance of the article by Murnane, Ford himself took pen in hand to produce his own account about a game of long ago. In a letter dated April 26, the 54-year-old Ford provided an account totaling 1,186 words about a game of baseball he said he had witnessed as a boy in his hometown of Beachville, in what was then known as the British colony of Upper Canada, today known as Ontario:

> Editor Sporting Life—The 4th of June, 1838, was a holiday in Canada, for the Rebellion of 1837 had been closed by the victory of the Government over the rebels, and the birthday of His Majesty George the Fourth was set apart for general rejoicing. The chief event at the village of Beechville [sic], in the county of Oxford, was a base ball match between the Beechville [sic] Club and the Zorras a club hailing from the townships of Zorra and North Oxford.
>
> The game was played in a nice, smooth pasture field just back of Enoch Burdick's shops. I well remember a company of Scotch volunteers from Zorra halting as they passed the grounds to take a look at the game.

Ford went on to name about dozen players from both teams.

> Were it not for taking up too much of your valuable space I could give you the names of many others who were there and incidents to confirm the accuracy of

Cooperstown, New York, and Beachville, Ontario (formerly Upper Canada), are separated by a border and about 350 miles of farm country. Many settlers from the British Isles paused in New England, New York and Pennsylvania before continuing west, pursuing cheap land in what became Canada. Author's collection.

the day and the game. The ball was made of double and twisted woolen yarn, a little smaller than the regulation ball of to day and covered with good, honest calf skin, sewed with waxed ends by Edward McNamee, a shoemaker.

The infield was a square, the base lines of which were twenty-one yards long, on which were placed five bags, thus:

At this point, he included a drawing that showed a "thrower" and "catcher" at one corner of the square, configured in such a way as to resemble a crude diamond, if turned on an angle. It depicted a first, second, third, fourth and home "bye," with the first and home "byes" separated by a few yards. The only dimensions specified on the drawing were the twenty-one yards indicated between the second and third and between the third and fourth byes. Ford's account continued:

The distance from the thrower to the catcher was eighteen yards; the catcher standing three yards behind the home bye. From the home bye, or "knocker's" stone, to the first bye was six yards. The club (we had bats in cricket but we never used bats in playing base ball) was generally made of the best cedar, blocked out with an ax and finished on a shaving horse with a drawing knife. A wagon spoke, or any nice straight stick would do.

Ford went on to describe some of the rules, noting that there were "fair and unfair balls," the former being "one thrown to the knocker at any height between the bend of his knee and the top of his head, near enough to him to be fairly within reach." He reported that the pitcher would try to throw "near his elbow or between his club and his ear." When a ball was struck, it constituted a strike. After three strikes, and misses, the batter was out "if the ball was caught [by the catcher, presumably] every time either on the fly or on the first bound. If he struck at the ball and it was not so caught by the catcher that strike did not count."

He added that the striker had to run if the ball was hit within the square, but anything outside it was a "no hit."

> There was no rule to compel a man to strike at a ball except the rule of honor, but a man would be despised and guyed unmercifully if he would not hit at a fair ball. If the knocker hit a ball anywhere he was out if the ball was caught either before it struck the ground or on the first bound.

Ford also noted that a base runner was out "if hit by the ball when he was off of his bye," a reference to the long-established practice of "soaking" or "plugging" runners. (A similar reference was deleted by A.G. Mills from the Cooperstown game described many years later by Abner Graves in another letter.)

After three men were called out, Ford reported the side was retired and when both sides were retired it constituted a complete inning. The number of innings, according to Ford, "was always a matter of agreement," usually from five to nine, and most often seven. He observed that a couple of old-timers recalled games in earlier days that lasted until the first team reached either 18 or 21 runs. He recalled that there was no set number of players, but mutual agreement generally produced from seven to twelve players aside:

> The object in having the first bye so near the home was to get runners on the base lines, so as to have the fun of putting them out or enjoying the mistakes of the fielders when some fleet-footed fellow would dodge the ball and come home. When I got older I played myself, for the game never died out.

The doctor recollected coming home from university one time and finding that several residents of the village were talking about a game played "down at or near New York" involving a "pitcher," "fouls," and a hard ball that contained India rubber. "You could knock it so far that the fielders would be chasing it yet, like dogs hunting sheep, after you had gone clear around and scored your tally," he wrote. Ford reported that not long after hearing about that game, he and some friends tried to play it that way. "The next day we felt as if we had been on an overland trip to the moon," he said. He then related another anecdote from Beachville and concluded: "I have played from that day to this, and I don't intend to quit as long as there is another boy on the ground. Yours, Dr. Ford."[42]

There it was. A lengthy account of a game from 1838 that the *Sporting Life* headline writer felt "closely resembled" the game being played in 1886. This letter from Denver had some similarities to a letter penned nineteen years later by another man from Denver. There was one significant difference: once Ford's story appeared, it was promptly forgotten.

# Four

## *The Doctor Moves On*

Who was Adam Ford? What prompted him to move to Denver, where he wrote a letter about a baseball game he witnessed as a young boy? As with Abner Graves, learning more about the man may shed some light on him and his motives. Unlike Abner Graves, however, Ford has not been subjected to ridicule or dismissed as a crank. Being ignored had some benefits.

Ford's life was similar in many ways to his fellow Denverite, the mining engineer, who put pen to paper and achieved baseball immortality. Both men clearly loved the game and they liked speaking and writing about it.

Adam Enoch Ford was born on August 26, 1831, on his father's farm in Zorra Township, Oxford County, in the British colony of Upper Canada, today known as Ontario. He was the last born of eleven children of Robert and Ann Ford. His father, a Protestant, had been born in 1779 in Enniskillen, Fermanagh County, one of the northern counties of Ireland. As a young man, Robert Ford was compelled to take up arms to help put down Catholic rebels during the "troubles" of 1798. Five years later, he sailed for America, settling in Pennsylvania where, in 1810, he met and married Ann Nelson, a native of the same county back in Ireland. Four daughters were born in quick succession: Elizabeth in 1812, Mary Ann in 1813, Catherine in 1814, and Priscilla in 1816. The Fords, who were farmers, opted to leave the new republic and join thousands of others attracted by the prospect of cheap farmland in the British colony to the north. Upper Canada had survived repeated American invasions during the War of 1812 and was actively recruiting settlers. The Fords settled first in York (later renamed Toronto) and then moved about one hundred miles west to Oxford County, settling on a farm near the tiny community of Beachville.[1]

Once again subjects of the British Crown, the Fords continued to expand their family. Rhoda was born in 1821, then Margaret in 1822, William in 1825, Robert and John Wesley in 1826, Lucinda in 1830, and, finally, Adam in 1831. Aside from toiling to feed so many mouths, Robert Ford was active in the Wesleyan Methodists and was known for his kindness in opening his doors to accommodate visiting ministers.[2] The Ford farm was just a few miles north-

47

west of Beachville, a crossroads hamlet that was the center for social activities often accompanied by baseball games. It was during a Militia Day muster that the game was played that Adam Ford wrote about witnessing during the summer he turned seven. Many of the settlers in the district had been born in the British Isles and lived for a time in New England, New York or Pennsylvania before deciding for reasons of lingering loyalty to the British Crown or, more pragmatically, the lure of inexpensive land in the colony. Some were even the product of happenstance having headed westward to Michigan, Wisconsin, Minnesota and Illinois only to like what they saw on their shortcut through the colony and decide to stay. The influx of American settlers transformed Upper Canada and by 1812, about sixty percent of the 75,000 colonists were known as "late loyalists," to distinguish them from the British loyalists who had fled the new American republic following the Revolution of 1776. Their continued immigration after the War of 1812 brought libertarian notions and political sentiments that helped fuel the failed Rebellion of 1837 against the colonial administration.[3]

Among the early settlers of Beachville was Lauriston Cruttenden, who had been born in Poultney, Vermont, in 1804. He established a general store on a main road linking the larger communities of Woodstock and London. It soon prospered, becoming a resting place, post office, and supplier of a wide range of goods. In about 1830, the successful young merchant married Permelia Dodge, one of five children of Daniel Dodge, a United Empire Loyalist, who had relocated with his family from New York state shortly before the hostilities of 1812–1814. There were soon six Cruttenden children to feed: Elizabeth born in 1831, Henry in 1833, Adelaide in 1835, Elsie Jane in 1840, Charles in 1842, and Alice in 1845.[4]

Cruttenden was imbued with a strong entrepreneurial spirit and was immediately interested when another man told him about new lands being offered for sale in newly surveyed Blanshard Township, to the northwest in neighboring Perth County. In September of 1841, Cruttenden made the thirty-mile trek along a trail blazed in the thick forest to a spot on the Thames River at its confluence with Trout Creek. The place was known as "Little Falls" because of the way the fast-flowing Thames tumbled about eight feet over a series of ledges along its limestone river bed. Two years later, Cruttenden, having purchased a number of lots in the new community now known as St. Marys, opened a general store on Queen Street. He had a knack for spotting opportunities to serve newcomers and St. Marys became a new focus for him while his family remained in Beachville with his original store. Cruttenden built a hotel in the new settlement at the falls and with a partner erected two flour mills, acquired a planing mill with another partner and established a general contracting business.[5] The presence of high quality local limestone saw many of the fine new buildings in the village built of the quarried stone and the distinctive appearance of the community soon earned it the nickname "Stonetown." By the time it was incorporated as a village in 1855, the population stood at 2,500.

The next year, Cruttenden moved his family to St. Marys and into a fine salmon-pink brick home he built for them on Ontario Street. Perched on a west-end hill, it provided a fine view of the river valley and the bustling little town the pioneer had done so much to get established. The Grand Trunk Railway arrived in 1857 and by the end of the decade the community's major industries of flour milling and limestone quarrying were flourishing.[6]

It was to the picturesque village along the Thames that Adam Ford was drawn after he graduated in medicine from Victoria College, Cobourg, Ontario, in 1855.[7] His brother William had settled there in 1845 and another brother, John, had also decided to relocate to St. Marys.

Ford liked the prospects of the community where he estab-

A portrait of Adam Ford as a young man in Canada. A family doctor and rising politician, he became mayor of St. Marys in 1877. Like Abner Graves in Iowa, he married the daughter of a town pioneer and played a key role in local affairs. Courtesy St. Marys Museum, St. Marys, Ontario.

lished his practice, becoming one of its first doctors. He chose an office in a fine stone building at the main intersection of Queen and Water streets and immediately threw himself into village affairs. One of Adam Ford's early interests in the community was the Mechanics' Institute, an organization dedicated to promoting wide public access to books and to knowledge, a forerunner of the public library. He and his brother William were among the earliest executive members of the institute. To promote the organization, on April 24, 1857, Adam Ford delivered a lecture about chemistry that was well received by a large audience. A reporter from the *Argus* newspaper was present and noted that the well-spoken doctor illustrated his subject with a series of experiments that "made clear the mighty labyrinth of nature.... Judging from the applause which was from time to time bestowed upon the learned lecturer, we would say that his remarks received the mental approbation of all."[8]

The slim bachelor had noticed the fine-looking Cruttenden girls upon

Adam Ford with sons Arthur and Leon in St. Marys, Ontario. When he left St. Marys for a new life in Denver, he took his sons with him. Courtesy St. Marys Museum, St. Marys, Ontario.

their arrival in town and, after an initial interest in an older sister, he turned his attention to Elsie Jane. The dark-haired girl, most often known as Jane, was about to turn seventeen, making her eight years younger than Ford. A whirlwind courtship ensued and on May 28, 1857, two weeks after his chemistry lecture, Adam and Jane were married at her family home on Ontario Street. The couple took up residence in a Regency-style cottage just around the corner at 157 Queen Street West.[9] It was built for them by the bride's father on land he owned. The young doctor was a rising star in the village, his prospects having improved as a son-in-law to one of pillars of the community. Three weeks after his marriage, Ford was best man for his friend Leon Clench, another native of Beachville. Clench, a lawyer had joined the migration to St. Marys, where he married Jane's older sister, Eunice.[10]

Ford was a man of boundless energy and he poured himself into local affairs as he and Jane began a family, starting with Julia in 1858. Arthur was born in 1860 and Leon in 1863, the latter's birth leaving Jane in frail health and unable to have more children.[11] Aside from his continued work with the Mechanics' Institute, Ford became associated with a number of other social and sporting activities. He and his friend Clench organized the St. Marys Brass Band, for which Clench acted as conductor. The pair spearheaded the first fundraising event for the Mechanics' Institute in late 1861, which featured the brass band and Ford as a soloist, singing "Dixie." Ford then performed in a duet with Clench, another with his brother John, then with Clench in a trio and in the quartet that ended the night with "God Save the Queen."[12]

Ford chaired the May 24th celebrations in town in 1864, an event that featured special community and sporting events. St. Marys, like other communities in the colony that had been known as Canada West since 1841, marked that date to honor Queen Victoria. Ford was a member of the board of directors of the St. Marys Driving Park Association, a post he held for five years. He sat on the managing committee of the local lacrosse club and, if that wasn't enough, he also played cricket. Ford had curled as a boy and he promoted the sport in St. Marys. In 1874, he became president of the St. Marys Curling Club and was instrumental in forming the Ontario Curling Association in 1874–75.[13] He drew attention to St. Marys in 1877 when his rink competed against large cities such as Montreal, Quebec City, Kingston and Ottawa for Lord Dufferin's gold medal in Ottawa.[14]

Ford's longest association with any sport, however, was with baseball. He played it as a boy and well into later life. Baseball clubs had spread across the colony in the 1850s and 1860s, although reports of games seldom made it into the newspapers of the day.

In 1854, the first formal baseball club was organized in Canada. The Hamilton Maple Leaf Club was established in Hamilton, about forty-five miles west of Toronto at the western end of Lake Ontario. It copied the form

The office of Adam Ford was in the fine Hutton Block building in downtown St. Marys. It is here that he administered poison to a drinking friend, the secretary of a newly established temperance society. The resulting scandal saw Ford flee the town in disgrace. Courtesy St. Marys Museum, St. Marys, Ontario.

of organization of the New York Knickerbockers, by electing an executive, imposing annual dues and establishing a home playing field.[15] In London, a newly incorporated city of 10,000, some eighty miles to the west of Hamilton, the first city directory in 1856 recorded the existence of the London Base Ball Club, headed by dry goods merchant J. K. Brown with Dr. J. Wilkinson as vice-president. The entry noted that the club "consists of 22 members, and days of practice are Tuesday and Thursday in the evening, at the Military Reserve."[16]

The first intercommunity game in Canada using the New York rules was played in 1859 when the Hamilton Young American and the Toronto Young Canadian clubs met. The arrival of railways in the 1850s ended community isolation in the colony and brought greater opportunities for competition and a need for standardized rules. The New York rules came to prevail because of cross-border competition that developed.[17] By 1860, baseball clubs were operating in communities near St. Marys, such as Beachville, Woodstock and Ingersoll, and farther afield in Stratford, Guelph and Dundas.[18]

In St. Marys, Ford was a key figure in club baseball and in 1876 was elected president of both the St. Marys Young Actives, an organization for youth in the community, and of the Beaver Base Ball Club, the town's senior

The home of Adam Ford on Queen Street in St. Marys, Ontario. Built in 1857, it still stands today. Ford left his wife and daughter behind there in 1880 when he and his two sons moved to Denver, Colorado. Author's collection.

baseball organization. His position as director of the Driving Park Association proved to be beneficial. The fifty-member Beaver Club was able to use the large infield of the driving park for its practices and for games because organizers could control admission and charge fees at the fenced-in horse track.[19] That same year, 1876, the *Argus* observed that baseball fever had gripped St. Marys, with seemingly everyone playing the game: "We doubt very much if even the snow will stop the devotees of this game next winter, so great a hold does it seem to have got upon this community."[20]

A likeable and social creature, Ford was also active in local politics. He was nominated for a seat on the St. Marys council as early as 1857, but he declined to let his name stand. In 1864, he was elected to council, representing the West Ward. The same year, St. Marys was incorporated as a town. Two years earlier, his father-in-law, Lauriston Cruttenden had been named municipal clerk, a position he held until he retired in 1879 at age 75. Meanwhile, Ford's brother-in-law and friend Leon Clench became town solicitor and Ford's older brother William served as tax collector and assessor. Adam Ford served on council again in 1869 and a year later told the press that he had decided against standing for mayor despite some pressure to do so.[21] The pioneer Cruttenden and his relatives exercised considerable power in the young town. The arrangement was not unlike one nearly a thousand miles west in Dow City, Iowa, where baseball fan, player and coach Abner Graves had married the daughter of the founding father of the community and he and his father-in-law held prominent positions in local government. Ford was known to discuss sport and politics late into the night at his downtown office, liquor always present to make good stories even better.[22]

The well-regarded doctor made an appearance before town council in late 1876, reporting on the death of Sarah Box, wife of mayor Richard Box, who had succumbed to smallpox. There had been some concerns that the disease might have spread and the council had heard reports that her coffin hadn't been sealed properly, so it ordered her burial to take place after 9 P.M., her home to be fumigated and the bedding burned. Ford assured the council that everything had been sealed properly and council then relaxed the decree and permitted her burial to proceed as planned.[23]

A taste for politics had returned for the busy doctor and he began mulling over a return to the political arena. He put his name forward for the post of mayor in late December for the 1877 term. The doctor, sportsman and community activist found he had the field to himself and the *Argus* wrote approvingly of his candidacy:

> For mayor, there are no names mentioned to oppose Dr. Ford, and we doubt not but that gentleman will be returned by acclamation. The doctor will no doubt fill that position with credit to himself and benefit to the town. He has served a good apprenticeship at the council board and is thoroughly tested in municipal matters, having been chairman of every important committee while in that body. We have an idea, too, that if elected he would be enabled to get that station of ours removed to a more convenient point. [This was a reference to the 1858 erection of the Grand Trunk Railway station at St. Marys Junction at the extreme northeast corner of the town, a situation which continued to inconvenience and annoy locals who wanted a station downtown.] If, as mayor, he could only do that, he would be entitled to the everlasting gratitude of every resident of St. Marys. The feeling generally is to elect the doctor without opposition....[24]

At the outset of January, Ford was acclaimed mayor for 1877. He might have expected a fairly smooth term on the ten-member council because several family members were in positions of support: father-in-law Lauriston Cruttenden was still clerk; brother W.N. Ford remained as assessor while friend and brother-in-law Leon Clench was town solicitor. But subsequent events would prove otherwise.

Also elected to the council for the 1877 term was another medical doctor, Thomas F. Guest. Dr. Guest was a son of Thomas B. Guest, the first reeve of the village of St. Marys and also first mayor after it achieved town status in 1864. The father and son were partners in several businesses, including Guest's Bank, housed in the fine new Guest Building downtown. In time, the father and son and yet another Guest would create turbulence for Adam Ford.

Council met in regular session on the second Monday of every month and, after the inaugural session in January, Ford and council got down to business. One of the first initiatives was to authorize a delegation headed by the new mayor that would meet with representatives of the Grand Trunk Railway to discuss relocating the train station.[25] At the April 9 meeting, Thomas F. Guest suddenly resigned, to be replaced on council by his father. The older Guest, now 60, had been mayor in 1864 during Ford's first term on council, so they were well known to each other. The minute books don't shed light on what may have prompted the 27-year-old Guest to step down. It may be that he and Ford, 45, had crossed swords on medical or political matters or perhaps Guest resented not being included in the popular late-night bull sessions at Ford's office over drinks.

Shortly after joining council, the older Guest made some waves. During a June 11 council session, when Ford was absent, Guest took the chair and persuaded council to appoint three members of council "to ascertain if William Box, [tax] collector has received or retained in his hands more of the municipal funds than he is entitled to."[26] Ford had acted as an advocate for the Box family on the burial issue and was likely annoyed when the honesty of the municipal tax collector was impugned in his absence. A second council meeting was convened on June 27 with Thomas B. Guest again in the chair. No further report appeared in the minute book concerning the tax collector at that time, but minutes from meetings later in the year suggest that he must have withstood any examination that was conducted, because he continued in his $200-a-year post.

Two days before that June 27 meeting, Dr. Thomas F. Guest, the short-lived councilor, and his brother Alfred angrily confronted Ford on the street in downtown St. Marys. The Guest brothers were charged with assault and the case was brought to court immediately, as was the practice of the day. Thomas B. Guest represented his sons before magistrates Richard Box (the former mayor) and Milner Harrison, a frequent member of town council over the years. Ford was sworn in and described the confrontation that the *Argus* reported this way:

> After taking my breakfast on the 25th inst., [of this month] was proceeding about nine o'clock to my office, when opposite the Registry office saw Dr. and Alfred Guest coming to meet me; they appeared very much excited; by what I had heard had reason to believe they were coming to attack me; in order to see whether it was so or not I went out on the road; they both immediately crossed over the road to head me off; having a lame hand I carried it in my breast; I presume Dr. Guest thought I had a revolver; he [Dr. Guest] said I have a revolver too; we have come to have satisfaction out of you; Alfred Guest, with various oaths, also said we are going to have it out with you; believe from what I saw that Dr. Guest had hold of the handle of a pistol; I still kept my hand in my breast; they both kept together; they followed me up; Dr. Guest said he could shoot as well as me and would blow my brains out, and also said you hit

my brother the other night when he was drunk and I will take satisfaction out of you; he [the doctor] then said "Go for him, Alfred and I'll see that you do it; I retreated; they started to run after me and pursued me; I told them there was a law for them as well as the poor man; I also told them I would not fight with blackguards in the street, but would give them the benefit of the law or words to that effect; both used a lot of low villainous language, asserting they would have it out of me if it was for ten years to come; I went in search of the constable, when I returned they were gone.[27]

Had Ford's brains been blown out by the Guest brothers that day, he never would have lived to tell his story about witnessing that baseball game in Beachville. It was another near-death experience for a man who would go on to write about baseball, although a bit less dramatic than the episode of Abner Graves defending his bank in Dow City.

In questioning by Thomas B. Guest, Ford confessed that he had felt fearful for his safety, expecting "blows from one and pistol wounds from the other." He added: "I consider one young man as bad as the other; had some idea my life was of some use yet," explaining why he fled.

The magistrates heard several witnesses to the confrontation who testified that they overheard accusations and who largely confirmed Ford's version of events. They included Ford's brother John, past whose house Ford had walked that morning. The Guest brothers did not testify, relying on their father to make submissions on their behalf. At the end of the trial, Thomas F. Guest was convicted of assault and fined five dollars and costs or 20 days in jail, while his younger brother was also convicted, fined ten dollars and costs with the same jail alternative.[28] It probably didn't hurt Mayor Ford's cause at the trial that one of the magistrates was the former mayor, the proper burial of whose wife Ford had helped to ensure. In any case, word that their popular new mayor had been involved in such a confrontation on the street with evidence of drunkenness, pistols and beatings must have been unsettling, if not shocking, for residents of the town. This was a small Ontario community that was conservative, God-fearing and far removed from the Wild West.

Decorum at St. Marys council must have been tested by the clash between Ford and the Guests. At its July 3 meeting, which the senior Guest missed, councillors voted to "revise the present rules of order in such a way as to have them enforced" and assigned that job to a subcommittee.[29] Guest attended a July 9 meeting but after that, his council seat remained unoccupied until December. In the interim, business proceeded as normal and in late September council adopted new rules of order and decided to print 100 copies. In October, council accepted the bond of the tax collector (not named, but no doubt Box) and he was authorized to proceed with collecting taxes.

On December 10, Guest returned to his council seat and immediately moved that council grant thirty dollars to "old Mr. Delmage" to help defray costs of taking him to his daughter's home in Chicago. The motion passed.

Shortly afterward, another councillor complained that "a member of council" had neglected to attend meetings for three months. This prompted Guest to jump to his feet to explain that he had been in ill health. Council, despite protests from three of its members, accepted Guest's excuse. One of them then tried to overturn the grant of thirty dollars to Delmage, arguing that it had been made by an illegal member of council. But, in the end, no vote was taken.[30] It was obvious that proceedings had become acrimonious as the council year drew to a close. In addition, the train station issue remained unresolved. At its December 28 meeting, with Guest again absent, council rescinded the grant to help Delmage get to Chicago.

In St. Marys politics of the day, elections were not strenuously fought contests; more often they were the result of an agreement among gentlemen. Traditionally, once elected to a one-year term, the mayor was unopposed for a second term. But Ford had ruffled feathers during his tenure and his battles with the Guests had cost him some support. At the end of December, Ford acceded to a request from ratepayers by calling a public meeting to discuss municipal business. A report of the event noted that "a few questions—mostly personal in their character—were discussed in a most acrimonious manner by most of the speakers."[31] Discussion turned to the upcoming mayoralty and several names were mentioned, including Milner Harrison, a merchant, former councillor and one of the magistrates who convicted the Guest brothers of assaulting Mayor Ford. But Harrison begged off, saying his health wasn't up to it. A show of hands by those present indicated strong support for long-time councillor David A. Robertson, urging him to oppose Ford.

At a nomination meeting several days later, Robertson and Ford were put forward for mayor. The two candidates and their nominators addressed voters who gathered for that purpose. Robertson announced "that he was the candidate of no clique," the *Argus* reported, and he promised to be impartial and fair. Ford replied that "he thought it strange that while other gentlemen had been allowed to fill the Mayor's chair for two years, that he should not enjoy that privilege, when even his enemies could lay no sin to his charge. He characterized the whole scheme of a clique who had 'axes to grind.'"[32] The paper said that both were good candidates and declined to endorse either man. In the ensuing vote, Robertson prevailed, winning 356 votes to 200 for Ford. The doctor was left to lick the wounds inflicted by voters and he was late for the January 14 meeting of council that concluded the last bit of business from the previous year.

Aside from the enemies he had created during his tumultuous year on council, Ford found that his lifestyle was running afoul of the growing temperance movement in St. Marys. His habit of late-night, alcohol-fueled gatherings at his office and evidence from the trial of the Guests about drunken beatings turned voters against him. The Rine Movement was on the rise in St. Marys and in other Ontario communities at the time with its gospel of temperance. It was named after a Pennsylvania Methodist preacher, David Isaac Kirwin Rine, known as the "Apostle of Temperance." Rine delivered a series of lectures across Southern Ontario and was attracting large and receptive crowds. His evangelistic railings against the evils of alcohol drew ever-increasing audiences on his return visits to St. Marys. Rine asked his followers to sign a pledge of abstinence and by late that same month the *Argus* reported "immense enthusiasm" for Rine and his cause, with 1,100 pledges having already been signed in town.[33] On the same page of the paper as success of the temperance crusade was reported, another article noted a permanent Rine Total Abstinence Club had been formed in town. The president was John E. Harding, the man who had nominated Robertson for mayor, while Robertson was first vice-president. Robertson, no doubt, had tapped the temperance movement to oust Ford. The doctor suddenly found himself on the wrong side of the anti-liquor tide that had swept into town.

With politics no longer on his calendar, Ford was able to spend more time curling that winter and was reported to have been skip (captain) of the St. Marys rink that lost narrowly to one from the Huron County town of Goderich.[34] In mid–February, it was reported in the *Argus* that Ford's oldest son, Arthur, had passed his primary examination to become a member of the law society of Ontario. The article said that the examination was difficult and that the young man "had no special training," providing testament to the quality of education being provided in St. Marys.[35] This claim of law society membership was in error, however, either because of assumptions made by the writer, or due to inaccurate information provided by the Fords. Arthur attended only one term of study at the Law Society of Upper Canada (even today, there is no Law Society of Ontario, because it still prefers the antiquated "Upper Canada" name). With such limited training, he could not become a member of the society and would not be allowed to practice law.[36]

That same spring, the Rev. Rine's temperance crusade suffered an unexpected setback. He was charged with indecently assaulting a young woman near the town of Mitchell, north of St. Marys. She complained that Rine, who was a guest in her house, entered her bedroom, kissed her on the lips and felt her breast. The minister was charged with indecent assault. On May 2, Rine was acquitted by a jury on a reduced charge of assault, but his name had been sullied and the case had caused a sensation.[37] Rine's effectiveness as a leading light in temperance was gone, although the anti-liquor movement continued to grow without him. In the following years, Rine showed signs of mental instability and moved to Detroit, where he became completely delusional. He died in a home for the insane in 1882.

Even greater sensation would strike St. Marys in just a few weeks and Adam Ford would find himself at the very center of it. Dawn broke Wednesday morning, June 5, and the town was soon abuzz with talk of the strange death of a young man the previous night. In his dying moments, he claimed he'd been poisoned by Adam Ford, it was being said. The dead man, it was soon confirmed, was Robert R. Guest, 21, a grocer, and the second oldest son of the late grocer Robert Guest who, in turn, was a brother of Ford's nemesis, Thomas B. Guest. The scandal gripped the town and theories were flying fast and furious as reporters for the daily newspapers in nearby London and Stratford raced to town. Rumors of all kinds were spread by citizens and correspondents alike, Ford's foes seizing on any bit of information to vilify him while everyone looked for some kind of motive. The coroner, a Dr. Harrison, immediately convened an inquest because of the suggestion of foul play. It began behind closed doors at 3 P.M. that same afternoon while the contents of Guest's stomach were sent to Toronto for laboratory analysis. The case broke too late in the week to be covered by the weekly papers in St. Marys, so the majority of news shared with residents was provided initially by the *Stratford Beacon* and the *London Free Press* and *London Advertiser*, the latter organ strongly in favor of temperance and its reports reflecting its bias.[38] Both London papers in their initial accounts headlined the case a "mystery," one hinting at foul play, the other at a "dark deed."

On Wednesday, Ford was arrested in London, where he had travelled to attend the horse races. Herrington, the chief constable of St. Marys, was assigned the task of bringing in the doctor. Upon his arrest in the death of Guest, Ford was reported to have said: "My God, you don't suggest me! We have been such good friends!"[39] Ford, it was suggested, had been "mixed up in many scrapes with females" and the poisoning of Guest might be connected to information the young man knew about the doctor. "The doctor is popularly represented to as given to drink and is said to have been fond of enticing young men into his office to drink, especially those who were correct livers," reported the *London Free Press*. Its reporter in St. Marys added that "there is strong excitement here over the matter. I hear that during the last year Ford had been gradually 'going to the dogs.'"

If the *Free Press* coverage was lurid and unhelpful to Ford, its rival, the pro-temperance *London Advertiser*, was absolutely brutal to him. It reminded its readers that Dr. Ford of St. Marys was someone with whom they should be familiar:

> During last year he occupied the position of Mayor of the town, and was held in the highest esteem. When the temperance agitation began, however, he sided with the liquor party, and this part caused such revulsion in the feeling concerning him that at the last election he was badly beaten. He seems to have taken this to heart a good deal, and he has since been drinking considerably, occasionally, as he is alleged to have told a lady friend, taking a poisonous drug to counteract the effect on his nervous system. Furthermore, it is alleged that he made special efforts to induce young men to violate their temperance pledges, one of these men being Guest, who was the secretary of a newly formed temperance society.[40]

The paper concluded that "there is not much reason to doubt but that the drug which caused the death of Thomas [sic] Guest was procured in the office of Dr. Ford."

If Ford had been trying to persuade Robert Guest to break his vow of abstinence, it wouldn't have been difficult. Several witnesses said that Guest was on good terms with Ford and testified that the young man had been at Kennedy's Hotel that night, where he consumed three glasses of beer before being seen on the street with Ford. After his arrest, Ford attended the inquest, which was a public affair. The evidence of a string of witnesses soon filled the papers. The *Advertiser* didn't restrict itself to the evidence from the inquest, reporting all of the local gossip:

> We have spoken of the apparent absence of a motive. All sorts of rumors are afloat, of course. It is said, for instance, that the parties were rivals for the affection of a female named Thorn, concerning whose character we would not care to print all that is said. It is also hinted that Guest was an important witness in a case of abortion in which Ford was concerned.... In addition to the stories concerning the dissipation of the doctor, rumors of eccentricities are floated, and it is claimed by some that he cannot be in his right mind.[41]

The inquest was held in a crowded church before a 15-member jury with the county's top prosecutor playing a key role in eliciting evidence. Key testimony came from Angus Bethune, a bank clerk and friend of Guest who saw him downtown near Ford's office, between 11 P.M. and midnight, gasping for breath and trying to vomit. Bethune testified that Guest said he had just come from Ford's office, where the doctor had poisoned him by putting something in his drink of rum or rye whiskey. "He continually complained bitterly of the Doctor giving him poison. Witness said he could not understand why the doctor should do so when they were such good friends," the *Advertiser* reported. Bethune was asked if he knew a woman named Ann Thorn and he said he didn't.

Some witnesses said Guest seemed cheerful and sober that night, while others said he was quieter than normal and not particularly sober. Bethune said he took Guest to the stricken man's home about 12:30 A.M., where Guest related to his older brother what had happened. The *Argus* reported the conversation Thomas Guest recalled under questioning this way:

> "Tom, I'm drugged"; "You have been to Dr. Ford's office, haven't you?" He was reticent but said "yes," and was groaning loud as if in pain. Repeated "I have been drugged," and when asked by whom distinctly said "Dr. Ford"; do not know when the Dr. and my brother became intimate—it is within the year.[42]

Thomas Guest conceded that the dead man had been seeing a young lady who was not of good character.

A Doctor Wilson testified that he was called to attend to Guest and that he was "cold, pallid, pulseless" and there was little that could be done for him. Guest, he said, died shortly after 1 A.M. The doctor testified that death was likely caused by "some irritant" in the patient's stomach. The inquest was then adjourned to await laboratory analysis of the contents of the victim's stomach. Ford was remanded to the jail in nearby Stratford, the county seat.

Upon resumption of the inquest on June 20, the jury heard from former town constable James Delmage, who insisted he had seen Guest leave Ford's office on the night of the poisoning and heard Ford's voice coming from his office, saying: "I'll teach you to come sneaking around here, prying into my secret, G_d d__n you!,"[43]

That damning evidence was offset when, under questioning, Delmage conceded that he was not on good terms with Ford. Delmage said he believed Ford had signed papers a decade earlier that confined him to a mental asylum in Toronto. "I never had any particular liking for Dr. Ford," he admitted. "I always considered him a scaly character and have a worse opinion of him now than I ever did before."[44] Delmage was recalled as a witness by the coroner later to answer questions about things he had been overheard to say after his testimony against Ford. But Delmage denied he told a man named Matthew O'Brien that he would do everything he could to get back at Ford; he denied he had claimed Ford was related to the chemist who analyzed Guest's stomach, and he denied he'd made derogatory remarks about the chemist and the jury."[45] His denials rang hollow and jurors would likely place little credibility on Delmage's testimony, given the grudge he seemed to bear.

The contents of Guest's stomach contained no poison, the jury had learned from the chemist, and then the coroner called the final witnesses. On June 20, the *Argus* printed an editorial in which it lamented the way in which reporters and citizens alike had portrayed the former mayor. "No incident or accident which has ever taken place in the town of St. Marys has given rise to so much excitement as the tragic death of Robert Guest," it said. The weekly expressed sympathy to his widowed mother and other family members and noted that the public anxiously awaited the outcome of the inquest:

> Highly colored and exaggerated reports have appeared, and all sorts of rumors are afloat, as may be expected. A good many names, especially those of females are dragged into the discussion. In the London and Toronto dailies articles paint Dr. Ford's character in blackest colors, and are not by any means limited in their charges against him, morally or professionally. Others take a warm stand in his favor.[46]

Ford declined to say anything on his behalf when given that opportunity by the coroner as the inquest concluded. The coroner then reviewed with the jury the evidence taken and on June 22 the case was placed in their hands. After 12 hours of deliberations, jurors reached a verdict shortly before midnight:

> This jury is of the opinion, from the evidence before them, that the deceased, Robert Guest, came to his death, on the 5th day of June, at St. Marys, from the effect of some irritant poison taken into the stomach; and the jury, from the evidence, and that the said poison was given by Adam Enoch Ford, M.D., but this jury is unable to discover from what motive, or that Adam Enoch Ford either premeditated or intended personal injury to the deceased.[47]

The finding, like the evidence brought before the inquest, left many unanswered questions. Most often asked was what would prompt Ford, a man apparently on good terms with Guest, to give him poison? A disagreement about a woman, or about the temperance movement? And if Guest was on the executive of a new temperance group, what was he doing drinking that night, first at the hotel and later in Ford's office? Had Ford simply shared with the young man the same kind of "poison" some said he was using on himself? Questions and insinuations continued to swirl for weeks and months.

Ford was kept in jail as officials prepared to bring him before a grand jury at the fall assizes of court. There, it would be determined whether there was sufficient evidence to try him for murder. On June 26, following arguments in the Court of Queen's Bench in Toronto, the doctor was granted bail of $4,000 and was again a free man after three weeks in custody.[48]

The *Argus* reported that the coroner's jury was "exceptionally intelligent" and had done its job conscientiously. It found a silver lining in the plan by prosecutors to take Ford before the criminal courts.

> This verdict seems hard on Dr. Ford but we think that it is really better for him. Had he been acquitted and allowed his liberty the stigma of the crime with which he is charged would have rested with him as long as he lived; but now that he is committed he secures the opportunity of defense, and is placed in a position to vindicate his character before a proper tribunal.[49]

Despite the confidence the weekly placed in the restorative powers of the justice system, Ford's character had been so thoroughly blackened in a public forum that it was doubtful that vindication was possible. The temperance movement was continuing to gain followers and the use of poison-laced liquor to kill a temperance organization's secretary would not soon be forgotten. One can only imagine the shame that weighed on Ford and his family once the doctor regained his freedom and was again able to walk the streets of St. Marys.

His appearance before a grand jury was delayed when his case could not be heard at the fall assizes. When the grand jury finally was convened, in March of 1879, it rendered a "no bill" verdict. That meant that it had heard insufficient evidence to warrant conducting a trial for Ford in the poisoning of Guest.[50] Ford was a free man, but a "no bill" finding behind closed doors was not as categorical as a "not guilty" finding in open court would have been. He could not escape the notoriety the entire sorry episode had produced for him. His fall from public grace had been dramatic, swift and complete.

As months went by, it became clear to Adam Ford that his name had been sullied beyond repair. The situation caused a rift in his family, with his wife Jane refusing to leave the town her father had helped build. After many hours of soul-searching and impassioned discussion, a decision was reached. The Ford men, Adam, Arthur and Leon, would head west for a fresh start. Julia and Jane would stay behind and try to tough it out. Sometime in 1880, Adam, Arthur and Leon Ford stepped off the train in Denver, Colorado, a world away from the troubles back in St. Marys.

# Five

## *Eleven Years in Denver*

Abner Graves's decision to relocate to Denver in 1894 is curious, to say the least. Certainly he would not have been sorry to get away from the faltering farm economy of western Iowa, where his multifaceted business empire lay in ruins. And it is true that Denver was a hub of activity for Graves's first love—mining.

But Denver, and indeed the entire state of Colorado, whose economic strength was based largely on mineral resources, had been hard hit by the "Panic of 1893," as it was known, a dramatic economic adjustment that marked the onset of one of the worst depressions in U.S. history. The depression proved both pervasive and persistent, lingering for most of the rest of the decade.[1]

For several years there had been signs of looming trouble. In agriculture, the wheat, cotton and corn belts had expanded throughout the 1880s, but overproduction led to low prices for agricultural commodities and inevitably to widespread foreclosures and tax sales.[2] A key to economic growth had been railroad construction—from 8,000 to 12,000 miles of track was laid some years as competing companies such as Southern Pacific and Santa Fe opened new lands to agriculture and provided access to mines and markets. But that blistering pace couldn't be sustained and by 1887 this major engine of economic growth began to sputter.[3]

In May of 1893, when collapse came with a resounding thud, railroad and industrial stocks plummeted and major businesses went bankrupt. Unwittingly, the federal government had contributed to the crash by adopting silver, alongside gold, to back U.S. currency. Washington had been pushed by a pro-silver lobby, the "Silverites," and by politicians in silver-rich western states and some farm interests. The Sherman Silver Purchase Act of 1890 required the government to buy silver and create coins in a ratio of sixteen ounces of silver to one ounce of gold. Initially, silver mining companies were happy about this development and so were farmers, the latter believing that inflationary pressure would let them pay off their loans in dollars worth less than the dollars with which those debts had been incurred.[4] But the value of silver had declined due to excessive mining and people opted to exchange their overvalued silver for

64

gold, weakening the U.S. Treasury's supply and harming American credit abroad, where gold was still considered the basis of U.S. currency.[5] Many western silver mines closed and commercial and banking failures became widespread. Among the railroads that went bankrupt were the Philadelphia and Reading, Northern Pacific, Union Pacific, and the Atchison, Topeka and Santa Fe.[6]

As the depression deepened, nearly twenty percent of the American workforce was unemployed, 15,000 companies failed and 600 banks closed.[7] Unemployed workers, begging for government assistance, marched on Washington but they were generally ridiculed and dismissed by the press and public. To deal with the crisis, President Grover Cleveland called Congress into session to repeal the Sherman Silver Purchase Act. But there was no quick fix and the economic misery would last for years.[8]

Nevertheless, the 60-year-old Graves left his wife Alma and young son Nelson in Dow City to start a new career as a mining consultant in the once-bustling Queen City of the Plains, a place struggling from the collapse of silver. He hung out a shingle as a mining consultant in the Bank Block building in downtown Denver at 17th and Arapahoe streets.[9] He must have liked the office because he remained there until 1920.[10] Five blocks away was the imposing new Masonic Building, where he could attend social events and meetings of the secretive fraternal order he had joined a decade earlier.

Unfortunately, what he found in Denver was an economy in shambles. Colorado had seen warning signs well before the crash of 1893. Railroads had expanded beyond good business sense, oftentimes underfinanced, and bankruptcies were not uncommon.[11] Ranchers were suffering from a combination of hard winters and overgrazing. Mine owners had expanded to the extent that by 1890 nearly sixty percent of America's silver came from Colorado. The oversupply saw silver prices fall from $1.05 an ounce on the open market in 1890 to 62 cents by mid–1893, leading to mine closures and job losses.[12] In Denver itself, residents panicked and withdrew their savings from banks, causing a dozen of them to fail in the month of July alone. The hard times even affected the richest man in Denver, silver mining entrepreneur and businessman Horace Tabor, a man with an extravagant lifestyle funded by a fortune believed to be about $5 million. His losses mounted and within three years he was forced from his mansion and into inexpensive quarters in a hotel.[13] Thousands of jobless miners joined the ranks of the unemployed as a tent-and-shack "city" rose on the banks of the South Platte River. Relief was in short supply and efforts to rid the city of transients included setting them adrift on barges and lowering the cost of one-way railroad tickets out of town. This did little to curb social unrest and at least two trains were hijacked by hungry, unemployed men as the situation deteriorated.[14]

The capital of Colorado had been a booming center of about 50,000 in the mid–1880s when one hundred trains a week steamed into town. By 1890, the population stood at 106,713, but the collapse of 1893 saw an exodus and by 1895 it had dipped to an estimated 90,000.[15] Denver's rapid growth had been fueled by the railways that made it a key transportation hub and the city serviced a vast mining hinterland. Its fate was closely linked to steel rails and the nearby gold and silver mines.

Understandably, Graves had an uphill fight to establish himself as a mining consultant at a time when Denver was going through so much upheaval. It can be no surprise that for a time in 1895 he was looking at prospects in California, where he dabbled in real estate, returning to the state where he had sought his fortune as a much younger man. In May of that year, he was in Pasadena and in August in San Diego.[16] There, he wrote a long letter to the editor of the *Los Angeles Times*, praising what he had seen in California. "This is my first visit," he wrote (overlooking his initial trip in 1849, return visit in 1865 and holiday in 1892), "and a four months residence divided between Pasadena, Los Angeles, Avalon and San Diego, has convinced me that Southern California is the ideal place for people to live, and has decided me to pull up my eastern stakes and come out here to stay."[17] However, things didn't pan out as Graves hoped and by the fall of 1896 he was back in Denver. He had returned "in the interest of some Chicago capitalists, his special purpose being to examine mines in Lake City, Hinsdale County. This trip resulted in making Denver his residence city," as was explained in a later history of Colorado personalities for which he provided biographical information.[18]

Clearly, Graves had decided that mining, despite the industry-wide turmoil, best suited his talents. His mining consultancy became headquarters for his property interests in Colorado, Wyoming, Arizona, Nevada, Oregon and Mexico.[19] He sold real estate as a sideline, despite frequent trips into mining country and back home to see Alma in Dow City and to visit friends and family in Cooperstown.

The newly established mining consultant/real estate salesman was constantly looking for new opportunities and by 1898, he had found one. The city directory showed that he was rooming on California Street and described him as vice-president of the Colorado Mineral Palace Car Company.[20] This venture was tied to the new Colorado Mineral Palace, opened in 1891 in Pueblo to house the largest collection of gems and minerals in the world, the basis of Colorado's wealth.[21] The magnificent building was considered one of the most ornate in the United States when it opened. Egyptian in style, it held thrones for King Coal and Queen Silver and glass cases featuring a vast mineral exhibit. The Mineral Palace became a centerpiece for a magnificent park created around it in 1897. That same year, a plan was devised for a train that would be a rolling showcase of Colorado's mineral wealth and a promotional vehicle for the Mineral Palace. Graves became involved in the venture but, despite his efforts, it never amounted to anything. A subsequent scheme, the "Colorado Train," was announced in 1902 in a bid to promote the state, its natural resources and attract investment and tourists. At that time, it was reported that the earlier scheme had foundered because of difficulty securing rolling stock related to the demands of the Spanish-American War of 1898.[22] The 1902 effort consisted of five railroad cars, including one specifically to promote the Colorado Mineral Palace that featured cabinets full of mineral specimens. But by that time, Graves was no longer involved. He was busy with a project in Mexico and with tending to his mining interests throughout the southwestern states.

In July of 1898, Graves attended the first International Mining Congress in Salt Lake City. The gathering brought together about two thousand delegates to consider the latest developments in mining and to press for national legislation to promote the industry.[23] Doubtless he would have been pleased that his attendance at the event, where he chaired a committee on credentials, drew widespread newspaper attention, including in the mining country west of Denver. It was reported that he called for members to vote in support of a revision of mining laws.[24] Graves also backed a motion to establish a federal department of mines and mining, moved to thank the various mining bureaus that helped stage the congress and formally moved adjournment at the end of the four-day gathering.[25] He raised his profile in Salt Lake City and promoted his services.

By 1899, the remnants of his business back in Iowa were weighing heavily on Graves's mind and he decided to pull the plug. According to a news report:

> Abner Graves of Dow City, formerly a banker and now engaged in civil engineering, has filed a voluntary petition in bankruptcy in the United States district court. Beyond a mortgage of $2,000 on his homestead, the petitioner is unable to give a list of his liabilities. His assets consist of real estate valued at $3,000 and personal property claimed as exempt, amount to $250.[26]

That same year, Graves and his wife decided that it was time for their son, Nelson, soon to turn 18, to conclude his studies and prepare to enter business with his father. Despite his many absences, Abner was close to his son. He took Nelson, at age five, for a vacation in Hot Springs, South Dakota, where they stayed in a large hotel, swam in the hot springs and rode horses. It was a carefree time of father-son bonding. Five years later, the family travelled to Catalina Island, California, where they enjoyed the sunny climate and fishing.[27] Nelson's only child, Mabel Claire, who was only about four years old when her grandfather died, remembered into her nineties that Abner Graves had "adored" her father.[28]

The Graves had found enough money to enroll their handsome dark-haired boy at Shattuck School in Faribault, Minnesota, founded in 1858 as an Episcopal military school for boys. Its goals were clear cut, as spelled out in a brochure aimed at parents:

> The scheme of life at Shattuck is designed so that each boy receives a well-rounded educational experience in religion, culture, leadership and social activ-

Abner Graves at his mine in northern Mexico, circa 1900–1905. Graves favored formal attire, even in mining country. Used by permission of Claire Strashun.

ity. Shattuck offers its boys a balanced general education at the secondary level, an education that will not only gain them entrance to college, but also prepare them to be intelligent members of the communities of which they will be a part. Shattuck believes that, through military training, it is performing a patriotic duty in addition to supplementing its primary function of preparing boys for college and civil life.[29]

Abner and Alma Graves may have been inclined to send their son to a military-type school as part of the heightened sense of patriotism that buoyed the country following the successful and short-lived Spanish-American War and the widely hailed military exploits of Teddy Roosevelt and his Rough Riders in Cuba. Whatever their reasons, it proved a good move. Upon his graduation in June of 1901, Nelson's certificate of honors standing recorded his overall grade average as ninety percent.[30]

As Nelson completed his studies at Shattuck, his father was constantly on the go. He made trips to mines in Mexico and continued to travel east to Dow City and Cooperstown. In 1900, Graves purchased a mining claim in Carbo in the northwest Mexican state of Sonora.[31] It took him a year to obtain clear title to the copper-bearing property and by 1902 he founded the Alma

Copper Mining Company to develop it.[32] Graves was excited about his prospects in the region and when interviewed by a reporter, his comments were laced with hyperbole. He claimed to have found a forty-foot-wide vein of eighty-percent pure copper in the Ures district bearing traces of silver and gold and to have begun sinking shafts to pursue it, one of them reaching 100 feet. "The vein is of such immense size and variety of stratas [that it] makes it little short of a marvel," he said. "This is the greatest mining country of the south and has a future before it second to no district in the world."[33] If Graves embellished his views to attract potential investors, he certainly wasn't the first mine promoter to do so.

Abner Graves and son, Nelson, at their mine in Carbo, Mexico, about 1902. Despite high hopes for the prospects in Mexico, by 1905 the venture had been largely abandoned. The father and son also worked together in Denver. Used by permission of Claire Strashun.

Plans were afoot for Nelson to join his father in the Mexican venture. When he arrived, the 19-year-old proved to be a big help, having become nearly fluent in Spanish.[34] Nelson kept watch over the operation at Carbo as superintendent, while his father left from time to time to investigate mining prospects elsewhere and provide opinions to those who retained his services. His Bank Block office in Denver remained the base of operations as he became active in the local chamber of commerce and the real estate community. Graves also developed some rich coal mining properties in nearby Wyoming and ran a rail line to service them.[35] Graves remained a man of boundless energy as he approached 68, an age when other men would have scaled back.

Despite his busy, almost hectic, life, Graves maintained his love of baseball and found time to visit the ballpark in Denver to cheer for the home team. A few years later, in a newspaper interview about his role in the first game of baseball at Cooperstown, the spry septuagenarian said he was planning to play in an upcoming game between the real estate exchange and the chamber of commerce.[36] The reporter ate up the story as embellished by Graves, but added his own observation: "Mr. Graves, who is a real estate dealer, is one of the most enthusiastic followers of the baseball game in the country. There are mighty few of them that he misses in Denver, and he is usually seen in the front row of the grandstand, yelling with all his might for the Grizzlies."

Tragedy struck early in 1902 when Alma died suddenly back in Dow City. Plans for Mexico were held back for a time as Abner wrapped up her affairs in Iowa. As the year progressed, Graves tutored his son in the science of mining as the operation in Mexico grew slowly. Graves continued to flit between his geographically diverse interests and beat the bushes to find investors willing to help him exploit the riches at Carbo. To raise funds, father and son created the Graves Investment Company in 1903, which they based in Des Moines, Iowa, a move that produced $100,000 for the mining venture.[37] By 1905, however, the Alma Copper Mine lay idle and by 1907 it had been abandoned entirely.[38]

\* \* \*

Sometime during 1902, Abner Graves acquired a new neighbor, an aging medical doctor named Adam Enoch Ford, who established his office a short block up 17th Street at the corner of Lawrence Street.[39] Ford had bounced around downtown Denver, with offices in at least nine buildings since his arrival in 1880. This time, the baseball-loving doctor landed mere steps from the office of mining engineer Graves, in a core area surrounded by saloons. Denver was recovering nicely from the economic collapse of the 1890s and by 1900 its population had climbed to 134,000 (helped along by some annexations) and the number of saloons had mushroomed to 334.[40] By comparison, Denver boasted 149 churches in 1900, 80 schools, eight hospitals, nine libraries and 11 banks.[41] The saloons were heavily concentrated in a six-square-mile area in the city core and were the most common businesses on many blocks of 15th, 16th, 17th, 18th and 19th streets.[42] The temperance movement remained weak and that was just the way Adam Ford liked it. Graves, no teetotaler himself, likely felt the same. He still carried a whiskey flask he'd had since his days in Virginia City and it comforted him on his trips to Mexico.[43]

The saloon culture was entrenched in Denver life as the twentieth century dawned. Nine of the sixteen wards in Denver city government were represented at one time or another by saloonkeepers.[44] Aside from political clout, the saloons carried financial force. The city licensed them and by 1900 liquor license revenue had risen to $215,538, an amount roughly equal to one-fourth of all the money Denver's city government spent that year.[45] Upon his election as mayor in 1904, Robert Walter Speer, whose growing political machine was reliant on the saloon lobby, quickly put temperance reformers in their place. "No effort will be made to make a puritanical town out of a growing Western City," he declared. "You must take people as you find them, and by firm and persistent policy, make conditions better gradually. Spasmodic and sensational efforts of reform will be avoided."[46] Speer fought tenaciously to keep speakeasies, with their associated vices of gaming and prostitution, in the downtown area during his years in office, but the suburbs could be dry.

Historian Thomas J. Noel, a professor at the University of Colorado, studied the city's saloon culture and wrote an entire book about it. He found that alcohol and related vices permeated the city which, even as it grew larger and more mature, was reluctant to change its ways. "Long after the frontier period passed, heavy drinking remained an expression of hospitality and of manliness," he wrote. "The obsession with virility, potency, body building, and sports that characterized turn-of-the-century America permeated saloons."[47] Men with stories to tell had a place to tell them in Denver and a ready, if not particularly sober, audience. No definitive proof exists that Abner Graves and Adam Ford met while quenching their thirst in one of the saloons that surrounded them in the three years their offices were so close. But it would seem likely.

The two men also may have met at the ballpark, given their shared interest in the sport. Denver has a long history of baseball, a first call going out for "gentlemen" to play the game two years after its founding in 1858.[48] Denver baseball historian Jay Sanford has researched and written about local baseball and about the Negro Leagues and was a consultant to filmmaker Ken Burns, introducing him to former Negro Leagues star Buck O'Neil of the Kansas City Monarchs. O'Neil's easy smile and vivid memories enlivened Burns' subsequent acclaimed documentary, *Baseball*. According to Sanford, those early Denver "gentlemen" ballplayers were among the leading lights in the young city. They included future mayor Baxter Stiles, along with the benefactor of a major hospital, the president of a bank, and others.[49] The local newspapers, Sanford found, chronicled baseball's rise in popularity as the gentlemen retired to the viewing stands and more accomplished athletes took their place on the diamond.

Across the Rocky Mountain region, the game grew rapidly in the 1870s and 1880s with teams fielded by towns and cities across Colorado.[50] In 1879, Denver had its first professional baseball team and by the mid '80s games were attracting fans who were the "movers and shakers" of the city, including the police chief. By 1886, a team named the Denvers joined the new Western League of professional baseball.[51] Subsequent teams adopted the name Grizzlies or Bears. Denver was caught up in the same love affair with baseball that was sweeping America.

Another Denver historian has documented the long-standing attachment between Denverites and all sports. According to Phil Goodstein, it continued into modern times as "people flocking to the city, knowing nothing of its traditions and customs ... found rooting for sport teams a means of identifying with their new community. Ruling Denver likewise adopted sports as its—and the city's—identity."[52] Goodstein observed that in the late 1800s, "locals regularly played baseball. Efforts at forming professional teams dated from the

1880s. The minor league franchise emerged as the Bears or Grizzlies. It frequently disappeared, hibernating for years at a time."[53]

Much was weighing on the mind of 71-year-old Adam Ford when he established his practice at 1705 Lawrence Street, a few saloon doors from the Bank Block building where Abner Graves toiled. The previous year, 1901, had been filled with business and family turmoil. Ford spent that year promoting his Washington Sanitarium, a treatment center for those addicted to alcohol and drugs, in Seattle. His son, Arthur, now 41, who had first-hand knowledge of substance abuse, was enlisted to help establish the center. Just a year earlier, Arthur had been an "inmate," one of seven persons listed as living at a treatment clinic operated by Dr. Daniel Stradley at 2100 Champa Street.[54] Stradley and his brother Ayres, also a doctor, operated a sanitarium there "for the treatment of persons afflicted with dipsomania [alcoholism] and nervous diseases."[55] The *Portrait and Biographical Record for Denver of 1898* reported that Daniel Stradley had successfully treated 800 or 900 patients by that time, receiving the "highest testimonials" from some of them. He also had been appointed by judges as "medical expert in lunacy cases." Arthur's alcohol and drug dependency was apparently more than his father could handle, even as Adam was planning to open his own sanitarium.

Once Arthur was released from the care of the Stradley brothers, Adam Ford put him to work and took him to Vancouver, British Columbia. That city, just across the border from Washington, would be the base of operations for the new venture as Ford brought together his family for the first time in years. The 1901 Census of Canada found him residing in Vancouver with his wife Jane, daughter Julia, 42, sons Arthur, 39, Leon, 35, and Thomas G. McPherson, 50, listed as an "assistant." Also there were two nephews, Armour and Harold Ford, listed as 30 and 19 respectively (although having been born in 1874, the latter in fact would have been 27). In January of 1901, Adam Ford incorporated the Washington Sanitarium Inc. in the state of Washington, with capital stock of $210,000 and issued 500 shares at $10 apiece to himself.[56]

Ford had always enjoyed public speaking as a raconteur and one-time politician, so he used this talent to promote his new venture on Second Avenue North in Seattle and to sell shares. An undated newspaper clipping, believed to be from a Vancouver newspaper shortly after the January 22, 1901, death of Queen Victoria, revealed that Ford had enlightened views about the treatment of addictions at a time in which such conditions were often blamed on moral failings:

Dr. Adam E. Ford, of the Washington sanitarium, Seattle, gave an interesting and instructive lecture last evening on "The Brain and Nervous System," with special reference to the diseases of the so-called habits, known as morphine, opium, cocaine and liquor habits. He explained that the use of alcohol, opium, morphine, etc., produced diseases of the brain, not by destroying the structures but by altering, over-exciting and then paralyzing the energies of the nerve centers. Being perversions of action only these diseases could be, and should be, cured. The idea that these "habits" are mere moral obliquities to be cured by moral suasion or exercise of will power and good resolutions was a grievous, often a terrible mistake, and the belief that the sufferer is to be made an outcast because he suffers from these diseases was cruel and inhuman. He closed with an eloquent and touching tribute to the dead Queen, "Victoria the Beloved," for which he received loud and long continued applause.[57]

Things soon soured for the Ford family and for the Washington Sanitarium. On February 26, a patient died at the facility and a coroner's jury concluded that it was due to strychnine poisoning.[58] Worse still, Arthur Ford, employee Charlotte Morgan and a man named Bert Chapman were blamed for the death. The case drew front-page headlines in Seattle. Maggie Hunsucker, the report said, was a morphine addict who had been persuaded by Chapman to attend the Washington Sanitarium for treatment by Dr. Ford. The report continued: "Arthur Ford, a son of Dr. Ford, according to witnesses, gave the Hunsucker woman an injection of pliocarfine[59] a short time before she died. He followed the injection by giving her a tablet of strychnine. Several hours after Ford left, the woman was seized with a convulsion and died."[60] The next day, Arthur Ford and the two others were charged with manslaughter.[61] The stress of the charges and the subsequent trial were hard on Adam Ford and his entire family and the bad publicity virtually ensured that the sanitarium was doomed. On April 8, a judge discharged all accused, noting that the state had failed to prove that strychnine was the cause of Hunsucker's death.[62] He added that no complete analysis of the dead woman's organs had been conducted by the authorities. But for the Fords, the damage had been done.

Heartbroken at the turn of events, an eerie echo of an earlier episode of poisoning and bad publicity, Adam Ford returned to Denver later that year with Arthur. Leon returned to the road to continue seeking his riches in the American West. Jane and Julia went back home to St. Marys, Ontario, and the nephews scattered. With all the sorrows he had experienced by 1902, Adam Ford had many reasons to be thankful that the temperance movement was still only a tiny voice in the Denver wilderness and that he could easily find solace in local saloons.

His dream of a sanitarium in Seattle had become a nightmare and a financial setback. But it was quickly replaced with a plan for another one closer to home when Ford learned of a big project that had become the talk of real estate and mining circles. The newspapers were reporting a plan to create a new mining community west of Pueblo: Custer City was to rise beside a new mine to be sunk in Custer County, about 140 miles south of Denver. The promoter was Francis I. Meston, one of Pueblo's prominent citizens, a developer who had attracted hundreds of thousands of dollars of Eastern capital to the city, where he owned a residential plot of land.[63] Meston established the Custer

Mining and Realty Company with business and financial partners to develop the project. The new city, like the county in which it was located, was named after General George Custer, who had lost his life in a battle with Indians at the Battle of the Little Bighorn in eastern Montana in June of 1876. A statue of the general was to be the focal point of the new community, which was to have an electric railway linking it to Pueblo, full street illumination, a bank, a hotel and other urban amenities. Plans were drawn up for a 32-block section of the new community and in June 1902, on the anniversary of Custer's death, an opening ceremony was held that included a former governor of the state. The unveiling of the statue was accompanied by speeches to a crowd of 3,000 from political and business leaders brimming with optimism.[64] Other events that day included a baseball game between the Custer Nine and the New Yorks of Pueblo, along with horse and burro races, fireworks and a dance at the brand-new hotel that night.[65] The local newspaper was swept up in the excitement and gushed about the new community and the gold mine to be established there. "The east end of the county will surely witness a boom this year, and it contains the ore to back up its boom," reported the *Wet Mountain Tribune* in nearby Westcliffe.[66]

Adam Ford saw a business opportunity now that the Washington Sanitarium was just a bad memory. Newspapers in Golden and the mining towns of Fairplay and Rifle reported in September: "Dr. Adam E. Ford of Denver proposes to build a sanitarium on the cottage plan near Custer City, in Custer County. Log houses will be occupied by distinct classes of patients, but the institution is intended for the care of those afflicted with consumption [tuberculosis]."[67] It seems Ford had decided to back away from treating addicts after the Seattle troubles. Sanitariums had sprouted up all over the state to provide relief for tuberculosis sufferers in the thin, clear, mountain air. But almost immediately the prospects for the heavily promoted new community took an unexpected turn. Meston died of heart disease in Pueblo's Grand Hotel on the morning of September 11 after a meeting the previous night at the townsite with "Eastern capitalists who were planning the development of Custer City."[68] The *Wet Mountain Tribune*, reporting his sudden death, observed that the "deceased was the promoter of the city of Custer in this county; which was but the incipient move in an enterprise of stupendous character, which meant much to our county and which will no doubt be carried out by others with whom he has been connected." The reins of the project were turned over to his associate, N.E. Guyot.

For several months the newspaper continued to champion the project and Guyot's activities. But by the following June, the newspaper's editorials had become exceedingly critical and Guyot responded in kind. The sniping continued well into the next year and, in the end, Meston's vision was never realized.

The name of Abner Graves did not crop up in the Custer City fiasco, no doubt because he and Nelson were still struggling in Mexico to make their Sonora operation successful. Or perhaps Graves had misgivings about the Pueblo-based real estate and mining promoters and could smell something that Dr. Ford, the wishful sanitarium promoter, could not.

\* \* \*

In the Denver city directories for 1902 and 1903, Arthur Ford was still listed with his father at the corner of 17th and Lawrence streets, his occupation identified as secretary of the Washington Sanitarium. But by 1904 and 1905, still at the same address, the directories call him a lawyer, no doubt based on information he himself provided.[69]

Finally free of the Seattle Sanitarium and with hopes dashed for one in Custer City, Ford immersed himself in his passion for politics and love of sports. Money was growing tight as he helped Arthur in his continued struggle with drugs and alcohol. The old doctor's renewed interest in sport came as an escape from his reduced circumstances as he continued to drink. One sign of his decline can be found in a letter sent to daughter Julia, living with her mother back in St. Marys. "I am in a great hurry to catch the mail," he wrote in a scrawl, dated June 15, 1904. "I got a $10 bill this morning and I feel so glad. I wondered if you might be as well pleased if I sent you half of it. So here it goes. All is well, with love, Father."[70]

While he was short in his letters to Ontario and in the amount of money contained in them, Ford had plenty of time to put pen to paper to write about curling, the sport in which he had excelled as a younger man. For three years in a row in the annual reports of the Ontario Curling Association, he described his curling exploits and triumphs in St. Marys. He wrote at length, his stories nostalgic and his prose often tinged purple.[71] He apologized in the introduction to his account contained in the 1905 annual report that he could not be more prolix. He still managed to fill five pages with his tale, dated October 1904:

> I send you this hastily written account of some of my reminiscences culled from memory's field—and the brief time in which I have to write it is flying fast. The great national contest here, during the last month in which I spoke 27 times to very large meetings took away from the time I should have spent in writing something worthy of your pages.[72]

The "national contest" Ford described was the U.S. presidential election campaign of 1904.

In his six-page missive for the 1906 curling association annual report, likely penned in late 1905, Ford wrote about introducing the game to his adopted city of Denver about 1881 or 1882:

> After my arrival in Denver and my conclusion to stay here on account of the climate, I sadly missed the roar of the "stanes" and the excitement of the royal

game. I bore it as bravely as I could for one year, but the "spirit of curling came mightily upon me" the next, and I sent east for two pair of stones. Accompanied by my son, we went down the Platte River and up Cherry Creek and finally discovered a sylvan nook with a bonny sheet of ice in the outskirts of the city, and there in the seclusion of the hills and in sight of the mighty peaks of the Rocky Mountain range, their snow-clad summits towering up into the blue, we played points with a good deal of enthusiasm and more or less skill—and as we wended our way home, one of us would often say: "Wha's like us?" This was in 1881, and *was the first curling ever played west of the Missouri River.*[73]

He went on to discuss curling in Denver and speaking engagements in which he promoted the game born in Scotland. Ford had harsh words, however, for a plan that saw a $20,000, three-story building erected in Denver for curling with an unacceptably uneven playing surface created on its second floor. He described the structure, then standing unoccupied, as "a $20,000 monument to the people who knew too much."[74]

Ford had a colorful way with words and his tone betrayed much nostalgia. His better-known account in *The Sporting Life* of 1886, describing the 1838 baseball game he witnessed as a young boy in Beachville, pales in comparison to his stories about curling.

\* \* \*

A mere six months before Ford penned those words about curling, Graves wrote his own infamous letter about the origin of baseball. His words would go on to make history and draw the sort of attention Adam Ford would have envied.

Historians debunked the story Graves told at the age of 71, noting the many reasons it was a piece of fiction that was seized upon by wily baseball conspirators determined to prove the game was unquestionably American in origin. A clue to the roots of his tale may lie in close scrutiny of his life and especially his time in Denver.

It is not the least far-fetched to suggest that the inspiration for his detailed account was Ford's piece in *The Sporting Life* in 1886. But that was 19 years earlier. More likely, he heard it in person from Ford himself. Graves may have been familiar with the story because he was familiar with the *storyteller*. Chances are strong that they crossed paths, based on an examination of their activities from 1894, the first year in which they both were residents of Denver, until early 1905, when the letter about Cooperstown was mailed. The shared interests and activities of Graves and Ford in those eleven years would certainly lead one to speculate that Beachville begat Cooperstown. A case can be made.

First, both men shared an interest in sport and were known to frequent the home games of Denver's baseball teams. Even before Graves came to town, Ford was there to watch his son sprint around the bases and play the game. For his part, Graves was described as a longstanding supporter of the Grizzlies, one of the names of the Denver clubs. Denver baseball historian Jay Sanford has little doubt that Ford and Graves met through their shared interests and circumstances:

> With Dr. Adam Ford's interest in baseball being evident, he would certainly have attended Denver's minor league games with others in the mining and medical industries. Dr. Ford's son, Arthur, frequently raced baseball players and track stars before Denver ball games, for purses of one hundred dollars or more. Arthur Ford also played baseball. The *St. Joseph Daily Gazette* of June 8, 1886 mentioned "Arthur Ford, son of Dr. Ford of Denver ... has been playing as a substitute in the Cincinnati Nine." With Abner Graves's arrival in Denver in 1894 and sharing Dr. Ford's interest in mining and their mutual involvement in Denver community functions, it would lead one to think that these men crossed paths, on occasion, if not on a regular basis, perhaps even at the ballpark.[75]

Then there was a possible connection through the Masons. Ford rented office space in the brand-new Masonic Building when it opened in 1890. He must have had friends and backers within the organization even though he himself never joined. The Masons, logic suggests, would ensure tenants in their magnificent new edifice were of good character and recommended by fellow Masons. Once Graves arrived in town four years later, the Shriner no doubt attended events there and may have met Ford through mutual acquaintances.

In addition, both men enjoyed spirits. Freemasonry was founded in taverns and drink was very much part of their social activities. The brotherhood later embraced temperance, but not until well after 1905 in Denver.[76] The city was full of saloons—talk of sport and other exploits were part of its culture, especially for two outgoing personalities who had a tendency to seek attention and tout their accomplishments

A Shriner, Abner Graves originally joined the Freemasons in Dunlap, Iowa, in 1889. He attended many conventions of the fraternal organization well into his old age. He likely connected with Adam Ford through the Masons. Used by permission of Claire Strashun.

The Masonic Temple Building in downtown Denver on Welton Street at 16th Street into which Adam Ford moved his medical practice in 1890. Courtesy Masonic Temple Association of Denver, Claud Dutro, president.

through letters to newspaper editors and to other publications. Both men were living the single life, with wives back east, and by 1902 Graves was a widower. The saloon presented a chance for conversation and fellowship.

Graves and Ford were both reasonably successful in business, Graves with his mining consultancy and real estate interests, Ford as a physician. They were professional men and while their names did not appear in the "blue books" of the Mile High City, they tended to operate in similar circles. Adam Ford was not involved in mining, other than through the short-lived plan to create a sanitarium in Custer City, but his younger son, Leon, was a mining engineer in many of the same places as Abner and Nelson Graves, including Sonora, Mexico, and California. Leon and Nelson may well have known each other and introduced their fathers at some point. Arthur Ford had strong connections to Leadville, the important mining town west of Denver and may have encountered Graves there or in Denver.

The most likely point of contact, however, comes from simple geography.

The home at 2942 Marion Avenue in Denver where Adam Ford and his sons Arthur and Leon lived during 1897. It is one of the few places where the Fords lived that is still standing in the city. Author's collection.

From 1902 until 1905, when the Cooperstown letter was written, Abner Graves had his office near that of Adam Ford in downtown Denver. Between them were three saloons.[77] Two professional men who loved talking about themselves and sport would tend to gravitate toward each other and saloons presented a handy opportunity for socializing. It is easy to picture them spinning their yarns over beers, or something stronger.

Based on Ford's account in a curling publication, if it is to be believed, he delivered 27 speeches to large political crowds in the latter part of 1904. Among his listeners may have been his neighbor the mining engineer, who also shared an interest in politics. And the talk, knowing Ford's penchant for self-promotion, may well have strayed beyond politics into matters of sport.

Abner Graves worked hard all his life and his granddaughter recalled that he was constantly seeking recognition.[78] He found it in an unlikely place: Akron. And he is remembered to this day because of the letter he penned there.

When he saw Spalding's published request for memories about early games of baseball, Graves recognized an opportunity to draw attention to himself and to his hometown in New York. Assuming he was familiar with Ford's Beachville story, all he had to do was a little tweaking to alter names of participants, some of the rules and—most importantly—change the location to a more acceptable American one.

Was it a clever piece of plagiarism?

One or two opportunities to interact between Graves and Ford in their Denver days might not a case of plagiarism make. But there were so many potential points of contact it creates a strong circumstantial case and leads to a hard-to-escape conclusion: the story about the origins of baseball in America likely had its roots in a similar story about a game from north of the border, in what was, at the time in which the earlier story was set, a colony of *Britain*.

The fine irony would be enough to make Albert Goodwill Spalding spin in his grave.

# 6

## *The Doctor Strikes Out*

Another Ford arrived in Denver in 1902. Adam's nephew, Harold Ford, 28, had decided to try his prospects in the booming Colorado capital. He was the youngest son of Adam's brother William, back in St. Marys, and he was determined to spread his wings after his training as a pharmacist.

Harold and his family often heard news about his cousins in Denver through Julia Ford, who tended to her mother in the white cottage on Queen Street. A steady stream of letters kept the Fords connected despite the vast distance that separated them. Harold was particularly intrigued by stories about life in the far off American West, a place full of cowboys and adventure that seemed so exotic to him. He and his oldest brother, Armour, were surprised to learn from Julia in 1900 that the St. Marys Fords planned to reunite with the Denver Fords in Vancouver, British Columbia, for a new business venture. (Vancouver was to be the family base as Adam established the Washington Sanitarium across the border in Seattle.) Harold and Armour, a lawyer, suggested that their skills might be helpful and Uncle Adam readily agreed. The two young men joined their extended family early in 1901 in Vancouver, but within a few months the new venture turned sour. Arthur's charge of manslaughter in the poisoning death of a patient gave the business a black eye that his subsequent acquittal did little to reverse. The bad publicity doomed the sanitarium. Collapse came as a keen disappointment to Jane and Julia, who had hoped the family unit would be restored and their shaky finances improved in the west coast city. In the end, the women returned to St. Marys, accompanied by Armour.

Adam Ford and his sons went back to Denver and persuaded Harold and his wife, Geddes, to go with them. Harold quickly found a position as a pharmacist at Morell's Pharmacy on East Colfax Street, a major thoroughfare. He stayed there a couple of years before moving to Corona Street, where he opened his Red Cross Drug Store.

When Harold took up residence in the Mile High City, his uncle had just found an office at 1705 Lawrence Street, just a block away from fellow baseball fan Abner Graves. Adam Ford was dealing with some significant anguish because of the legal troubles of Arthur and the failure of the Seattle sanitarium upon which he'd pinned his hopes and in which he had invested heavily. California beckoned Adam's younger son Leon, who returned to his mine engineering and geological and exploration work there. Meanwhile, older son Arthur continued to struggle with alcohol and drug addiction, despite his father's best efforts. Adam Ford, the nephew observed, was still vital and outgoing, but it was obvious that Arthur's problems weighed heavily on him. Adam began talking about another sanitarium he was considering in Custer City, just west of Pueblo. As Harold saw it, his uncle seemed busy enough with his practice but never seemed to have much money, constantly spending it in efforts to wean Arthur off the liquid and chemical demons that controlled his life.

Adam Ford was keenly interested in the welfare of his brother William, who was now in his mid–70s and was beginning to slow down after a long career as town assessor and collector of customs. The Mechanics' Institute had established a library in the new St. Marys town hall and William was seeking a Carnegie grant to build a new library. He had learned that nearby Stratford was seeking one and felt St. Marys should make a request as well.[1] Andrew Carnegie, the U.S. steel-baron-turned-philanthropist was donating money for libraries and William saw an opportunity that others in town dismissed as an impossible dream for a small Canadian town. Given his own early support for the Mechanics' Institute, Adam was gratified that his brother was carrying on the good work of the organization. Harold told his uncle about William's long service as a school trustee and his membership in the Masonic and Oddfellows orders, where he held high offices.[2]

One bright light for the doctor was the sporting scene in Denver, particularly the professional baseball club, and he often took Harold and Arthur to their games. Harold found that his uncle enjoyed talking about baseball games, curling matches and the cricket games he played as a young man. Adam was particularly anxious to learn about the welfare of some of the old-time players he had known and the success of local sports teams in more recent times.

Harold couldn't help but notice how nostalgic his uncle became when talk turned to memories of sport from days gone by. The doctor had begun sharing his recollections of curling in St. Marys with the Ontario Curling Association, which he helped establish nearly thirty years earlier. The first of three stories he wrote for the curling association annual reports appeared in the 1903 edition. The editors introduced Ford that first year, accompanied by a large photo, reporting that they were pleased to share his stories "about curling in Southwestern Ontario and elsewhere in 1848, 1860 and 1878. The doctor's memory appears to be good, his style is vehement, and his pen graphic. He has given us a capital story and we hope will send us more."[3]

Ford recalled that his first experience with curling was on the Thames River in Woodstock, just east of Beachville, in 1848 [at age 16 or 17] "and the peculiarity of the game makes me feel like making a record of it. Scottish curlers had settled in Zorra Township, and had evidently played the game somewhere up in the township." His account was apparently well received and he was back again with two more annual installments.

Ford's accounts about his curling adventures in Canada showed that he could still spin a good story, suggesting that his speeches were likewise entertaining. In the 1905 annual report, for instance, Ford, the former "skip" (captain) of a very successful St. Marys team, recalled competing for Lord Dufferin's Gold Medal in Ottawa against rinks from Quebec and Montreal in 1877. He wrote that upon filing scores of preliminary matches with curling officials, it was learned in town that:

St. Marys led the Dominion [of Canada] with its score of 143. This was the first time that these nabobs of the curling world had ever heard of St. Marys. They had yet to learn that the sons of the hardy pioneers of Western Ontario were men of brawn and brain, whose strength and skills made them worthy foemen on any field.[4]

Ford described playing before Lord and Lady Dufferin, who watched proceedings from behind a glass partition. Toward the end of the match, the Quebec rink's rock was lying "shot" (closest to the center button, thereby making it the winner) and it was well protected from the opposition, he wrote. As skip, he had the last shots to try to dislodge that rock. Ford recalled that he and his rink were handicapped by having to use a heavy iron stone thirty pounds heavier than the granite ones to which his team was accustomed:

I poised myself for a single instant and away went the stone. People saw it coming and jumped up on the boards—only [deputy skip] John [Weir] stood there like a statue, never moving until the stone flashed by him and just grazing the guards, cracked a whole basket-full of eggs on the nose of the winner, sending it spinning like a top, and on and on and out of the house. Cheer?—well, yes, and utterly forgetful of the august presence of our semi-royal hosts, a cyclone of bonnets and brooms flew wildly into the air, and the welkin rang with a good old British cheer. His Excellency and the Hon. Allan Gilmour (the umpire) came up and shook hands with me; when a tapping at the glass partition behind us made us look around, and there was the Countess [sic], who had done the tapping with a fan.... She graciously held out her hand to me with a smile that was partly a gleam—saying: "We all watched that shot. I didn't think you could do it—it was grand."[5]

The recognition from Lord Dufferin and his appreciative spouse was a real feather in Ford's cap. Lord Dufferin was the British peer who had been appointed Governor General of Canada in 1872, a post he held until 1878.[6] As Governor General, he was the representative of Britain's Queen Victoria in Canada and therefore head of state for the newly independent dominion.

Among his non-political accomplishments during his posting to Canada, Lord Dufferin created the Governor General's Curling Trophy and also encouraged the sport of shooting.[7]

Ford recounted in great detail other matches against rinks from Montreal and the Ontario cities of Guelph and Sarnia. Ford liked seeing his own words in print, and so, too, did the Ontario Curling Association. His mind was still sharp into his seventies.

Upon his death, an "in memorium" salute to Ford appeared in the curling publication. It lamented that "the game of curling lost one of its keenest devotees in the death at Denver, Colorado of Dr. Adam Ford, who was for many years associated with the game in Ontario." The tribute to him continued:

> [He had] taken an active part in all the memorable contests in which his club engaged, and how as skip, he was always a tower of strength on the ice. No one was so much the life of the evening as Dr. Ford with his singing and telling well the curling anecdotes. There were few, if any better after-dinner speakers in the province, and he gave freely of his talents for the benefit of others. In his writings for the curling annuals his articles and tales were always spicy and interesting.[8]

In curling circles as well as others, Ford was seen as the life of the party. Cricket also felt his presence.

During his years in Denver, Ford maintained his interest in cricket. The English game was played for many years in the city and reports about the sport appeared from time to time in the local papers. The *Rocky Mountain News* carried an account of the first social event held by the Denver Thistle Cricket Club in 1885, complete with Scottish dancing accompanied by an orchestra and bagpipes.[9] The game went through its ups and downs in a city that came to embrace baseball. By 1899 and 1900, a reorganized Denver Cricket Club was on a definite upswing, with reports of local games carried by the papers. Judging by one account, enthusiasts of the game were getting downright cocky by early 1900 when the club challenged all comers:

> Any cricket team in the world that thinks it is able to force the Denver team to osculate the dust of defeat is invited to come to Denver; and if it succeeds in that endeavor it will be rewarded with a handsome cup. This worldwide defi was issued by the Denver Cricket club at its annual meeting last night. The trophy will be a valuable one. It was at first proposed to confine competition for it to state teams, but it was finally decided to throw down the bars entirely. The cup will be open to a challenge always, but it must always be played for in Denver.[10]

The world might have been surprised to be challenged for cricket supremacy by Denver, a town not associated with the game. Albert Goodwill Spalding, who wrote that cricket appealed more to the slower witted and less manly British than to the average American, would have been surprised at the existence of the game in a town known more for saloons than English tea rooms. The bold challenge must have raised some eyebrows. In any event, the cricket world didn't beat a path to Denver's doorstep and it's not known what happened to that handsome cup.

Adam Ford no doubt watched local cricket matches. With his outgoing personality and love of all sports, he made friends there easily. The Denver Cricket Club appreciated his support and on November 9, 1904, the day after the landslide presidential election victory of Teddy Roosevelt, it granted Ford a certificate of life membership. The document was presented and signed by club president Walter Fairbanks.[11]

In 1905, Ford vacated his office on Lawrence Street and relocated with Arthur to what was termed a "health cottage" on Tennyson Street, in a northwest Denver residential area known as Berkeley. It's likely that Dr. Ford, about to turn 74, wanted to get Arthur away from the downtown saloons to a less tempting environment. The move did little for Arthur, however, who turned 45 in September. He continued to rely on morphine, cocaine, opium and alcohol, rendering him unable to work. With Dr. Ford's practice in decline, the father and son found money was in short supply.

The spring of 1906 was cool and wet in Denver and Adam Ford, who had developed a chronic cough, was becoming impatient about the arrival of the baseball season. He had been feeling unwell during the winter for days or even weeks at a time, often feeling too ill to get out of bed. But he would rally and seem fine, with Arthur there to help when his mind wasn't fogged by drug or drink. Adam continued to correspond with Julia back in St. Marys, where she and her mother had become recluses. Years earlier, Dr. Ford had signed the house over to Julia, who struggled to make ends meet while tending to her asthmatic mother. The Ford ladies appreciated it whenever Adam or Leon could send cash to help them pay the bills and keep the white cottage's roof over their heads. At times, in desperation, Julia had to borrow from relatives to pay for fuel as tradesmen began to decline to extend credit to her.[12]

From his new place on Tennyson, Adam Ford sat down on May 3, 1906, to compose a letter to Julia in which he enclosed a small sum for her, apologizing "I am sorry I could not send some sooner but I simply could not." He continued:

> I am anxious to hear further from Leon but I only expect to hear from him through you as he is too busy to write anybody.... A hundred questions come up but you will tell me what you hear without asking. It is still cool and showery here and no growth to speak of, baseball being the only unstinted [sic] crop.[13]

The two-page note concluded with some comments about friends of the Fords and an upcoming marriage. In closing, Ford wrote about a mutual friend who "was representing some firm in San Francisco and escaped with difficulty when the disaster occurred, but got safely away. It might be well to drop me a note on receipt of this. With much love to you both, Father." At the end of the note, he added a short postscript: "I have written to Leon."

Ford's concern about his youngest son was understandable. Leon Ford was in San Francisco on April 18 when a massive earthquake struck, laying waste to the city of 410,000. The quake, centered at the south end of the city, struck shortly after 5 A.M., sparking one of the worst disasters in American history. The quake and the estimated 60 fires that broke out in its aftermath wrought great damage to the hastily constructed city that had become the cultural and economic hub of the west. More than 500 city blocks were destroyed, more than 3,000 inhabitants died and another 250,000 were left homeless. Damage was set at about $500 million.[14]

Leon was staying with his aunt, Alice Stoddart, the youngest sister of Jane Ford. Alice had married patent-medicine promoter and pharmacist Archie Stoddart in St. Marys. Stoddart, a smooth-talker, had grand plans and what proved to be questionable ethics. He and Alice moved to Buffalo, New York, then on to Kansas City, Missouri, while he developed and sold various concoctions under the impressive-sounding name of Liebig World Dispensary and International Medical and Surgical Institute. Archie began claiming to hold a degree in medicine, without the benefit of the requisite education. He was not unlike his nephews Arthur and Leon Ford in inventing phony credentials and achievements. Constantly on the road throughout the American west before settling on San Francisco as his base of operations, one of his principal products was the "Dr. Liebig Invigorator," a restorative tonic of dubious value. Given his ability to think big and stray from the truth to advance himself and his products, more than one observer wondered if the Liebig name was a sly joke by a snake-oil salesman. After all, he called himself a doctor and he told big lies.

A serial philanderer while on the road—and he was always on the road— Stoddart became intimate with another woman and married her in 1890 without bothering to divorce or advise Alice. Five years later, he obtained fraudulent divorces from Alice and wife number two and promptly married a third, all the while sinking deeply into debt. Stoddart declared bankruptcy in 1901, a lengthy legal proceeding which was interrupted by the quake of 1906 when important documents were lost. After his death in 1910, Stoddart's estate was found to be $40,000 in debt.[15]

Alice Stoddart had been abandoned by a husband she believed to be a man of substance. His letters home had always been full of stories about his expanding business empire and opening of new dispensaries. After his death, Alice became embroiled in litigation with another of his wives as both fought for Archie's money. But after several years, the two Stoddart widows discovered there was no money in the estate after all and they gave up the fight.

Throughout her various troubles, Alice drew support from her brother

Charles, who also had moved to San Francisco. For years, Alice happily played host to other members of the family from back east. In about 1890, her sister Jane, along with Julia and Leon, stayed with her for several months. In fact, the well-dressed Leon was one of her most frequent visitors. He found that the city provided him ready access to the mining country of northern California, whose riches had transformed San Francisco. Staying with Aunt Alice was much less costly than hotel accommodation in the booming city by the bay.

In letters sent back east by Alice and Leon, relatives learned how they survived the disastrous earthquake. Leon was with Alice when the earthquake destroyed her home, but neither was hurt. The first night they huddled with other homeless refugees, seeking shelter from a chilly breeze in the shadow of the wrecked Flood mansion in the fashionable Nob Hill district. Leon reported that he helped some friends bury valuables in a bank cellar and covered them with concrete blocks and dirt. When they returned a week later, they found nothing but ashes from the fires that had swept the area. Alice wrote that he had filled two blankets with clothes and other personal items and lugged them around for three days, helped by soldiers who had been dispatched to aid homeless civilians. With the support of Leon and her brother, Alice found new accommodations, but by 1920 the aging widow decided to return to St. Marys, where she moved in with her niece Julia.[16]

On May 17, 1906, at about 8 P.M., Adam Ford passed away in his sleep at his little health cottage on Tennyson, with son Arthur in the next room. He was 74. Arthur sent a terse telegram to Julia in St. Marys: "Father died from grippe eight o'clock tonight notify Leon his address unknown."[17]

The *Denver Post* carried a story about his death on the front page. In an era of yellow journalism and fierce circulation wars when accuracy often took a back seat to both melodrama and embellishment, the paper published this report:

Once Wealthy,
> Dr. Ford Dies
> Alone in Want
> His Son, a Yale Man, Is a Morphine Fiend, and Fails to Get Physician
> WORK OF DRINK AND DRUGS
> A Pioneer of the State and Once Worth Half a Million Dollars, His Career Closes in Pitiful Poverty
> Worth at one time more than $500,000, and one of the best and most prominent physicians of Denver in early days, Dr. Adam E. Ford died last night in his little "health cottage" at 3940 Tennyson street, penniless, alone and vainly crying for the assistance that did not come. Not even one of the many friends he had was present to smooth the pillows or bring him a glass of water.
> Dr. Ford was more than 80 years old, and most of his later life had been devoted to trying to find a cure for his son, Arthur, who, at 45 years, is a hope-

less wreck. Morphine, cocaine and opium have ruined the younger man and this worry over his son's habits hastened the father's death.

Several months ago Dr. Ford sold out his large house on Curtis street and bought the cottage he died in. This was fitted up into a small hospital or sanitarium, where his son was treated.

On the first of last March the son escaped from the house and, securing morphine, spoiled the cure which had almost been effected. He was arrested on Eighteenth and Market streets and tried before Justice of the Peace Hudson, who sentenced him to ninety days. Through the efforts of his father, Ford escaped serving this sentence and returned home. He continued using the drug, however, and the broken-hearted father could do nothing for him.

Last Sunday, Dr. Ford was taken ill and since had been gradually sinking, until, last night, about 10 o'clock, death relieved his sufferings. A few minutes before he died his son was with him. He went out in search of a doctor, but was so demented from the drugs that he either forgot what he was looking for or lost his way. This morning he could not be found anywhere, and Coroner Rollins is holding the body of his father until he can be located.

Adam E. Ford came to Denver in the early 60s. Young and just out of college, he soon made a name for himself here. Wealth and marriage followed and soon afterward a son. The son was sent to Yale University when 18 years old, but did not take the entire course. He returned to Denver and became interested in athletics. He broke the record for the 100-yard dash at the old D. A. C. Park in 1895 and won many sporting trophies.

His father owned considerable property in Denver and the son, taking advantage of this, did not do much work. He soon became a drunkard. Drugs followed and then the death of his broken-hearted mother.

The father then took to drink and his property gradually slipped from his hands, and today he leaves nothing. He had rich relatives in London, from whom he has been receiving allowance mostly to support himself and son. Coroner Rollins will notify them if the son cannot be located, and the body will probably be shipped to England for burial.[18]

It made for a highly readable story, but most of the purported "facts" were fiction. One can only wonder what Arthur's "dead" mother must have thought upon reading it. Adam Ford's age, his reported wealth and fine home on Curtis Street, his arrival year in Denver, his son winning sprints at age 35 and his wealthy relatives in London provide the most interesting blend of fact and fiction. It's not surprising that the reporter decided to send Ford's body to England, when the less-glamorous London associated with Ford's family was actually located in Canada, not far from St. Marys. Ford had again achieved front-page coverage and some notoriety that embarrassed his family. Worse, this was in a city to which he'd moved 25 years earlier to escape front-page nightmares back in Canada. His grieving family, heart-broken at his death, must have been distraught at how the sad event was portrayed.

Coroner Rollins, who signed Ford's death certificate, placed the time of death at 8 P.M. on May 17 and attributed it to "senility." He noted that the burial was in Fairmount Cemetery, Denver.[19]

Two days after his father's death, Arthur composed a lengthy letter to Julia and his mother to share with them details of Adam's final days.

Father has been a sick man all winter, no question about that and many a stretch of a few days at a time I've had him on my hands to nurse. This time he was in bed 3 days and as you may surmise there was no way to judge him likely to succumb any more than at any other time. He would announce himself to be dying time without number and yesterday gave strong evidence that he had passed the worst and was on the mend. I got him to sleep near noon and he slept fitfully to the end. I really believed him at the point of death the day before and worked for an hour over him fanning and rubbing etc., so he came through all right. I was in the next room much of yesterday and had looked in 2 or 3 times the last time finally went up close to find him lifeless and had passed away while he slept.[20]

Arthur explained that he had only five dollars cash on hand and that the current month's rent had not been paid on the cottage, so he would not send another telegram to Julia. He reported that burial was planned for the following morning and that his cousin, Harold Ford, and Harold's wife Geddes, had been helpful and supportive. "For the present there is presented an aspect of much cash needed and no available assets," he wrote. "I will eventually realize something out of the worn old furniture odds and ends." He concluded with:

Poor father, much at fault often was yet of lofty caste amid the crowd, wrought of the finer metals, walking with head and shoulders high ... seeing above the massed millions in our so-called educated civilization.

On May 21, Leon arrived from San Francisco and immediately dashed off a note to Julia and his mother. He reported that he had found Harold at his drugstore and that his cousin had briefed him on the situation:

Learned that father was buried yesterday at Fairmount, with everything in proper and respectable style. It was rather a keen disappointment for me to be late but then, it was probably for the best as seeing him could have done no good and as it is I have been saved a good deal of the emotional side of this trouble. Harold and his family have been most kind and hospitable, and friends have all been good in their care and attention to the dead and to Arthur ... Arthur came over this evening and we had a good visit. He is in much better condition than I expected and we will make some arrangements for him to continue on and obtain his needs.[21]

Harold Ford also sent along an empathetic letter to Julia and his Aunt Jane, expressing his condolences and assuring them that there had been "nothing undone after your father's death." He wrote that Adam's passing had come as a surprise: "I regret very much that I was not aware of uncle Dr's illness in time to do something. I feel that something could have been done if we had only known."[22]

Adam Ford was buried in an unmarked grave in a southern section of the sprawling Fairmount Cemetery in east Denver. Arthur could never afford a marker stone and his father's resting place remains unmarked to this day.

Adam Ford died without ever hearing the Abner Doubleday story fabricated by Abner Graves. But two years after he was laid to rest, *Spalding's Base Ball Guide* of 1908 was published and promoted the story that Graves had concocted about baseball's conception in Cooperstown. Spalding had his cherished American origin and Americans accepted it at face value. The myth was on its way into the textbooks of schoolchildren and a place in the hearts and minds of baseball fans. Had he been alive, Adam Ford would have been surprised at this turn of events. And, had he spied Graves in one of his old haunts, he might be forgiven for shooting a look at the mining engineer and challenging the fiction.

Arthur Ford continued to battle his demons now that he had only his younger cousin Harold to keep an eye on him. Arthur's behavior became increasingly erratic and in 1910, after observation at the City and County Hospital in Denver, the hospital superintendent William A. Sheriff swore out an arrest warrant for him on March 11. Ford was brought before a Denver County court judge and jury, who found him insane and ordered his detention. A citation for lunacy was filed on March 25 and he was incarcerated at the mental hospital. On June 20, his treatment apparently successful, Ford was ordered freed. He was placed on parole and put in the custody of a W.F. Gettis at the request of attending physician Ed Delehanty.[23]

Little more is known about Arthur Ford and the struggles that continued to plague him. His life continued to spiral downward and in 1917, newspapers reported that he had taken his own life. The *Denver Post* hadn't hired any fact-checkers since its lurid story about the demise of Adam Ford eleven years earlier. More melodrama and mangled information was provided its readers:

"Here goes the wreck of a misspent life."

Arthur B. Ford, 54, Princeton graduate, one time nationally known as a baseball player and foot racer, but of late years a pitiful victim of the drug habit, scrawled the foregoing epitome of his sentiments on a scrap of paper in his room at the Bristol Hotel, 1848 Larimer street, shortly after 11 o'clock this morning, and then sent a bullet crashing into his brain.

Ford's career was as picturesque as his end was tragic. He was born in Canada, of wealthy parents. His father, Dr. John Ford, was one of the leading practitioners of the Dominion. He was graduated from Osborne Hall, St. Mary's Ontario, and later studied law at Princeton university. During his college career he gained a reputation for himself as a ball player and sprinter.[24]

Wrong father, wrong education and exaggerated claims about his prowess on the ball diamond and race track, but at least it was mercifully brief, reducing the chance for further embellishment and misinformation. The *Spokesman Review* of Spokane picked up the story a few days later and noted that Ford would be remembered in that city as a former manager of the R.G. Dun & Company credit reporting agency and as a fine billiard player. It reported that Ford had left Spokane in about 1894 because of his drug habit and had moved to San Francisco, where his father, a Canadian doctor, found and cured him of the habit: "Until the father's death a few years ago Arthur Ford had enjoyed the best of health, but again took up the habit that led to his suicide."[25]

Arthur was buried in an unmarked grave about 50 yards west of his father in Fairmount Cemetery in Denver. Leon Ford continued to chase his dreams, billing himself as a geologist as he promoted gold and other mineral ventures in California and neighboring states. He tried oil exploration in Louisiana and Texas from 1917 to 1919 but by 1923 he was back in California in the Grass Valley district, where he was listed as consulting geologist for Grass Valley Extension Mines. The venture had an option on 1,700 acres of land next to mines that had produced more than $300 million worth of gold. In a prospectus promoting investment in the mine, Ford wrote that he was "deeply impressed with the possibilities for production" based on vein formations. He predicted that early and energetic development of the property "will result in making a mine of high value and long life." After his glowing report, Ford was made a director and consulting geologist for the venture.[26] But as with virtually all the projects with which he became associated, the much-hyped opportunity failed to live up to expectations and became little more than a mining footnote.

Throughout his travels, Leon Ford kept sister Julia apprised of his activities, sending money when he could and always expressing optimism that his latest or his next project was bound to make him a success. He invariably dressed the part of the successful man he aspired to be. Even when he returned home to visit Julia in St. Marys, Leon favored formal attire, complete with cane and gloves, and when children saw the exceedingly dapper man on the streets of his hometown, they referred to him behind his back as "Lord Ford." But real financial success eluded him and upon his death in 1946 in Los Angeles, his estate amounted to a mere $82.[27]

Adam Ford's widow, Jane, passed away quietly at home in 1914 at age 74, leaving Julia alone for a time before she agreed to take on and care for her Aunt Alice. Financial struggles continued in the home built for the Ford family. Alice died in 1937, aged 91, followed by Julia in 1948 at 90.

The life and times of Adam Ford and his family made for a tragic tale. Touched by poison, death, manslaughter, success, failure, alcohol and baseball, it was a real-life melodrama no newspaper needed to embellish. With those ingredients, it is eerily similar to the life story of Abner Graves, the more famous teller of a story about baseball, who also made Denver his home.

# Seven

## *Filling a Need*

In 1874, American professional baseball, still in its infancy, organized a tour of England and Ireland. The group was led by Harry Wright, manager of the Boston Red Stockings, who proclaimed that the purpose was to showcase the game and the "virtues of the American way." The tour, featuring players from the Red Stockings and the Philadelphia Athletics, failed to generate much interest or revenue and was considered a failure.[1]

After that tour, which Spalding helped arrange at the request of Wright, Spalding was of the view that baseball's roots lay in England.[2] But the constant assertions of a British origin by Henry Chadwick, who by 1881 was editing Spalding's popular baseball guides, so irked him that he sought American roots. A rising tide of American national pride no doubt played a role in his change of heart and in 1888 he decided to organize another world tour to again spread the gospel of American values and of its game. As Spalding's biographer Peter Levine put it, "although less aggressive and more modest than other late-nineteenth-century adventures in American imperialism, Spalding's gambit clearly aimed to extend an American presence in the world."[3] Besides, by then, baseball was his business, and he was determined to travel as far afield as Australia, he told a reporter, "for the purpose of extending [his] sporting goods business to that quarter of the globe and to create a market for goods there."[4] Baseball had been very good to Albert Goodwill Spalding and he was going to use the game to further his sporting goods empire.

The tour lasted from October 1888 to April 1889 and included players from the Chicago White Stockings, of which Spalding was president. He also brought along players from other National League teams so the Chicago team could play against a league all-star league team as the tour circled the globe. They headed to San Francisco, playing a number of games between themselves and exhibition matches with local teams along the way before sailing for Australia. After finding mixed results Down Under, the tour visited Colombo, Ceylon, for a heat-shortened game before continuing west to Egypt and a game beside the pyramids in Cairo. Italy was the next stop, where a game was played in Rome, but Spalding failed in his efforts to arrange an audience with the pope and a game in the ancient Colosseum. Then the tour traveled north for games in Florence and in Paris. Crossing the English Channel, Spalding's "All Americas" played 11 games in England, Ireland and Scotland, where the reception was warm for the players, but less so for the game they played. On the bright side, they met and played before British royalty.

On April 6, 1889, the tour sailed into New York harbor, having played 42 games around the globe before about 200,000 people during the previous six months. Parades and banquets greeted the returning heroes and Spalding soaked it all in. He told a reporter that after meeting royalty, seeing the sphinxes, admiring the beauties of Paris and sampling worldly delights, "I am proud to be called an American."[5]

A highlight of post-tour celebrations was a gala all-male banquet held at Delmonico's banquet hall in Manhattan on April 8. Delmonico's, the most fashionable restaurant in New York, staged one of the most elaborate events in its history for the globetrotters. On hand were 300 celebrities, including Theodore Roosevelt, the author, adventurer and former New York State assemblyman who was a rising star in Republican politics and still a dozen years and an assassin's bullet from the U.S. presidency. Also present were Mark Twain and famous actor DeWolf Hopper, known for his theatrical performances of "Casey at the Bat," who recited it yet again.

The host of the event was A.G. Mills, the former president of the National League and a good friend of Spalding. He saluted the players that night as "gladiators ... covered with their American manhood." Mills insisted that the game they played for the world to see was baseball and that "patriotism and research had established that the game ... was American in origin." His assertion drew thunderous applause and chants of "No rounders! No rounders! No rounders!"[6]

Twain, whose days as a cub reporter in Virginia City were long behind him, delivered a rambling but well-received speech in which he spoke about the Sandwich Islands, now known as the Hawaiian Islands. He praised the ballplayers for having "ploughed a new equator round the globe, stealing bases on their bellies." Twain declared that they had "carried the American name to the uttermost parts of the earth—and covered it with glory." The now-famous writer saluted baseball as "the very symbol, the outward and visible expression of the drive, and rush, and struggle of the raging, tearing, booming nineteenth century."[7] Twain's apparent enthusiasm for American expansionism was in stark contrast to the strong anti-imperialist tendencies he was developing. In just a few more years he became prominent in a movement that decried American imperialism. Meanwhile, Roosevelt, a fellow diner that night, would soon become a leading proponent of pushing American interests far beyond its borders.

The final stop was in Chicago, where the city feted Spalding and the sports entrepreneur drank in the praise and tried to overlook the fact that he had lost $5,000 on his world tour.[8] Despite the financial setback, Spalding took heart that his missionary effort to link baseball to American interests in the minds of the outside world had met with some success, even if other countries failed to embrace the game itself.

But Spalding was increasingly confounded by the ongoing claims about baseball's parentage from his editor, Henry Chadwick, who insisted the game was derived from rounders—despite those loud chants at Delmonico's. The doughty Chadwick could have been fired by Spalding, but Spalding kept him on. In the ensuing years, as the United States shifted its gaze to matters overseas and became determined to advance its national interests, Spalding grew ever more determined to prove that baseball was an American invention.

Chadwick, as we have seen, used the 1903 edition of *Spalding's Official Base Ball Guide* to espouse his view that there was "no doubt" baseball's predecessor was rounders. In late 1904 or early 1905 Spalding came up with the idea of establishing a commission, a specially appointed group of men to pursue the origins of the game and prove its American conception. He carefully picked its members in a bid to ensure that its findings would coincide with his own opinion. To act as secretary and solicit information from the public, he appointed James E. Sullivan, president of American Sports Publishing Company, publisher of *Spalding's Official Base Ball Guide*. As such, Sullivan had been his employee. Spalding persuaded A. G. Mills, his longtime friend and former president of the National League to chair the commission. Also named to the group was Morgan G. Bulkeley, first president of the National League in 1876, and Nick Young, the first secretary of the league, who followed Mills as its president. Rounding out the group were former star players Al Reach and George Wright (and more recently, business associates of Spalding). United States Senator Arthur P. Gorman, who had been associated years earlier with baseball in Maryland, was also appointed but died before the commission could issue its findings.[9] With this group, chaired by Mills, who had declared back in 1889 at the Delmonico's banquet that "patriotism and research" had already established America's claim to the game, Spalding was certain his friends and associates would see things his way. Then, when the commission reached the pre-ordained conclusion, Spalding could claim that his view had been endorsed by a blue-chip panel that had left no stone unturned in its efforts.

Spalding, in his continued speeches and newspaper articles, asked listeners and readers to submit their early memories of the game to commission secretary Sullivan. Over the next two years, hundreds of letters and documents were received by the commission. It was relatively early in the existence of the inquiry that Abner Graves spied Spalding's appeal in the Akron newspaper. It's not known when Spalding first saw Graves's letter, but historian David Block surmises it must have been forwarded by Sullivan to Spalding at his new home at the Theosophist colony in Point Loma, California, an article appeared in a Theosophist newsletter there in August telling the Cooperstown story. The article noted that the late Abner Doubleday, the Civil War major-general and prominent Theosophist had named, invented, and developed baseball. And it attributed the revelation to Denver mining engineer Abner Graves.[10] The Theosophist newsletter quoted from Graves's letter and also reminded readers of the significant contribution to baseball made by another well-known Theosophist, A. G. Spalding. It was no doubt Spalding who leaked the Graves letter to the publication.

The same day the story about Doubleday appeared in the newsletter, Spalding fired off two letters drawing attention to it. He sent one to an old-time player, Albert Pratt, in upstate Ticonderoga, New York, to see if the Cooperstown story rang true to him. The other went to Sullivan at the Special Base Ball Commission, urging him that the "Doubleday Cooperstown tip is worthy of careful investigation and corroboration."[11]

For some reason, Spalding took several months before contacting Graves about his story. He had ready access to Graves's address through his man Sullivan, so perhaps Spalding was waiting for some sort of confirmation from old-timer Pratt, who lived about 140 miles northeast of Cooperstown. Or maybe he was awaiting something supportive of the Graves tale in the hundreds of submissions that Sullivan was going through. Nothing materialized.

In a letter dated November 10, 1905, Spalding advised Graves that he was seeking further information about the Cooperstown story. The letter asked the question: "Who was Abner Doubleday?" Spalding knew full well that Graves had claimed it was the Civil War major-general, so it would seem to be a strange question. Unless, of course, Spalding was feigning ignorance as some sort of test of Graves's mind. Spalding then asked for Doubleday's age at the time of the embryonic game. And he sought clarification of the year because Graves's reference to the "log cabin and hard cider campaign" of General William Henry Harrison meant that it could have taken place anywhere from 1839 to 1841. "Could you give me the name and address of any persons now living in Cooperstown, New York City, or elsewhere, that could substantiate your recollections of Doubleday's invention or his first introduction of the game of Base ball?," he asked. Spalding also wondered if Graves could share any more recollections that he may have omitted from his letter.[12]

Graves didn't waste any time in replying. In a letter dated November 17, 1905, he responded that he believed all the players from 65 years ago were dead, except for two aged men, one living in Cooperstown, the other in Cleveland. Graves added that there was virtually no chance any diagram made by Doubleday had survived. He recalled that Doubleday was about 16 or 17 years old and living in Cooperstown when he invented the game. Graves also claimed that he remembered a game in which the inventor played catcher for Otsego Academy. Doubleday, he wrote, drew a diagram of the positions in the dirt for Graves and some other boys who had been playing marbles in front of a tailor's shop. The mining engineer failed to clear up any confusion about the year and provided little more about Doubleday. He concluded with an editorial comment: "Just in my present mood I would rather have Uncle Sam declare war on England and clean her up than have one of her citizens beat us out of Base Ball."[13] Graves may have been referring to Henry Chadwick and his rounders theory. While Spalding likely admired Graves's patriotism and determination, he was doubtless unhappy that the response failed to provide any corroboration for his tale. Graves did include a diagram he created to show "Abner Doubleday's plan of 'Base Ball,' made in Cooperstown, N.Y. 1839 -40 or -41." It showed eleven men and their positions on a diamond-shaped field. Five of them were infielders, three at the bases, with shortstops between first and second and between second and third base. Also depicted were a pitcher, a catcher and four outfielders.[14] The game had all the hallmarks of the New York game played at the time.

Another letter written by Graves about the same time describing Doubleday's invention of the game appeared in *The Story of Cooperstown,* a book published in 1917 by Ralph Birdsall, Rector of Christ Episcopal Church in Cooperstown.[15] It is unclear how Birdsall obtained the letter or whether it was sent to Spalding, but it contains further information that Graves felt compelled to share about Doubleday. According to Birdsall:

"Abner Doubleday," writes Graves, "was several years old than I. In 1838 and 1839 I was attending the 'Frog Hollow' school south of the Presbyterian church, while he was at school somewhere over the hill. I do not know, neither is it possible for anyone to know, on what spot the first game of Base Ball was played according to Doubleday's plan. He went diligently among the boys in the town, and in several schools, explaining the plan, and inducing them to play Base Ball in lieu of the other games. Doubleday's game was played in a good many places around town: sometimes in the old militia, or training ground, a couple of hundred yards southeasterly from the Court House, where County Fairs were occasionally held; sometimes in Mr. Bennett's field south of Otsego Academy; at other times over in the Miller's Bay neighborhood, and up the lake.

"I remember one dandy, fine, rollicking game where men and big boys from the Academy and other schools played up on Mr. Phinney's farm, a mile or two up the west side of the lake, when Abner Doubleday and Prof. Green chose sides, and Doubleday's side beat Green's side badly. Doubleday was captain and catcher for his side, and I think John Graves and Elihu Phinney were pitchers for the two sides. I wasn't in the game, but stood close by Doubleday, and wanted Prof. Green to win. In his first time at bat Prof. Green missed three consecutive balls. Abner caught all three, then pounded Mr. Green on the back with the ball, while they and all others were roaring with laughter, and yelling 'Prof. is out.'"[16]

While Spalding may never have seen this letter, its style suggests that it was, in fact, penned by Graves. And, with a local man of the cloth quoting from it, it would seem to be genuine. For his part, however, Spalding must have felt that there was little more to gain from additional correspondence with Graves. There was no further exchange between the two men and Spalding looked in vain for corroboration. In the end, he set aside any misgivings he might have had and accepted Graves's story about the game's invention by an American military hero and fellow spiritualist.

Throughout 1906, Sullivan continued to receive letters from old-time ballplayers and writers recalling the early days of the game. Among the submissions received were some insisting that the game was American, but none of them provided any proof. One such letter came from John M. Ward, a former shortstop for the New York Giants, who had participated in Spalding's 1888–89 World Tour. He based his opinion on interviews with old-time players. Henry Chadwick gamely laid out his rounders theory yet again, although he must have sensed that the fix was in and that his boss' hand-picked commission would never accept it. The work of the commission continued, but no bombshells or revelations were unearthed as the months dragged on. A three-year mandate had been given the Special Base Ball Commission when Spalding set it up in early 1905, so a report was expected by the end of 1907.

In July of 1907, with the deadline looming, Spalding put his own oar in the water with a long letter to Sullivan at the commission in which he denounced Chadwick's rounders theory and endorsed the Cooperstown tale of Graves. "I am very strongly inclined to the belief that Cooperstown, N.Y., is the birthplace of the present American game of Base Ball, and that Major General Abner Doubleday was the originator of the game," he wrote.[17] He sent the letter from his home in Point Loma. He did not disclose his connection to Doubleday through the Theosophists. This was unlike the course taken by his friend Mills, who freely conceded his personal ties to Doubleday. In his final report on behalf of the commission, published in Spalding's 1908 Guide, Mills readily admitted his relationship with the Civil War hero through the Grand Army of the Republic.

In October, commission secretary Sullivan sent a package of selected submissions to committee members to get their thoughts as the inquiry began to wind down. He described it as "the gist of the information so far received" and it included the letter from Abner Graves. Sullivan asked members to be discreet as they pondered the materials:

> There is considerable public interest in this question, and to avoid premature publication and discussion I would suggest that this whole matter be treated in confidence until a decision is finally reached, and then it can be promulgated in some systematic way that will be satisfactory.[18]

There is little doubt that the "systematic way" had already been decided by the puppetmaster on behalf of the commission. The findings would be published in the next *Spalding Guide*, which is exactly what happened in the spring of 1908. In the end, it was left to lawyer Mills, the old friend of the late major-general, to write the report of the commission's findings.

* * *

The push to cast baseball as a product of American ingenuity came as the nation was trying to redefine itself in increasingly urbanized and industrial times. Life was becoming complicated. Questions arose about how to cope and answers were sought in new directions. Many of them were provided by reformers known as progressives. The Progressive Era, as it was known, began in about 1890 and lasted about 30 years. It promoted the value of education and scientific methods in history, economics and political science. The era saw efforts to eliminate corruption in politics and steps toward busting or regulation of trusts. Social and moral reforms were pushed, as well as improved working conditions, a ban on child labor and introduction of food inspection. Progressives challenged the old ways of doing things and sought a better way. A muckraking press helped them expose inequities and abuses committed by governments and business.[19]

Baseball's popularity grew rapidly during the Progressive Era as millions flocked to the ballparks. One observer described the connection between the country and the game this way:

> The Progressive ethos framing baseball's emergence as a national sport was of inestimable value in establishing baseball's status as a cultural icon. Baseball grew up with America's cities, its teams becoming a focus of civic pride and energy. At the same time, baseball's fields and parks, the leisurely pace of the game, and its becoming an outdoor, daytime spectacle invoked rural and pastoral associations that were particularly evocative to a generation of Americans confronting an increasingly urbanizing and industrializing environment.[20]

The country had become more complex as agricultural and rural interests gave way to the rise of cities and industry. Americans, no longer tied to the land and farm animals, had more leisure time to pursue and follow sports. Baseball was there for them and it hearkened back to simpler times. When a story emerged that baseball had its roots decades earlier in a small town in upstate New York, Americans embraced it. It was perfect. It made so much sense and it filled a need in the hearts and minds of those who heard it.

* * *

That Spalding, Mills and his fellow commissioners would be anxious to conclude that baseball was purely American was no surprise, given the rampant jingoism and patriotism of their time. America was on a roll and baseball was its game.

In 1901, when Theodore Roosevelt was sworn in as president upon the assassination of William McKinley, he became the most powerful man in what had become the most powerful nation on earth. As one of his biographers noted:

> For several years both he and the world had been aware that the United States was the most energetic of nations. She had long been the most richly endowed. This first year of the new century found her worth twenty-five billion dollars more than her nearest rival, Great Britain, with a gross national product more than twice that of Germany and Russia. The United States, with seventy million citizens, was already so rich in goods and services that she was more self-sustaining than any industrial power in history.[21]

America's manufactured products were shipped around the world and Wall Street was booming as investment flowed in from Europe. "Even the Bank of England had begun to borrow money on Wall Street. New York City seemed destined to replace London as the world's financial center," it was noted.[22] So it wouldn't do that the popular national pastime of this robust new world power was derived from a game played by English schoolchildren. Just as Daniel Webster had sought to make the language of the English more American, Spalding and company felt the need to ensure baseball had an American identity. America was emerging as a military power and tying baseball's birth to an American military leader like Doubleday was just what the country needed. As one writer explained the situation:

> Besides the military connection, the Doubleday story also helped the U.S. dispel its lingering sense of inferiority to Great Britain. In the absence of having a native language and people (with most Indians now killed off), having a home-grown sport was important for America's national identity. And beyond shaking off *inferiority*, baseball's creation tale was instead used to proclaim America's *superiority*.[23]

So it was important for America to lay claim to its favorite sport as the nation arrived on the world stage. Increasingly, militarism and expansionism fit the mood of the day. The country was awash in pride over the swift and successful Spanish-American War of 1898, when Teddy Roosevelt and his volunteer Rough Riders captured San Juan Hill in Cuba. That war provided overseas possessions in the Philippines and Puerto Rico and, for a brief time, Cuba. An assertive president was in the White House and he was outward-looking. Roosevelt took steps to dramatically expand the navy, he took over construction of the stalled Panama Canal and he mediated a peace treaty between Russia and Japan and a dispute between France and Germany over Morocco. He espoused the Roosevelt Corollary to the Monroe Doctrine of years earlier, which had insisted that no European nation should intervene in the Americas. His corollary reasserted that no European nation had any business interfering in countries to the south of the United States, but added that, under certain conditions, American intervention might be warranted. He settled the lingering Alaska boundary dispute with Britain and he ordered the voyage of the Great White Fleet, the first circumnavigation of the globe by any country's naval forces. When he was U.S. Assistant Navy Secretary in the 1890s, Roosevelt readily conceded that he was an expansionist, but had rejected the derisive "imperialist" tag bestowed by people like Mark Twain and the Anti-Imperialist League. Roosevelt was forging a new, more aggressive role for America in the world and he enjoyed wide public support.

When American forces went to other lands, they took baseball with them. The game, which had been played by soldiers during the Civil War, became incorporated in military programs and into military education at West Point and the Naval Academy. The annual Army-Navy baseball game began in 1901.[24]

Baseball's connections to the military had been recognized long before Spalding touted them in *America's National Game,* where he argued: "Base Ball is War!," adding pointedly, "The founder of our national game became a Major-General in the United States Army!"[25] Surprisingly, one of the first had been Henry Chadwick, the Brit, who in 1889 published *How to Play Base Ball* and laid on the military metaphors with a literary shovel. The prolific sportswriter wrote about a "well placed attack" in the game, with tactics drawn up and coordinated by the captain or "commander of the field." Chadwick noted that the battery of pitcher and catcher is "what the battery of a regiment is to the line of the infantry." The pitcher, he wrote, fires at the opposing team's "home base." Chadwick insisted that the success of the "field corps" (infielders) depends on the ability of the catcher "to stand the hot fire of the pitcher's delivery." For his part, the batter faces "hot fire courageously" from a pitcher who wants to "capture" him.[26] Little could Chadwick have known that he was helping to prepare the ground for a story about an American origin of the game in which an American military leader would get credit for inventing it.

Chadwick went on, noting that to win games, teams must become "a nine who work together with machine-like unity ... [making practice a] kind of West Point drill." He also observed that, like soldiers in a long war, baseball players prevail in pennant races who "can best stand the costly wear and tear of the campaign."[27]

In 1906, the *Chicago American* observed: "Baseball is one of the reasons why American soldiers are the best in the world—quick witted, swift to act, ready of judgment, capable of going into action without officers."[28] It was not the first time sport was linked to military exploits. Rugby played on the fields of Eton had been credited with forging the character of British soldiers.

Writer C.H. Claudy issued a book in 1912 called *The Battle of Base-Ball,* in which he likened baseball to war and its players to soldiers. "Base-ball is a battle," he wrote. "It has its generals, its captains, its lieutenants, its rank and file. It has its grand strategy, its tactics and its drill. It has its battlefield, its arms and its equipment." He went on:

In war the individually brilliant and brave man frequently performs some remarkable act, and lives forever as a hero, as Pickett at Gettysburg, or Hobson at Santiago harbor. [Richard Hobson, a rear admiral was decorated for his courage at the Cuban harbor during the Spanish-American conflict.] But it is the men who think first of the good of the entire army, and the success of the campaign, who win the battles.... Just as the nerves of an army are its signals, so the nerves of a base-ball team are its signals or signs by which the captain or manager directs the play, and by which players inform each other what is about to be done.[29]

Claudy, Chadwick and Spalding reveled in the military metaphor, which today may seem foolish since another American sport is far more like war. Baseball, in retrospect, seems an odd sport to connect to war. After all, how many military victories have claimed by an army that ran around in more circles than the enemy? And where the object of the game is to successfully reach "home"?

Football would seem to be a more fitting sport to be tied to the military. Its players wear helmets. Football teams march down the field to take territory from the enemy. They have on-field generals in quarterbacks and they clash in hand-to-hand combat, not unlike trench warfare. Over the combatants' heads, the quarterback may throw a "bomb" during an aerial assault. Football is a game of gaining territory to reach a "goal."

George Carlin, the late American comedian, made these hilarious but insightful comparisons between the two sports:

Baseball is a nineteenth century pastoral game. Football is a twentieth century technological struggle. Baseball is played on a diamond, in a park. The baseball park! Football is played on a gridiron, in a stadium, sometimes called Soldier Field or War Memorial Stadium.... In football, the specialist comes in to kick. In baseball, the specialist comes in to relieve somebody. Football has hitting, clipping, spearing, piling on, personal fouls, late hitting and unnecessary roughness. Baseball has the sacrifice.[30]

Carlin went on to observe that football is often played in dreadful weather, while baseball games are cancelled if it rains. He noted that military lingo pervades football in phrases like "blitz" and ground attack" and in punching holes in defensive lines. Meanwhile, the object of baseball "is to get home, safe."

So why did the military embrace baseball—not football—as America strode onto the world's stage? The simple fact is that baseball was ready; football wasn't. Baseball had been played professionally since 1869 and by 1901 the two major leagues drew 3.6 million spectators. By 1905, when Graves wrote his letter, attendance had grown to nearly six million. Baseball was booming, just like the country. Football, however, was struggling to survive. A game played at colleges and by amateur clubs, the game was still evolving and would not become professional until the 1920s. By 1905, when the Cooperstown baseball story surfaced, there were calls to ban football entirely because that year saw 18 players die, three of them at the college level. In addition, another 159 were injured, some of them paralyzed.[31]

Football was a violent, brutish sport at the time. As far back as the 1820s Americans had played the game. Princeton and Harvard students played early variations of football and, although it faded out for a time, it returned after the Civil War. For several decades the game was rife with brute force that was used to break up offensive formations. Rutgers, Princeton, Columbia, Cornell and Harvard were all fielding teams. As a young Harvard freshman in 1876, Theodore Roosevelt saw his first football game when Yale prevailed over Harvard. Roosevelt remained a fan of the game for the rest of his life, although the athletic but slightly built and bespectacled man never played it.[32] In late 1876, the Intercollegiate Foot-Ball Association was formed to create a standardized field of play of 140 yards by 70 yards and establish universal rules. (Until then, captains met before games to set the rules for the match.) Football at the time bore little resemblance to the game of today. Rugby-like scrums were used, but eventually a line of scrimmage was developed and the position of quarterback created, although no passing was allowed. The concept of "downs" was eventually adopted. As experimentation continued, the flying wedge was adopted as a mass formation to move the ball forward. By 1893, Harvard was using 60 variations of it. But the formation took a toll on the players it mowed down because they wore virtually no protective equipment.

Some colleges began talking about banning football because of the frequency of serious injuries and some newspapers backed the call. Even longtime fan Teddy Roosevelt realized that there was a problem, but he didn't want it banned. "The brutality must be done away with and the danger minimized," he wrote in *Harper's Weekly* in 1893. "The rules for football ought probably to be altered so as to do away with the present mass play, and, I think, also the present system of interference, while the umpires must be made to prevent slugging or any kind of foul play."[33]

Charles Eliot, president of Harvard, Roosevelt's alma mater, was a constant and harsh critic of the game. In an early 1905 article titled "The Evils of Football," Eliot wrote that he disliked how it made otherwise civil men behave. He denounced the roughness of a sport that saw players "disabling opponents by kneeing and kicking, and by heavy blows on the head and particularly about the eyes, nose, and jaw." Eliot despised its war-like quality: "The common justification offered by these hateful conditions is that football is a fight; and that its strategy and ethics are those of war ... the barbarous ethics of warfare."[34]

When it appeared that the threat to football's continued existence was real, Roosevelt summoned representatives of Harvard, Yale and Princeton to the White House in 1905. He urged them to take steps to reform the game, so as to make it safer, rather than face a ban. In early December, thirteen institutions gathered to consider changes and on December 28, 1905, in New York City, a larger gathering of 62 college and university officials was convened to undertake reform. This group would become the National Collegiate Athletic Association.[35] Roosevelt, by intervening when he did, is credited with saving football as a sport by using the same powers of persuasion that allowed him to mediate a peace accord between Japan and Russia at roughly the same time. He was awarded the Nobel Peace Prize for that effort a year later.[36] It was ironic that the warrior of San Juan Hill was an international peacemaker at roughly the same time that he was fighting to keep gridiron warfare alive domestically.

A rules committee brought in changes intended to reduce deaths and injuries in football. These innovations included introduction of the forward pass, doubling to ten yards the distance needed to gain a first down and a ban on all forms of mass formation and gang tackling. Injuries were immediately reduced, but deaths, after a dip to eleven in 1906 and 1907, increased to 13 in 1908 and spiked at 26 in 1909, with ten of those victims being collegiate players. It took many years before deaths were brought down significantly and permanently.[37] So while decidedly more warlike than baseball, football was still experiencing major problems that caused it to run afoul of college administrators, the muckraking press and others.

Roosevelt and others of his day viewed baseball as "too soft," something Spalding seemed to acknowledge. However, "the Doubleday myth allowed the sport to fight back. It helped baseball establish its military credentials and sign on for empire," Robert Elias asserts in *The Empire Strike Out*. He cites baseball historian Harrington Crissey's take that although "serious baseball research has refuted the [Doubleday story, it did] not diminish the relationship that developed between baseball and the military over the last century."[38]

Elias went on to describe the symbiotic relationship between baseball and a newly confident nation at the outset of the twentieth century this way:

> Baseball signed on early in support of America's imperial ambitions, partly because it had similar aspirations. The sport was drafted by the nation's empire builders, and it also eagerly enlisted. As the United States has projected its dominance worldwide, baseball lent a hand—bolstering the military, boosting the nation's global reach, and proselytizing for the American way. As the United States expanded, conquering new frontiers, so did baseball. Each found multiple uses for each other. And for the most part, all seemed well.[39]

Baseball had aligned itself with American interests generally and with the American military in particular. Given this relationship, when Abner Graves came up with a story about a Civil War major-general inventing the game, its appeal was irresistible. Baseball needed the Doubleday story and it filled an even deeper need in America.

# Eight

# *The Myth Promoted,*
# *Exposed, Adopted*

**Baseball,** a popular sport in the United States, of such general interest as to be known as "the national game." It had its origin in the old English game of "rounders," but developed on American soil into a very different sport. In Philadelphia an early form was played under the name of "town ball," and a similar game was known in Upper Canada as early as 1838. It was in the neighborhood of New York, however, that baseball received its greatest development, regularly organized clubs contesting in the "Elysian Fields," at what is now the site of Hoboken, N. J., as early as 1845. It was not until 1857, however, that the first baseball convention was held for the purpose of framing uniform rules out of the various methods of each district and club, and in the following May the first "National Baseball Association" was organized.[1]

So began a lengthy entry about baseball in the 1905 edition of the popular *Encyclopedia Americana*, its sixteen volumes published by *Scientific American*. Sources given for the entry included *Spalding's Base Ball Guide*, Henry Chadwick's 1886 book *The Art of Pitching and Fielding, Batting and Base-Running* and J.M. Ward's *Base Ball* of 1888. This was the prevailing wisdom about the origins of the game before Abner Graves and Albert Spalding perpetrated their mischief. The encyclopedia was barely off the press when Graves penned his letter about Cooperstown in April that same year.

Baseball history was about to be rewritten by the Special Base Ball Commission chaired by A.G. Mills. Months went by as Sullivan compiled and sorted the evidence he received. With the end-of-1907 deadline approaching, the dutiful secretary shared with all commission members the gist of what he had received. That included Spalding's promotion of the Doubleday-Cooperstown story and Chadwick's argument about rounders. Then it was handed to Mills, the able lawyer, to pull it all together in the group's official finding.

Mills barely met the deadline. In a letter dated December 30, 1907, Mills delivered his conclusion to Sullivan. In slightly less than 1,400 words, Mills

Abner Graves (right) in his office in the Bank Block, downtown Denver, circa 1910. Note the rock samples in the glass case to the left. One of his visitors, at rear, inspects a chunk of rock while Graves studies some documentation. Used by permission of Claire Strashun.

delivered the opinion that baseball was American in origin and that the "best evidence obtainable to date" was that Abner Doubleday devised it in 1839 in Cooperstown.

The letter lacked clarity and precision, suggesting that Mills was pressed for time and had spent little time revising it. In its second sentence, Mills wrote: "I cannot say that I find myself in accord with those who urge the American origin of the game as against its English origin as contended for by Mr. Chadwick, on patriotic ground."[2] That was a strange assertion from Mills, the master of ceremonies at the famous Delmonico's banquet of 1889, where he'd wrapped himself in the flag to declare that "patriotism and research" had demonstrated that the game was American to its core.

Then, in an apparent effort to cushion the blow of what followed to Chadwick and others who pushed a British origin, Mills added that "our Anglo-Saxon kinsmen" should be praised for fostering field sports. Mills insisted that if the facts had shown that baseball's origins lay in England, "I do not think it would be any the less admirable or welcome on that account."

He went on to observe that "until my own perusal of this testimony, my own belief had been that our game of Base Ball, substantially as played today, originated with the Knickerbocker club of New York...." More than once in his report, Mills referred to evidence received by the commission as "testimony," giving it status beyond its worth. As a lawyer, Mills would have known that by using that term he was adding inappropriate weight to the submissions received. In fact, the letters and other items he reviewed had not been taken under oath.

Next Mills returned to "Father" Chadwick and his assertion about rounders. Mills dismissed the English game's similarity to baseball as limited to tossing a ball or "striking it with some kind of a stick." Such implements, Mills noted, were employed in games that were played in ancient Greece and Rome. He went on:

> I do not, myself, see how there can be any question that the game of Base Ball originated in the United States and not in England—where it certainly had never been played, in however crude a form, and was strange and unfamiliar when an American ball team first played it there.

Mills then re-stated his earlier personal belief that the Knickerbocker club originated the game in New York in 1845:

> but, in the interesting and pertinent testimony for which we are indebted to Mr. A. G. Spalding, appears a circumstantial statement by a reputable gentleman, according to which the first known diagram of the diamond, indicating positions for the players, was drawn by Abner Doubleday in Cooperstown, N.Y., in 1839.[3]

Mills described Doubleday's military career and his death in 1893. "It happened that he and I were members of the same veteran military organization—the crack Grand Army Post," he wrote. Mills reported that he had been in command of the military escort and guard of honor as Doubleday lay in state before his interment at Arlington National Cemetery.

While Mills made no effort to hide his connection to Doubleday, one is left wondering about the relationship between the two old warriors. If they had been close, wouldn't Mills have already known that Doubleday invented the sport? Social occasions in veterans' organizations would have been an ideal time for the old major-general to talk about baseball. Wouldn't Mills have included some reference to Doubleday's assertions to further buttress the story from the "reputable gentleman"?

Mills readily assigned credit to Spalding for the discovery of the origin tale, yet omitted the name of the "reputable gentleman" for some reason. Mills was overstating Spalding's role, no doubt to acknowledge his friend of forty years as the driving force behind the commission. One wonders why Abner Graves was not named. And why Mills described him as "reputable." Was this an embellishment on the lawyer's part to address the lack of corroboration?

Mills went on to note that for schoolboys in Doubleday's time, injuries were common because of collisions between players when so many were allowed on the field. Injuries also resulted from the practice of having to strike base runners with the ball to record an out:

> I can well understand how the orderly mind of the embryo West Pointer would devise a scheme for limiting the contestants on each side and allotting them to field positions, each with a certain amount of territory; also substituting the existing method of putting out the base runner for the old one of "plugging" him with the ball.[4]

Here, Mills clearly misstated the story shared by Graves. In his letter to the commission, Graves wrote that even after Doubleday's improvements "anyone getting the ball was entitled to throw it at a runner and put him out if he could hit him." Mills's true intention here is unknown. It might have resulted from some confusion considering all the documents he had seen. But he could have corrected it had he taken the time to review and revise before submitting it. Perhaps he felt that by eliminating "plugging," seen by some as evidence of a more primitive game, the Doubleday game would seem more modern and connected to the game of the early 1900s.

Mills dismissed as inconsequential the fact that Graves had reported that eleven players were used at Cooperstown, instead of nine. He noted that they were placed on the field "in the manner indicated in Doubleday's diagram." Here again, the lawyer was being careless with the facts and it would seem yet again he was gilding the Cooperstown story. There was no Doubleday diagram only a sketch made by Graves on the back of his letter to Spalding that was said to resemble Doubleday's. Had Mills been open to cross-examination, the shortcomings in his decision would have become apparent.

Mills concluded by stating that he had been trying to get more information about the Knickerbocker baseball club, but had decided that he could wait no longer for it and felt compelled to issue his report. He noted that a "Mr. Curry" had spoken about a diagram brought to the Knickerbocker baseball field one day by a man named Wadsworth that might be traced to Doubleday's diagram—and the modern field layout of 1907. Attached to Mills's report were the signatures of commission members Morgan Bulkeley, Nick Young, Al Reach and George Wright, indicating that they unanimously agreed with the decision rendered.

There it was. Baseball's special commission had anointed Abner Doubleday as the inventor of the game. Misgivings about the story and the only person to ever tell it were swept aside as it was shared with baseball and the country, where Americans seemed willing, if not eager, to accept it. The rushed effort suggested that Mills's heart had not been in the report. Further evidence of that came three years before his death. In February of 1926, Mills attended a banquet in New York marking the fiftieth anniversary of the National League. The former league president was joined by a handful of men who had played in the inaugural season. At one point that evening, Mills was asked what evidence he had for his conclusion that Abner Doubleday invented baseball in Cooperstown. He replied: "None at all."[5]

In late March 1908, the conclusions of the commission were published in *Spalding's Official Base Ball Guide*. It was the last *Guide* with Chadwick as editor. He dropped a good-natured note to Mills in which he described the lawyer's handiwork as "a masterful piece of special pleading, which lets my dear old friend Albert [Spalding] escape a bad defeat.... I was so sure of my case that I failed to present more detailed evidence. The fact is, The whole matter was a Joke between Albert and myself, for the fun of the thing."[6] Chadwick died a month later at the age of 83.

In the months and years to come, the Cooperstown story gained currency among the general public, certified genuine as it had been by the Special Base Ball Commission, A. G. Spalding and his *Official Guide*. Fifteen years after his death, Doubleday's status as a Civil War hero received a boost with his additional fame as the purported inventor of baseball. His accomplishment would soon be recorded in school textbooks and marked in other ways.

Within a year of the release of the Mills Commission report, two critics, both sportswriters, came forward. Writing in *Collier's* magazine in May 1909, Will Irwin insisted that a game called baseball had been played in England long before rounders or Abner Doubleday. And, he noted, in 1839 Doubleday was a student miles away at West Point. Veteran baseball writer William M. Rankin wrote in a 1909 letter to Alfred Spink, founder of the *Sporting News*, that while he agreed the game was American, it actually originated with Alexander J. Cartwright of the Knickerbocker Base Ball Club of New York in 1845. He dismissed the Doubleday story as "the latest of all fakes.... The records of West Point, N.Y., and the War Department at Washington, D.C., were the means of exposing his fake."[7] In fact, it would be learned that Doubleday enrolled in the United States Military Academy at West Point in 1838 at age 18, and that he took no leaves of absence during 1839 or 1840.

Irwin and Rankin failed to turn the tide against America's latest hero and the tale of his invention became part of popular folklore. Spalding, baseball and the American public were in no mood for the facts provided by naysayers determined to poke holes in the creation myth. When Spalding died in 1915, he had every reason to feel comfortable that he'd proven to himself, to baseball and to America that the game was a homegrown sport. Further challenges to the Doubleday story would not emerge for decades. In the meantime, millions of Americans continued to flock to professional ballparks now armed with the confidence that the game was unquestionably theirs.

* * *

In Cooperstown itself, news of the Mills Commission findings made it to the front page of the weekly *Freeman's Journal,* the local paper in the village of about 2,000. Under the headline "Home of Baseball," the story began: "Cooperstown is the birthplace of baseball." The newspaper drew attention to the letter Spalding sent to the commission backing the story of Abner Graves that the game had been invented by Abner Doubleday. "Personally, I confess that I am very much impressed with the straightforward, positive and apparently accurate manner in which Mr. Graves writes his narrative, and the circumstantial evidence with which he surrounds it," Spalding was quoted, adding:

> It certainly appeals to an American's pride to have had the great national game of Base Ball created and named by a Major General in the United States Army, and to have that same game played as a camp diversion by soldiers of the Civil War, who at the conclusion of the war, disseminated Base Ball throughout the length and breadth of the United States, and thus gave to the game its national character. The United States Army has certainly played a very important part in the early development of Base Ball, and in recent years the United States Navy has become the emissary that is planting the seeds of the game in every foreign land, which must result in making the American national game of Base Ball the universal field sport of the world.[8]

After scratching their heads at this revelation, some Cooperstown residents began puffing their chests with pride. Previously, the village's most famous son had been writer James Fenimore Cooper, author of *The Leatherstocking Tales* and *The Last of the Mohicans*, who was also the son of the founder and namesake of the community. Now Abner Doubleday, with his twin military and baseball accomplishments, would also bring attention to the picturesque village at the southern tip of Otsego Lake. The account went on to point out that it was at Duff's Military School, where a private home now stood, that the seminal game was likely played. It added, "Many Cooperstown people remember Major General Doubleday, and he has some relatives of the same name in this vicinity now." The fact that Doubleday himself was born in Ballston Spa near Albany and as a boy moved to Auburn, near Syracuse, and never actually lived in Cooperstown—despite Graves's assertion—was never addressed.

The story then quoted from an account from the *New York World* which praised the conclusions of the baseball commission:

> Their report settles an old controversy and is entitled to the respect of all investigators of the origin of the horse or discoverers of "missing links." Base ball is thus proved to be, like poker, a genuine American product. It did not come "out of the mysterious East," like our religions and languages, like chess and cards, peaches and sherbet. It was not played in ancient Rome, like hop-scotch and jackstraws. It is native, indigenous, all our own, and the fact is a just subject for pride. Has Doubleday a monument? He is now shown to have been illustrious on two fields. Cooperstown has acquired a second famous son whose achievements will deserve centennial commemoration.

Cooperstown residents apparently needed time to digest the village's new-found status as the cradle of baseball, since little was done to capitalize on it in the near term. The lack of response underlined the fact that fame was not something Cooperstown had sought; rather, that fame had been foisted upon a village that was completely unprepared to deal with it. Several times during the next few years it was suggested that some sort of monument to the first game of baseball was needed, but nothing came of it. The sleepy village remained sleepy for awhile yet. As Rowan D. Spraker, the longtime editor of the *Freeman's Journal*, put it:

> The fact that Cooperstown had been designated as the birthplace by the Committee [Mills Commission] had little effect upon the community when it was announced in *Spalding's Baseball Guide of 1908*. Cooperstown did not vie for this designation and it had little, or no, effect upon the community. The *Freeman's Journal* ... carried a story on the decision of the Commission and that was the last that Cooperstown thought about the situation for a number of years.[9]

The memory of residents was jogged in 1912 when the *Freeman's Journal* carried an account of an interview with Abner Graves that had appeared in the *Denver Post*. Graves, approaching 80, told that paper that he actually had played in the first game in Cooperstown and had added that he expected to play again in an upcoming game in Denver. The story from the *Post* was submitted to the *Freeman's Journal* by J. Arthur Eddy, of Chattanooga, Tennessee, who suggested that a monument marking the first game should be erected in Cooperstown.[10] The following week, the paper carried a tongue-in-cheek suggestion from Eddy, that some monument with a torch of enlightenment, not unlike the Statue of Liberty, should be erected along the shore of Otsego Lake: "While the poetic feature of a beautiful goddess holding aloft a torch may be substituted by a gifted gabby baseball fan threatening the umpire with a bat; these are but minor details which must be worked out to best grace the shrine of the future mecca of the baseball fiend."

In 1916, the dedication of the new Delaware and Hudson railroad station drew some high-powered visitors to Cooperstown. They included John Tener, president of the National League and former governor of Pennsylvania, Harry Hempstead, president of the National League's New York Giants, and Col. Jacob Ruppert, president of the American League's New York Yankees. Tener was an interesting character with strong credentials in baseball and a connection to the late Albert Goodwill Spalding. A lanky minor league pitcher, Tener had been picked up by Cap Anson of the Chicago White Stockings in 1888, just in time to join Spalding's World Tour, for which he served as treasurer. Tener jumped to the upstart Player's League in 1890 and soon afterward ended his playing days. He went on to win election as a Republican member of the U.S. House of Representatives, then as governor of Pennsylvania.[11] Because of his connection to Spalding, it would have been expected that he'd have a special interest in venerating Cooperstown. In anticipation of the arrival of the powerful figures in baseball, the *Freeman's Journal* reminded its readers about the village's claim to baseball immortality. In a report in advance of the visit, the paper added Alexander Cartwright, of Knickerbocker fame, to the first game in Cooperstown along with the two Abners, Doubleday and Graves. The story pinpointed the site of that game as being at what was known as "Phinney's lot," a former military training ground: "It is probable that the matter of erecting a suitable marker on this spot will be discussed during the stay of the baseball men this week."[12] The visitors did not disappoint, with *Freeman's Journal* editor Spraker noting: "These men were loud in their praise of the field and suggested that it be made a memorial to General Abner Doubleday of Civil War fame."

Just before Christmas, 1916, a letter from Abner Graves appeared in the *Freeman's Journal*. He wrote in response to another article that had appeared in the paper suggesting that the village ought to do something to mark the centennial of the birth of Abner Doubleday in 1919. Graves introduced himself as among the "boys that Doubleday showed his completed diagrams and plans of the new game and whom he instructed as helpers to play the first game and test of his plan, and I helped in those as one of the players." He suggested that a game similar to Doubleday's could be played to mark the occasion "and if such is done I wish to enter my name now as one of the players." He conceded that many years had passed since 1839, "but I expect to be able to run and dodge the balls the opposing players throw at me sufficiently well so as to make a 'home run' under those old rules of the game."[13] At the time, Graves was about to turn 83 and was apparently enjoying the limelight. He also saw fit to elevate his status from mere observer who was too young to play to participant in the history-making first game of baseball.

The next year, 1917, Cooperstown found itself in an odd crisis. The village faced the prospect of losing the only real ball field it had, which would have been an ironic turn of events for the newly christened cradle of the game. For generations, a field along Fair Street had served as the community ballpark and youngsters who played there had gone on to the major leagues.[14] The property had been sold so that it could become the site of the new Mary Imogene Bassett Hospital. The loss of the field prompted city fathers to look around for a replacement and "Phinney's lot" immediately became the prime candidate. It was centrally located and games of "scrub" had been played there for years. Besides, it was the spot identified by Abner Graves as the site of Abner Doubleday's first game. The property wasn't ideal, however, because it was bordered by a creek that often overflowed in springtime. The Cooperstown Chamber of Commerce decided to take up the cause and spent considerable time considering options. Some farsighted businessmen realized the potential of exploiting the village's newfound reputation. It wouldn't do for the birthplace of baseball to be without a baseball field and the place where the game purportedly had been invented was the only logical place to locate it. But Cooperstown became distracted when the United States joined World War I and the area's young men marched off to participate in the war intended to end all wars.

The preferred site was owned by Alexander Stewart Phinney. By 1919, a "playground committee" established by the chamber had been authorized to lease the property from him for a term of two years. The rent was $100 annually and at the end of two years, the chamber would have the option to purchase it for $5,000. The field was leveled and put in playing shape for the latter part of the 1919 season. However, in the village election of 1920, voters turned down spending the $5,000 to buy the property. The setback was unexpected, but only temporary.

A few days later, *Spalding's Official Baseball Guide for 1920* included an article arguing that a suitable monument to Abner Doubleday ought to be erected in Cooperstown. This prompted the "playground committee" of the chamber to swing into action by undertaking a public fundraising campaign to which residents and former ballplayers contributed. Approaches were made to the National League and other interests in New York, but these initially proved unsuccessful. The sparkplug of the fundraising campaign was a man who had an entirely appropriate surname for a baseball fan: Dr. Ernest L. Pitcher. His tireless efforts gradually met with success and money began to arrive in contributions of as little as twenty-five cents. More good news came in August of 1920 when National League President John A. Heydler wrote: "I am very interested in the project you have in mind of securing Doubleday Field." Heydler was replying to a request from Pitcher for a National League umpire to work the inaugural game at the new field on Labor Day. Heydler replied that because of a close league championship race that year he couldn't spare any umpires, but he added that he'd be prepared to discuss things further once the World Series was over. On September 9, Heydler appeared in the village and umpired an inning in that first game before turning the rest of it over to National League umpire Barry McCormick, who had accompanied Heydler. Pitcher had found a friend in a high place for Cooperstown. The doctor's fundraising efforts continued to bear fruit and in September 1923, Phinney's old field, now known as Doubleday Field, became village property.[15]

The support of Heydler for the Cooperstown venture was important and proved to be ongoing. Heydler had been born in 1869 in La Fargeville, New York, about 140 miles northwest of Cooperstown, where he developed a love of sandlot baseball. He became a printer and then a sportswriter, while also umpiring college and semi-pro baseball games. In the late 1890s, he had a stint as an umpire in the National League before returning to sportswriting. He rejoined the league in 1903 as its secretary, where he compiled its official statistics. In 1909, he was appointed president of the league upon the suicide of Harry Pulliam. After serving for a year, Heydler was not reappointed and he pursued other interests for several years before returning to his job as league secretary in 1914. Four years later, National League president John Tener, who had been among the baseball dignitaries in Cooperstown for the opening of the train station, suddenly resigned. Tener's replacement was Heydler, who served as league president until his retirement in 1934. During his lengthy tenure, Heydler faced many crucial challenges: he had to deal with the Black Sox game-throwing scandal following the 1919 World Series, he supported the appointment of Judge Kenesaw Mountain Landis as commissioner of baseball and he promoted the designated hitter rule. In his later years in the post, he advocated strongly for the Hall of Fame.[16]

As National League president, Heydler stayed in touch with Pitcher and had to keep reminding the doctor that more should be done to celebrate the community's connection to baseball. In a letter of September 13, 1920, for instance, Heydler wrote:

Dear Doctor: I wish to thank you for your letter of September 8th, and also for the interesting little history of Cooperstown. I know I shall enjoy reading it as soon as we finish the championship season and have the World's Series back of us. In going casually through it I notice the author fails to refer to Cooperstown as the birthplace of the National Game ... I am glad your fund has grown to $3,500.[17]

On May 2, 1928, Heydler sent Pitcher a note praising his efforts at preserving the ball field in the community and added:

I have looked over the pictures of the Cooperstown scenes on the Chamber of Commerce letterhead. It is certainly a beautiful spot but I believe they made a mistake in not taking more notice of the fact that the first baseball diamond was laid out here in 1839. Next to its historic value as the Fenimore Cooper country, I believe Cooperstown's claim as the birthplace of our national game is the most important.[18]

Yet again, the push for Cooperstown to celebrate something it had never claimed for itself was coming from outside. Moreover, the source was one of the towering figures in baseball of the day.

In the midst of the efforts to secure a new ball field in 1919, Abner Graves entered the fray, suggesting that the village needed something to commemorate the 1839 game he had described. This item appeared in the *Freeman's Journal*:

Abner Graves of Denver who played in the original baseball game as planned by Abner Doubleday has suggested to the *Journal* that he would return to Cooperstown to participate in the dedication of a national park for baseball and play his old position.[19]

Even the originator of the Doubleday story was nudging the village along, this time toward a "national park." The report did not include his age at the time he made the offer to return to the diamond for a good cause. In fact, he was now 85, yet no one seemed to question his ability to remember so many details from the watershed moment that purportedly occurred when he was a lad of just five years old.

# Nine

## *An Unhappy Ending*

In 1907, Abner Graves pulled the plug on the Alma Copper Mining venture in Mexico and Nelson rejoined him in Denver. The Carbo mine, which just five years earlier Graves had touted as "little short of a marvel," had failed to live up to his expectations as he directed operations from Denver and sought capital to exploit it. Instead, the active widower had developed some coal mining properties in Wyoming and was offering opinions about mining prospects throughout the west.[1]

Denver was approaching a population of 200,000 and was firmly entrenched as the commercial, agricultural, manufacturing and amusement hub of the region. The political elite was tied into the saloon culture, which still flourished in the city and which maintained Denver's reputation as one of the wildest cities in the American west.[2] Mayor Robert Speer, elected in 1904 with the support of the city's tavernkeepers, vowed to keep prohibitionists at bay, although Denver's suburbs were allowed to be "dry" areas. A progressive, he worked diligently to improve the appearance of the drab town that had grown so rapidly. But Speer was defeated in 1912 amid charges of corruption and ties to the underworld. In late 1914, Coloradans voted for statewide prohibition to begin January 1, 1916. A cleaned-up Speer returned to office in 1916, but by then the political and social landscape had changed. The saloon doors that slammed shut in 1916 did not reopen until prohibition was repealed in 1933. Prohibition marked the end of an era for the Mile High City. As one Denver historian noted, "the saloon as a major social, political and economic institution was closed for good."[3] The long-popular institution had also, no doubt, brought together Adam Ford and Abner Graves. Without those Denver saloons, baseball history might have been different.

As James E. Sullivan continued to receive information about early baseball at his New York office and Spalding promoted Graves's story about Cooperstown, the Denver mining engineer was a busy man. In the summer of 1907, he was in southwest Colorado offering an opinion about a mining prospect there, attracting the attention of the local newspaper:

Mr. Abner Graves, an eminent mining expert and engineer, whose headquarters are in Denver, is spending the day in the Telluride the guest of Mr. E.L. Davis who is showing him through the Liberty Bell and Smuggler milling plants, and other points of interest.

Mr. Graves is well along in years, his locks white with age, and he has experted [sic] and examined all the principal mines in every mining region of any note in the whole world. He has just spent several days at Rico his errand being an expert examination of the Rio Dolores properties for the purpose of advising the company as to future operations, and incidentally he looked the camp over generally, examining the principle mines. As a result he enthusiastically declares that Rico is destined to make one of the important mining districts of the world, and listening to his explanation of the theories on which he bases this conclusion one is impressed with the conviction that he is right in his diagnosis.[4]

The boosterish news item continued with Graves's description of the promising rock formations found in the area. The report concluded that the newspaper had heard similar sentiments from other mining experts, "but has found none so enthusiastic as Mr. Graves, as to the future of the district." Graves's enthusiasm may have been why mining companies kept calling on him—his reports were used to help them raise capital for development work, so the more glowing his reports, the better. Graves's assertions were as well received by mine promoters as one about baseball had been by the sport's biggest promoter.

Also in 1907, Graves established the Nevadian Mining and Milling Company at Battle Mountain, Nevada, near where he'd fought in the Shoshone Indian Wars some forty years earlier. Nelson was named general superintendent of the copper mining property and kept the books for it while based in the Denver office.[5] By 1910, the father and son were no longer involved, suggesting that Abner's well-documented enthusiasm had deserted him even sooner than at the Mexican operation.

About the same time they took over the Nevadian mine, Abner moved from a fine mansion on Humboldt Street in the western core area of Denver to a large home at 1535 Logan Street, in the Capitol Hill area, a short distance northeast of Colorado's capital building. The move was part of a trade that saw him also acquire some ranch land near Byers, just east of Denver.[6] Capitol Hill had once been the city's premier neighborhood and was still solidly middle class by the time Graves moved in. It was not uncommon in the early years of the twentieth century for residents to rent parts of the larger homes in the area to boarders and Graves did the same.[7] Graves was living there in 1908 when Nelson, who had followed him into Freemasonry, became a Master Mason, having worked his way steadily upward in the fraternal order.[8]

The next year, at age 75, Abner married Minnie Latham, a Virginia native who at 34 was less than half his age. It's not known how they met, or where, but Graves put the house on Logan into Minnie's name, for reasons that are likewise unknown. Nelson continued to stay in the fine home, and, following the neighborhood custom, lodgers lived upstairs.[9] That same year, 1909, Abner established the Graves Investment Company and he placed an advertisement announcing it in the city directory. The ad listed the company business as including real estate, stocks and bonds, as well interests in "homes in sunny Colorado, irrigated lands, lands in the 'rain belt,' Denver city property, colonization tracts, special sales agency, Northwestern Land and Iron Company, [and] Denver, Laramie and Northwestern Ry. Co.," all at his Bank Block offices.[10]

The mining engineer/real estate agent/entrepreneur kept in touch with his friends and former family in Iowa, where he was fondly remembered. A few weeks after his wedding, the *Dow City Enterprise* noted that town resident S.A. Dow had just returned from Denver. "He reports Abner Graves being recently married. The *Enterprise* extends congratulations."[11] Dow may have been discussing business prospects with him and Graves was known to make business trips back to Dow City. Around 1911, Graves became partners with his former brother-in-law, William Dow, in opening a hotel in Dow City.[12] S.A. Dow may have acted as a go-between in the transaction. That same year, 1911, the Denver city directory listed for the first time a firm called "Hydro-Engine Power & Irrigation Co.," with Abner Graves as president, Felix B. Tait as vice-president and Nelson D. Graves as secretary-treasurer. The address, yet again, was Graves's office in the Bank Block building.[13] For a man some historians have dismissed as a mental case, Graves was able to balance a wide portfolio of business interests well into his seventies.

At the outset of the 1912 baseball season, the Denver Chamber of Commerce and the Real Estate Exchange announced they were going to play an exhibition game. Proceeds from the match were to go toward advertising Denver as an ideal destination for tourists traveling by automobile. An enterprising *Denver Post* reporter got wind that one of the attendees would be the Denver man who gave the world the Cooperstown story. Under the headline, "Denver Man Played First Baseball Game in History of Sport," Abner Graves shared his story, which he embellished far beyond the version he gave the Mills Commission. Atop the article was a photograph of the cigar-chomping Graves waving a Denver Chamber of Commerce pennant.

> "You know, they don't play ball like they used to. Why, I played in the very first game of ball that was ever played. And that game—well, it was some baseball, young man."

> Then Abner Graves began to reminisce. With his half-smoked cigar in his mouth, and holding the book, "The American National Game," [sic] which he was reading when his interviewers entered his office, the septigenarian [sic] grew interested in his review of the early baseball games in which he participated.

"I was a student at Green college in Cooperstown, N.Y., at that time," he continued. "Abner Doubleday, the man who invented the game, if you call it an invention, came to our school and interested us boys in his idea. We went out on the college campus, and Doubleday drew the diagram of his game in the sand. It was much like the diamond of today, but the distance between bases was longer, and the distance from pitcher to batter was shorter. We played eleven men in those days; two shortstops and four outfielders.

"That was in 1840, and the boys of that college played the first game of baseball in the history of the great American game. But, oh, it was so different from this strenuous game of today. We would go to bat and wait for a ball to be pitched that suited us. The pitchers didn't try any curves or anything like that. They never attempted to fool a batter by throwing a ball, but always tried to throw a good one. We could stand at the bat until a ball came along which we thought we could hit, and then we would bing at it. If we 'ticked' it or knocked what is now called a foul ball, a strike was not declared. We could stand at bat, waiting, for as long as we chose. If, however, we struck at the ball three times and missed, we then ran to first base. We were safe unless the ball was thrown and hit us, or we were touched in some manner by the ball.

"The same thing applied when we got a hit. No matter where we knocked the ball, either in the hands of a player or after it was thrown at us. A one-bagger was, in that way, often stretched to a home run. The boys became expert at dodging the ball, and usually succeeded in making a score on a hit.

"The bat we used was about four inches wide, and the ball was fairly soft, being made of rubber and twine.

"It was not until 1845 that the first ball club was organized. It was called the Knickerbocker club, and was in New York. After that I organized a club and we had some great games. No admission was ever charged to those games.

"Yes, sir, I played in the first baseball game ever played in the United States. I am very proud of it, and I expect, Saturday, to play in the game between the chamber of commerce and the real estate exchange. I guess I'll be shortstop or something like that."

Mr. Graves who is a real estate dealer, is one of the most enthusiastic followers of the baseball game in the country. There are might few of them that he misses in Denver, and he is usually seen in the front row of the grandstand, yelling with all his might for the Grizzlies.[14]

This was quite the story, for a number of reasons. Graves had changed his story in a key respect, but in others areas he held steadfast to the story he shared with the Mills Commission, despite the tinkering Mills had done with it. In this 1912 telling, Graves claimed—for the first time—that he played in that first game. And he left the impression he was a college student at the time. Pretty good for a boy aged five, on both counts. In this version he was at "Green College," but no such thing existed in Cooperstown. In one of his 1905 letters, the one referenced in Birdsall's 1917 *Story of Cooperstown*, Graves maintained that he had been attending Frog Hollow School at the time of Doubleday's invention. Hugh MacDougall, official historian for the town of Cooperstown, has done a nice job sorting out the school situation in the village in 1839 and 1840. Frog Hollow, he found, was an elementary or common school, the kind of district school established by law in every community. Attendance was not compulsory and fees were required to attend. Education and conditions were very rudimentary. As MacDougall found, the next step up in the hierarchy of schools was the "select" school. These profit-oriented schools charged tuition and could choose the students they would accept, hence the name "select." By 1839 and 1840, there were two select schools in Cooperstown:

In Denver, Abner Graves was an enthusiastic booster of the Denver Chamber of Commerce. This photo, from 1912, accompanied a newspaper account stating that he was planning to play in an upcoming game between the chamber and the Denver Real Estate Exchange. Denver Post in Western History Collection, Denver Public Library, Denver, Colorado.

Otsego Academy and Major Duff's Classical and Military Academy. Boys at Major Duff's Academy were known locally as "Duff's Greens," possibly because of the color of their uniforms or Duff's Irish roots. MacDougall suggests that this is the school Graves dubbed "Green's Select School" in that first letter to the Mills Commission and which he said Doubleday was attending.[15] In Graves's *Post* interview it had morphed into Green College and Graves now claimed that it was he himself who attended it. Was Graves trying to embellish his age and education along with his role in the game itself? Or was his memory becoming hazy? Regardless, Duff's Academy still wasn't a college in the modern sense of the term, just an elementary school operated for a profit.

In two other aspects, the *Post* story showed Graves differed from the Mills Commission. It would seem that he hadn't brushed up on his story as contained in *America's National Game*—the book that he was conveniently reading when interviewers arrived at his office. Grave told the paper that the first game was played in 1840, not 1839, as Mills had arbitrarily decided. More importantly, Graves reiterated the contention from his first letter that the practice of hitting players with the game ball to put them out was a key part of the game. In his final report, contained in *America's National Game*, Mills specifically credited Doubleday with "substituting the existing method of putting out the base runner for the old one of 'plugging' him with the ball."[16] So on the latter issue, particularly, Graves stood by his original story. But the most interesting part of the newspaper account was the new claim that Graves had played in the original game. It went unchallenged and the aging raconteur might be forgiven for basking in the limelight, especially when no one was still alive who could contradict him. It wouldn't be the last time that he would claim to have been one of the players.

Graves was given a free ride on both his account of the old game and his assertion that at age 78 he was ready to play shortstop in the contest between the chamber of commerce and the real estate exchange. Whether it was laziness or age-related deference on the part of the reporter for the *Post*, Graves was not challenged. The old man told a good story and that seemed to be good enough. The reporter was in good company: Spalding and Mills had felt the same way.

In 1913, Graves was included in *The Semi-Centennial History of the State of Colorado*, along with others viewed as prominent at the time. In his entry, no doubt based on information Graves provided, it noted that he was "largely interested in mines and real estate through the west and a well known resident of Denver." It traced his early history in Cooperstown, reporting that he "received his education in the public schools and at Otsego Academy" before joining the California Gold Rush at age 15. This is the first indication that Graves attended Otsego Academy, a competitor for Major Duff's (Green) Academy and a step up from Frog Hollow school.

The entry for Graves also indicated that he arrived in Colorado "in the fall of 1896 ... in the interest of some Chicago capitalists, his special purpose being to examine mines in Lake City." This is two years later than evidence suggests he actually came to Denver, the city described as "the headquarters for his extensive mining interests in Mexico, Nevada, Arizona, Oregon, Wyoming and Colorado." It mentioned his first marriage, but not his second. Reference was made to Graves's son, and also to his Republican politics and his high rank in Freemasonry.[17] His reasons for changing the year of his arrival in Denver and omitting his second wife remain mysteries.

The year 1913 was a big year for Abner and Nelson Graves on the social front when an event important to Freemasonry took place in Denver. The Triennial Conclave of the Knights Templar, a philanthropic order within the Masons, saw hundreds of delegates from all over the United States stream into Denver for parades and fellowship. Nelson, a rising star in the organization, was a member of both the hotel, and the accommodations and entertainment committees for the event, which filled four days in August.[18]

Abner turned 80 in early 1914 and still showed no signs of slowing down. He continued to assess mineral deposits and when he traveled he invariably also packed his enthusiasm. In late 1915, he was reported to be in Boulder County, northwest of Denver. "A field rich in tungsten and gold ore which may be a sensation in the mining reports of the year has been discovered in Boulder county, according to Abner Graves, veteran mining engineer," reported the *Fairplay Flume* in its wrapup of news items from across the state.[19]

Through friends and relatives back in Cooperstown, Graves monitored how the village was responding to the national spotlight he had been responsible for turning on it. He noticed a letter in the *Freeman's Journal* in late 1916, suggesting that something should be done to mark the one hundredth anniversary of the birth of Abner Doubleday in 1919. Graves fired off his own missive, reminding readers that he was one of the "boys that Doubleday showed his completed diagrams and plans of the new game and who he instructed as helpers to play the first game and test out his plan, and I helped in those games." This was the second time he had asserted that he was not just an observer, but an active participant. Graves wrote that a game played like the original one would be an ideal commemoration and that if that were to occur, "I wish now to enter my name as one of the players." He noted that he was more than seventy years of age (he was actually eighty-two), "but I expect to be able to run and dodge the balls the opposing players throw at me sufficiently well so as to make a 'home run' under those old rules of the game."[20] Graves was still clinging to "plugging" as an integral part of the seminal game, despite Mills's claim that Doubleday had eliminated that anachronism. When it appeared that nothing was being done to mark the centennial of Doubleday's birth, Graves again wrote to the newspaper, early in the 1919 ball season, offering to play in a game at a national park that he felt should be created in the village.[21]

At age 35, Nelson Graves married Edith Larrabee in June of 1918 in a quiet ceremony that came as a surprise to their friends. After a honeymoon in the east, the couple returned to Denver and took up residence at 1511 Logan Street, a few doors away from Abner and Minnie. On January 30, 1921, Abner Graves became a grandfather when Edith gave birth to Mabel Claire Graves, the only child Nelson and Edith would have.[22] The following year, Nelson left his father's employ and became a salesman for the McMurtry Paint Company.

In 1922, at age 88, Abner Graves drew attention as the oldest Shriner to attend the organization's annual convention, held that year in San Francisco from June 13 to 15. A newspaper noted that he was so old that he had first come to California in the Gold Rush of 1849, some 73 years earlier. That made Graves "one of the few living pioneers" from that time. His travel to California

**Abner Graves in front of his fine home on Logan Street in Denver, about 1920. It was here that he later shot and killed his second wife. Used by permission of Claire Strashun.**

and prospecting in the Auburn area were described. The report then turned to a revealing snapshot of the mining engineer in 1922:

> Although far past the age of average activity, Graves insists upon working all the time, and at present he is general manager of a large coal company in Denver and is sponsoring the construction of a railroad that will tap his extensive coal fields.
>
> He attributes his longevity to abstinence from all excesses and careful living and the conservation of energy. By careful living Graves explains he does not mean "total abstinence from alcoholic beverages or smoking, because he has done both until recently; but that a person cannot attain a high age through overindulgence." He pointed out that since a youth he was served liquor with adults and smoking was then, as now, a common habit, and that he is still an ardent admirer of "Lady Nicotine."
>
> "I do not drink anymore, because for one thing it is against the law, and then the stuff circulating these days is not the same furnished pioneers in the olden days."[23]

He might have acknowledged genetics as a factor in being so active as he approached the age of ninety, but Graves still seemed sharp mentally. He had obviously become comfortable with reporters and seemed to enjoy basking in the spotlight when they were around.

On February 27, 1924, he turned ninety and the *Rocky Mountain News* in Denver decided to salute the landmark for the aging local character. Accompanied by a photograph of the bright-eyed Graves lighting a mass of candles on his birthday cake, the headline read: "Denver Man, 90, Celebrating Birthday Smokes Five Cigars for Health's Sake." The article reported:

> One of the original '49ers in the gold rush to California, a pony express rider in the days when mail was carried across the continent by means of horses, a participant in the first game of baseball ever played, held in Cooperstown, N.Y., in 1839, Abner Graves, pioneer real estate, mining and cattle man of Colorado and Denver, yesterday celebrated his ninetieth birthday at his home at 1535 Logan street.
>
> Mr. Graves celebrated by arising at 3 o'clock yesterday morning to start work on his autobiography, in which he will include many facts pertaining to the early history of the West. Later in the day he took a walk, circling the block in which his home is located several times, and to show his high regard for Lady Nicotine, smoking five cigars before nightfall and also consuming four cups of coffee.
>
> In spite of the weight of the passing years, Mr. Graves declared in an interview yesterday he felt strong and spry.
>
> "I fully expect to live to be 135 years old," he said. "And there is no reason why I shouldn't. All my life I have worked hard out in the open, prospecting for gold for many years in California, and engaging in the profession of mining engineer for fifteen years after that. I feel almost as fit and hearty now as I did fifty years ago."[24]

The story went on to describe his childhood and his graduation from Otsego Academy for boys, his Gold Rush trek, his work as a pony express rider, his time in Iowa, his arrival in Denver and his longstanding involvement with the Masons and Shriners. Clearly Graves could still spin a story and his assertion that he expected to live to 135 showed a playful side.

A bit less than four months later, Graves was again in the Denver papers. This time, however, it was front page news. "Denver Invalid, 90, Shoots Wife," screamed the *Denver Post* headline. "Denver Man, 90, Shoots Wife After Quarrel," read the *Rocky Mountain News*. "Denver Man, 90, Shoots Wife, 48, Woman is Dying," reported the *Denver Express*.

The *Post* had the most lurid coverage.

> Abner Graves, 90 years old and so crippled he cannot walk without the aid of his crutches, shot and probably fatally wounded his 48-year-old wife, Minnie L. Graves, in their home at 1535 Logan street, Monday evening.

The shooting climaxed a quarrel which grew out of the refusal of Mrs. Graves to sign a bill of sale for their home. Graves was sitting in a chair at the time of the shooting and fired four shots into his wife's body as she stood only a few feet away.

Tuesday morning, Mrs. Graves, mortally wounded and unconscious, lay in a ward in the general hospital gasping her life out. With her last conscious breath she had sent a message of forgiveness to her aged husband.

In an adjoining ward, Graves, a physical and mental wreck, lay muttering, "I hope she dies."

"I had to do it," Graves told police. "One of us had to go."

He explained this by saying that his wife had tried to kill him by putting poison in his coffee Monday evening. After being questioned at police headquarters, Graves was removed to the general hospital where a stomach pump was used on him. Officials said they could find no trace of poison in his stomach.[25]

The account went on to explain that Mr. and Mrs. H.H. Hatch and Evelyn and Marie Helsey, the Graves's upstairs tenants, heard shots that evening and rushed downstairs, where they found Minnie lying in a hallway. They dragged her upstairs, locked themselves inside and called out the window for police. Officers could not enter the home by a door and had to smash a window and crawl inside.

Graves was found standing behind a table in a bedroom. Before the menace of the drawn revolvers of officers he surrendered and sank back upon the bed. His weapon was found on the bed. The gun contained two exploded and three unexploded shells. Officers have not yet discovered whether Graves had a second gun in shooting his wife or whether he partially reloaded the weapon after the shooting.

Mrs. Graves was partially revived after her removal to the general hospital and made a statement to Assistant District Attorney Kenneth W. Robinson.

"I didn't give him any cause to shoot," she is reported to have said. "He was quarrelsome during the evening and as he has a quick temper, I didn't cross him. But he wanted me to sign a bill of sale for our house and I wouldn't do it.

"I didn't know he had his gun near him. I went to get him a drink and I guess he got the gun while I was out of the room. Then when I brought the drink to him he accused me of putting poison in it. He got abusive and when I tried to quiet him he jerked out the gun and fired. I staggered out into the hall and that's the last I remember."

In making what she believed to be her dying statement, Mrs. Graves several times asked Assistant District Attorney Robinson to "tell Abner I forgive him." Her last words before she lapsed into a state of coma were forgiveness for the man who shot her down.

The prosecutor met with a different reception when he called upon Graves.

"Why did you shoot your wife?" Robinson asked when he entered the ward where Graves lay on a cot.

"You never mind, sir," replied the aged man. "It's no business of yours. I only protected myself."

"You know you tried to murder her," declared Robinson.

Graves flew into a terrible rage struggling to get off his cot to attack Robinson.

"I'll get you," the old man shouted in his frenzy and it was some time before he could be quieted. Only a few minutes before he was approached by Robinson, Graves slapped a policeman who tried to get a statement from him.

The report indicated that when police arrested him, they had to carry Graves from his house because he was unable to walk. It also noted, "according to relatives, Graves and his wife had quarreled frequently." The article then switched to Graves's background, his life in Cooperstown, his part in the California Gold Rush, and his playing in the first game of baseball. His involvement with the Shriners was mentioned and the fact that his son Nelson also lived on Logan Street.

The *Rocky Mountain News* carried a similar account and added a few details. It noted that a real estate agent had been visited by Graves earlier that day and that roomers reported that an argument between Graves and his wife ensued when she wouldn't agree to sign a bill of sale. It reported that Graves had suffered some sort of hip injury that forced him to use crutches to get around:

> Nelson Graves, son of the aged man, declared that he believed the shooting was done when his father was in a fit of temporary insanity.
>
> "My father has often told me that he and his wife did not agree," the son said.
>
> "He would come to tell me of their quarrels and I attempted to calm him as much as I could. I believe it was her constant nagging that brought about this condition in his mind and I do not think that he was mentally responsible at the time the shooting occurred."[26]

The account noted that Abner Graves "is the owner of extensive coal mining properties in Wyoming, just north of the Colorado state line, and in 1922 constructed a shortline railroad from his mines to Medicine Bow, Wyo." It added that he "had led an active life and the enforced inactivity occasioned by the injury to his hip is said by neighbors to have caused Graves a great deal of worry."

The *Express* reported that "the two had quarreled often, the woman living in fear for her life, neighbors say. Often she had run from the house, taking refuge in the homes of neighbors," they told police after the shooting.

> Sometimes, she had remained with neighbors all night, to escape the fury of her aged husband, her friends say.
>
> Police were called about two years ago and found Abner choking his wife. But Mrs. Graves forgave him, agreed to be kind to him, because she knew he was old.[27]

The paper noted that about 10 P.M. a real estate agent had left the Graves home after a loud discussion on the front porch. Abner and Minnie entered the home and the loud quarrel drew complaints. "Damn you, I'll kill you," neighbors overheard Abner shout. The upstairs lodgers quoted the wounded Minnie as telling them, "I knew it was going to happen. I knew he would shoot me some day."

Minnie Graves succumbed to her wounds the next night. Before she passed away, she dictated a will to assistant district attorney Robinson from her deathbed. She was no longer in a forgiving mood and she disinherited Abner and Nelson, leaving her property to others. It was predicted that her action might lead to a bitter legal fight, with the *Rocky Mountain News* observing, "Graves is said to be wealthy. It is not known whether any of the property bequeathed by Mrs. Graves includes any money he may have given her since their marriage fifteen years ago."[28]

Two or three days later, with Graves still under police guard in hospital, he was charged with first-degree murder, the oldest man in Denver history to face the charge. This followed a coroner's inquest which determined that the gunshot wounds he inflicted on Minnie were responsible for her death. Before the charge was laid, Graves was visited in hospital by *Express* reporter Sam Jackson. Under a headline "Abner Graves, 90, Killer of Wife May Not Hang," he filed this extraordinary report with its glimpse into a troubled mind:

They'll never hang Abner Graves.

He killed his wife—she died last night in General hospital, after his brutal fusillade—but if "murder" implies any moral responsibility, Graves is not a murderer.

I have just talked with Graves at his police-guarded bedside in the hospital.

He is a ship without a helm, a clock without a hairspring, a man of out-worn, clanking parts without a governing head.

In the middle ages in England they had a law that any cartwheel that ran over a man should be burned.

That's just the way the hanging of this 90-year-old automaton would impress you.

They might as well hang a runaway freight engine that has killed somebody, or jail a meteorite that has beaned an innocent pedestrian, or assess a fine on a Tennessee tornado.

Graves has lived too long.

That resourceful mind than made him a successful 49er, a famous pony express rider, a good baseball player on the first team ever organized anywhere—well, it isn't a mind at all, any more.

It is the battleground of impetuous impulses that rush unannounced from the different alleys of his cerebrum.

There is no umpire. The strongest idea wins and takes possession of his tongue or his limbs.

That tragic Monday night suspicion, hate and the homicidal mania that alienists [psychiatrists] tell us is common in senile dementia, formed a phalanx and swept all restraint before them—and he fired.

And with all pity for his victim, it is surprising that the 48-year-old wife would have lived with this walking keg of dynamite.

I'd rather live with Leopold and Loeb—they could be reasoned with.

"Yes, I've been here since Saturday night," the old fellow cackled when I approached him today. "Maybe it's a week or ten days, I don't know."

He finally decided it was Saturday that he was taken to the hospital, and no argument would convince him it was Monday night—the actual time.

It was quite impossible to elicit any memory of the shooting.

"They put me in a wagon—two of them—and hurt my hand. See there? They were pretty rough.

"Now the house is all open and unless the woman's there all my specimens will be gone. There are some I've had for 75 or 100 years."

"Don't you remember having a quarrel with your wife? Don't you remember shooting her?" was asked.

The old man struggled, shook his head.

"They were trying to tell me something about that," he said. "I don't remember it. I don't believe it. They're always trying to fool me.

"My wife's in the other room there.

"I heard her yelling last night and they tried to tell me it was a cat. They can't fool me."

Graves was quite unable to recall anything about the tragedy except the officers putting him into the patrol wagon. Even this had been forgotten when it was reverted to a few moments later.

A nurse has told him his wife was dead, but he didn't seem to understood [sic] quite what was meant.

"Yes, we quarreled a lot," he admitted. "She was always trying to get my money. She got a lot of it, too.

"But she didn't get deeds to any of my real estate. No, sir. I didn't fall for any fake real estate agents and deeds."

Asked his age, Graves replied that he guessed he was about 100. He complained because his son and lodge members had not come to see him.

In certain ways the old man is acute.

Evidently investigators have represented themselves as former friends to get him into conversation, and he related with great amusement how he penetrated the frauds.

He is not aware that he is under arrest, although an officer sits at his bedside.

"If they'd just bring me my clothes I'd get out of here, but they won't give me my clothes."

With that, he wept.[29]

This was the last that a reporter or the public would hear from Abner Graves. In his darkest hour, Graves was still talking to a reporter. It appeared that after 90 years of a busy and full life something had snapped. He had become scrambled mentally raising the possibility that he had suffered a stroke.

Two psychiatrists, Dr. Edward Delehanty and Dr. Cyrus Pershing, were appointed to assess the state of his mind. They found Graves "mentally incompetent" in a report that was presented to a jury. In court for his competency hearing on June 25, the chief witnesses were his son, Nelson, and Dr. Delehanty. Graves, Delehanty testified, had a "childish distinction between right and wrong easily dispelled by excitement." He diagnosed Graves as suffering from dementia and reported that he still did not realize that he had killed his wife.[30]

The jury rendered a verdict of insanity and Graves was committed to the state hospital for the insane in Pueblo. The finding meant that he escaped the death penalty. In Pueblo, he was a model inmate and was often visited there by Nelson and his young granddaughter, Claire. Graves died there on October 4, 1926, at age 92. News of his passing was revealed months later in the *Denver Post* on February 2, 1927, which reported that he had been buried in Dow City, Iowa. His death certificate indicated the cause of death to have been "valvular insufficiency of the heart."[31]

On February 16, 1927, the will of Abner Graves was presented in probate court in Denver. It was learned that his estate was valued at $10,500. The will, dated July 7, 1921, named his wife Minnie as one of the lesser beneficiaries. "The will is an odd document," the *Denver Post* observed. "It sets forth when Graves was born, gives a bit of his life history and emphasizes the possibility of one meeting death thru accident."[32]

Graves's will was indeed an unusual document. Perhaps because he never completed the autobiography he claimed to have been working on, he felt the need to tell his life story in his will. On a typewriter, he tapped out on a long sheet of paper a tightly spaced "testament," riddled with the same typographical, spelling and spacing problems that marked his letter to the Mills Commission:

> I, Abner Graves, writing this "of my own free will and accord" (the half of first line herof [sic] being quotation of phrase I have often used in certain work that will be understood my most of my friends and by them testified as characteristic of me), I will herin [sic] state that this is or will be, my first and last will and testament, altho several times when going on some risky expedition, I have written a few lines as partial direction in case of accident but not witnessed therefore could not be called a "WILL OR TESTAMENT in accord with laws of Colorado."
>
> I was born at six o'clock A.M. On February 27th, 1834, at the home farm in Cooperstown, New York, and being now at this writing on July 7th, 1921 a little over Eighty-Seven Years and Four months of age, and of good health and sound in mind and body; feel that as I have in view extensive trips away in the country, riding an Automobile (commonly designated as a "FORD OR a

FLIVVER"), and on Steam Cars and otherwise, there are possibilities of deathly accidents occurring, therefore believe it may be wise to cover contingency of such possibility, by making this my will so as to guard against any serious scraps over possessions.[33]

Graves described his son Nelson as "my full business partner in every way" but added that he had put most of his business documents in his own name because of the amount of time Nelson spent in Mexico, making it difficult for his son to sign business papers back in Denver. He noted that Nelson had received some Iowa real estate from his mother and had sold some property his grandmother gave him, placing $8,000 of the proceeds into the Graves company, so he was entitled to receive it back. After the $8,000 to Nelson, $1,000 to Nelson's wife Edith and $1,000 to their child Claire, the balance of his estate was to be split between Nelson and Minnie. One senses that as much as three years before he shot Minnie, Abner felt that, as the owner of their home, she needed little more in terms of assistance.

As with most things he wrote during his long and interesting life, Graves had an interesting way of assembling words and presenting information. He had accomplished so much in his 92 years and seven months of life in a variety of places, pursuing all sorts of interests. Overall, his life could be considered successful with the notable and tragic exception of the event at the end of it. Perhaps, as the newspaper reporter concluded, Graves just lived too long. The pity is that he didn't need to turn to embellishment or invention when he spun his stories because the true story of his life was sufficiently interesting and didn't need decoration. And yet it is for his invention about an invention that Graves is best known and remembered.

# Ten

## *Cooperstown Prevails*

After the village of Cooperstown purchased the land for Doubleday Field in 1923, minor improvements were made to level and improve the playing surface of Alexander Stewart Phinney's old cow pasture. The next year, a new grandstand was erected, and in 1926 voters approved spending $3,000 to acquire the Mitchell lot adjoining the field to be used as a parking lot. Doubleday Field was beginning to draw visitors, and "Lately the parking spaces on Main street had become entirely inadequate to meet the demand so that motorists driving to the village for trade were often compelled to drive some distance to locate a spot in which to leave their cars."[1]

The Great Depression struck upstate New York along with the rest of the country and Cooperstown was not immune. Emergency work relief rooms were operating by 1932 as government flour was distributed to needy families. Signs of trouble were everywhere. The Southern New York Railway discontinued passenger service and on March 4, 1933, the three banks in Cooperstown closed as part of the "bank holiday" declared by President Franklin D. Roosevelt. One of the three, Cooperstown National, never resumed regular business and was later dissolved. In early 1933, a survey conducted by the American Red Cross found that 320 families needed assistance to get through the winter, a sizable number in a village of about three thousand.

In time, Doubleday Field began to benefit from the depression as government relief money was applied to upgrade it further. In late 1933, extensive grading was undertaken under the "temporary emergency relief program." The village contributed $1,000 toward the project, which also attracted funding from the National Civil Works Program, part of President Roosevelt's sweeping New Deal. Good news came late in December, when the local chamber of commerce learned the National and American leagues planned to take part in the celebration of baseball's centennial in Cooperstown in 1939. Commissioner Kenesaw Mountain Landis, American League president William Harridge and National League president John Heydler, Cooperstown's booster and friend, were named to a committee to oversee the effort.[2]

The year 1934 proved to be pivotal for Cooperstown as the depression continued to grind on. In early July, further improvements were made to the field under another relief program to which Cooperstown contributed $1,937, with the balance in state and federal funds for a total of $10,255. The entire playing surface was regraded, two tennis courts at the western boundary of the field were removed, the grandstand was given a new roof, a new fence was erected in left field and a concrete-and-stone bridge built across Willow Brook at the entrance to the park. A crowd of more than 2,000 attended the reopening ceremonies on August 3 when the park was dedicated by New York Lieutenant-Governor M. William Bray. A baseball game marking the event went eleven innings before the hometown Cooperstown nine prevailed over a team from Oneonta.

A train ride taken that same year by a man named Alexander Cleland was vitally important for Cooperstown and its fortunes. Not much of baseball fan, but aware of Cooperstown's claim to fame, Cleland came up with the notion of a baseball museum in the village while returning to his home in New York City after a visit to Cooperstown. He'd been meeting with his boss in the village and afterward witnessed the work that was underway on Doubleday Field. Cleland thought that a museum should be erected nearby to salute baseball's past, giving an additional boost to tourism and complementing the field. Cleland shared the idea with his boss, Stephen Carlton Clark, the richest man in Cooperstown. Cleland, a native of Scotland with a passion for social work, had met Clark in 1931 when Cleland became director of Clark House in New York City. Funded by the Clark Foundation, which was headed by Stephen Clark, the Clark House provided services to newcomers to America by helping them find jobs and temporary housing. Cleland became Clark's personal aide and that was why he made his fateful visit to Cooperstown. Upon his return to New York City, Cleland wrote a memorandum to Clark and suggested that a museum could include items such as bats of famous players, "funny old uniforms," and baseballs thrown by presidents on opening days.[3] The idea appealed strongly to Stephen Clark and he had the drive and wherewithal to do something about it.

Clark oversaw a family fortune amassed by his grandfather Edward Clark, a lawyer who became partner with Isaac Merritt Singer, inventor of the Singer sewing machine. Edward Clark had a home in New York City and an estate at Cooperstown, the hometown of his wife, upon which he bestowed a great variety of gifts.

Edward Clark had teamed up with talented and eccentric inventor Singer in 1848 and helped focus his genius on a product that would be sought worldwide, an early success story in the industrial revolution. Born in Pittstown, New York, in 1811, Singer went to work in an older brother's machine shop in Rochester and, after marrying, became a mechanic and found himself in Cooperstown by 1833. He developed a machine to drill into rock and moved to Chicago where he obtained a patent for a machine to carve wood and metal.

Buyers for his inventions were few, however, and by 1849 he was working at a Boston machine shop. There, he improved upon the troublesome Lerow and Blodgett sewing machine at the request of the shop owner, who was tired of repairing the crude device. Singer made it more simple and reliable, and obtained a patent that would lead to riches when he pitched his machine to women with an innovative advertising campaign. His lawyer, Clark, helped him get through a patent infringement suit that nearly drove Singer bankrupt. Personally, Singer was a complex and creative character. He had a weakness for the stage, repeatedly trying to become an actor but without much success. And he was a serial philanderer who married women without bothering to obtain divorces. By the time he retired to a 115-room mansion in the south of England in 1863, Singer had 24 children and several former wives.[4]

Singer's scandalous personal behavior while president threatened the company reputation, so Clark, a straight-laced New York lawyer, created the Singer Manufacturing Company and persuaded Singer to retire with forty percent of the company stock. The two men had clashed frequently and by then thoroughly despised each other. Upon Singer's death in 1875 (leaving an estate of $13 million), Clark became president of the company, expanding it to Europe, South America and Southeast Asia. Clark extolled the virtues of the device with brilliant advertising campaigns and helped even the poorest women to acquire Singer sewing machines by providing easy payment plans. The Singer sewing machine was one of the first mass-produced products in the world and it made both Singer and his lawyer fabulously rich. Upon his death in 1882, Clark left an estate estimated at as much as $40 million to his only son, Alfred Corning Clark. The Clark family retained interest in the firm until 1959.[5]

Stephen Clark was born in Cooperstown, one of four sons of Albert Corning Clark, who left them about $120 million. A graduate of Yale, Stephen Clark was elected to the New York State assembly in 1910 and for a time published a newspaper. He directed Clark family enterprises through the Leatherstocking Corporation and went on to become a noted collector of art, including pieces by Rembrandt, Hals, El Greco, Picasso, Renoir, Cezanne and Van Gogh. He was a trustee of the Museum of Modern Arts and a director of the Metropolitan Museum of Art.[6] Best of all for Cooperstown, he was constantly contributing to local causes and doing his best to make the village a better place. A brother, Edward Severin Clark, was also very active working to improve Cooperstown and built a mansion called Fenimore House, the Otesaga Hotel and the Alfred Corning Clark gymnasium, a recreational facility and meeting house for the village. Edward used Clark family funds to help build the hospital that doomed the town's original ball field. A cow barn he acquired became a tourist attraction today known as the Farmers' Museum. Two other brothers, F. Ambrose and Robert Sterling, let Edward and Stephen tend to Cooperstown and its needs while they pursued other interests, including thoroughbred horses.[7]

Toward the end of 1934, Clark was among a group of local residents who incorporated the Otsego County Historical Society and opened a museum in the Village Club building on Main Street.[8] Sometime in late 1934 or early 1935, Clark learned that an old baseball had been found in a trunk in the attic of a home three miles west in the crossroads village of Fly Creek. A contractor there planned to demolish the house where Abner Graves reportedly had once lived. Local lore was that the tattered relic had been used in the first baseball game played by Doubleday in 1839. Clark quietly picked it up for five dollars. Although reported to be the property of Abner Graves, it soon became known as the "Doubleday Baseball." The artifact attracted great interest because it seemed to confirm the connection between Doubleday and baseball and Cooperstown. Now that the village had finally persuaded itself that it was the birthplace of baseball, here was some "proof" of Graves's story and a fine exhibit for the new museum.

Clark then "lent" his aide Alexander Cleland to the newly formed National Baseball Museum in February 1935 to act as its secretary as the 1939 centennial of the Doubleday game approached. From his base in New York City, Cleland lobbied baseball officials and sportswriters to try to convince them of the need for the museum. In Cooperstown, he was helped by Walter Littell, editor of the *Otsego Farmer*, which in 1924 had merged with the *Freeman's Journal*. The village board of trustees unanimously voted to have Cleland act as secretary of the Cooperstown Baseball Committee and on behalf of the village to plan centennial activities.[9] The still-struggling village was solidly behind the effort to turn baseball to its economic advantage.

In April of 1935, the Doubleday Field Association was created during a meeting of citizens in the gymnasium named in honor of Stephen Clark's father. Directors of the new association included Clark and Dr. LeRoy Pitcher, son of dentist E. L. Pitcher, the pioneer fundraiser for Doubleday Field, who had since moved to Albany. At the gathering, Clark formally donated the "Doubleday Baseball" to the baseball museum for which he would serve as chairman.

Cleland, with significant help and encouragement from his employer Clark, went to work lobbying Major League Baseball for donations of exhibits for the new museum. The pair found a receptive ear in Ford Frick, the new president of the National League. Frick liked the idea of a museum and came up with the notion of a permanent hall of fame associated with it to showcase the star players of the game.[10]

Clark continued to support the village's efforts to create a suitable shrine for baseball and a first-class facility at Doubleday Field. In 1937, he presented the village with a deed for more Phinney property on the easterly edge of the field and later acquired adjoining parcels along the left field area from a handful of other property owners.[11] In 1938, Clark gave $1,955 to the village to acquire further land around Doubleday Field from five owners, including Alexander

S. Phinney, whose cow pasture had been the first tract acquired. Also in 1938, village trustees applied to the Works Progress Administration (WPA) to further improve Doubleday Field. Federal funds of $23,401 to cover labor costs were allocated and the village came up with $17,300 for materials and rental of necessary equipment. Lumber was acquired for a new grandstand while a serviceable older grandstand was obtained from the Otsego County Fairgrounds. As work neared completion, the village borrowed $36,000 to ensure that the field would be ready for the centennial in 1939.[12]

In mid–1935, with Ford Frick firmly on board, plans for a Baseball Hall of Fame were announced within the new National Baseball Museum. On December 23, it was announced that thirty-three players had been named by the Base Ball Writers Association of America as candidates to be considered as the first inductees into the Hall of Fame.[13] As a later account explained,

> While Frick could never have envisioned the dramatic and significant impact of his idea [for a hall of fame], he understood history and the importance of baseball in American society. No longer just a school boy's game, it had become the national pastime. In the minds of many fans, years were measured by championships and individual performances. The game had also become a big business and, lamenting this development, Frick felt that it needed more sentiment. When he was ultimately elected to the shine in 1970, he stated that "we need a little memory of what has gone in the past if we are to have hope in the future and intelligent planning today.... Baseball helps to supply a continuity in this age of chaos."[14]

Frick, a native of Indiana, had played semi-professional baseball in Walsenburg, Colorado, in 1916 while teaching high school. Not long afterward, he moved to Colorado College in Colorado Springs, where he was an assistant professor of English. After the First World War, Frick became a sportswriter for the *Rocky Mountain News* in Denver before returning to Colorado Springs and starting an advertising agency while writing editorials for the local paper.[15] He left Colorado for a sports reporting job at the *New York American* in 1921 when his abilities were recognized by an editor there. His time in Denver, the same city in which the tellers of two important baseball stories resided, coincided with the twilight years of Abner Graves. In New York, Frick embraced Graves's story of Cooperstown for reasons beyond simple nostalgia. He was looking for ways to reinvigorate baseball, which had struggled through the Great Depression, leaving several franchises at risk of collapse. By saluting baseball and looking forward to a centennial celebration, he felt the game would benefit financially.

As 1936 dawned, seventeen public works projects employing 334 men in Otsego County were underway, with two more programs approved under New York State's "temporary emergency relief administration." Most of the projects involved public works such as highways. Clark himself was funding another project—extensive changes and additions to the Village Club building because of space needed by the historical society and the new National Baseball Museum also housed there. In February, the first five inductees into the hall of fame were announced: Ty Cobb, Babe Ruth, Honus Wagner, Christy Mathewson and Walter Johnson. In July and August, the National Baseball Museum and Otsego County Historical Society Museum in the Village Club quarters attracted more than a thousand visitors, about one-third of the population of Cooperstown. In October 1936, the National Baseball Museum was incorporated as an entity separate from the historical society and among its directors was the ubiquitous Clark. Late the following month, the baseball museum took formal possession of the baseball relics from the society and shortly after the new year it received the bronze plaques from Major League Baseball for the first five Hall of Fame inductees.[16]

On July 1, 1938, the National Baseball Museum and Hall of Fame officially opened in its fine new quarters. That same year, Henry Chadwick, the Brit widely known as the "Father of Baseball," was enshrined in the hall of fame. A year later, in the "centennial" of the game, his friend, employer and the man responsible for Cooperstown being anointed the home of baseball, Albert Goodwill Spalding, was similarly honored.

Acquiring items to display in the museum proved more difficult than Cleland had expected, but one early item helped justify the Doubleday story. It was well understood that baseball had been played during the Civil War and that when soldiers returned home afterward they carried the game with them, which helped spread it to a wider audience. A large colored print was acquired that showed a game played by Union prisoners in 1863 in Salisbury, North Carolina. It had been drawn by Major Otto Boetticher, one of the captives, an artist, and had the distinction of being the earliest known image of the game. The print was provided by a descendant of one of the prisoners. This find helped reinforce the story that a Cooperstown boy and Civil War major general had invented the game a bit more than two decades before the outbreak of the bloody conflict.[17] Also acquired were shoulder straps from Abner Doubleday's army uniform. By the time the hall opened, it featured many items, including baseballs, scorecards, bats, old photographs, books and other memorabilia. Cleland's perseverance was largely responsible.

As war clouds gathered in Europe, 1939 marked a time to celebrate one hundred years of baseball in America and Cooperstown attracted the attention of a nation. It was a time to mark a simpler, happier time and American values. Baseball again draped itself in Old Glory with a return of some chest-thumping nationalism like that espoused by Albert Goodwill Spalding thirty years earlier.

In February, James A. Shanley, a member of the House of Representatives, a Democrat from Connecticut, asked Congress to mark the centenary by introducing a national baseball day. According to a summary of his comments:

Alluding to the troubling events taking place in Europe, he contended that the game had saved the country from the "excess prevalent among nations abroad" and therefore deserved an honored place on the calendar. His bill authorized President Roosevelt to proclaim June 12th a baseball holiday during which flags would be displayed on public buildings. Shanley felt that "baseball best exhibits the American ideal of true sportsmanship, has contributed most to the development of the American temperament and has been the nation's safety valve." For the past century it has been the country's "pastime and passion," and in the process it "brought despair to Mudville—joy to Middletown." The entire country should "rejoice and thank God for a game that for 100 years has built Americanism."[18]

Shanley had a personal connection to the game, having played centerfield for Yale. His grandfather had been a pitcher during the Civil War. Given the times and his history, Shanley's hyperbole can be understood. Doubts about the validity of Graves's claim to fame for Cooperstown were largely overlooked as the country was swept up in patriotic fervor. Major newspapers, newsreels and broadcasters were planning coverage for centennial activities such as the Cavalcade of Baseball on June 12, which was to accompany the formal opening of the hall of fame. Cooperstown prepared to bask in the national spotlight.

Doubts about Cooperstown's claim as baseball's cradle had emerged in the writings of sportswriters Irwin and Spink not long after the publication of Spalding's *America's National Game* but nothing came of them. However, the announcement in 1935 of a hall of fame and museum for baseball prompted a renewal of the debate. One challenger was Bruce Cartwright Jr. of Honolulu, who contacted Cleland to claim that his grandfather, Alexander Cartwright, had been known as the "Father of Organized Baseball" because of his efforts with the Knickerbocker Base Ball Club of New York in 1845. "My grandfather told many local people that he organized it, drew up the rules they played under and also laid out the first 'base-ball diamond' which was officially approved by the Club and the measurements used by all other clubs for years," he claimed. He added that Alexander Cartwright joined the Gold Rush of 1849 and spread the game across America on his trip to California. In his letter, Bruce Cartwright offered to provide some items relating to his grandfather to the museum. Cleland replied that he'd be happy to accept any items Cartwright might donate and noted that the St. Louis Baseball Club had recently been seeking information about Cartwright. (Cleland had advised the St. Louis club, but not Cartwright, that Abner Doubleday had earned the honor of inventing the first game.)[19]

As word of preparations in Cooperstown continued, Cartwright kept lobbying for recognition of his grandfather. He enlisted the support of John Hamilton, manager of the Honolulu Chamber of Commerce, to promote Alexander Cartwright as father of the game. In a letter to Cleland, Hamilton suggested that the Abner Graves story was in error. "We desire to ask your

IN MEMORY OF

MONROE F. AUGUR    GEORGE H. CARLEY
DR. HARRY L. CRUTTENDEN    LORA J. GROSS
DR. ERNEST L. PITCHER

WHOSE JOINT EFFORTS IN THE EARLY 1920'S LED TO
THE DEVELOPMENT OF DOUBLEDAY FIELD ON THE SITE
WHERE ABNER DOUBLEDAY INVENTED THE GAME OF
BASEBALL IN 1839

This plaque at Doubleday Field shows that the village of Cooperstown, which owns and operates it, is still encouraging the notion that baseball was born in the central New York community. Author's collection.

further consideration and if necessary, further study in order that the records may be kept straight for the future."[20]

Faced with this, Cleland turned to Ford Frick of the National League for advice about how to respond to such queries. Frick told Cleland that the centennial was about a game, not individuals, and that "so far as the records show, the first baseball diamond in history was laid out in Cooperstown." He stressed that there was no intention to slight Cartwright for his role in the game and added that he "certainly will be included among the immortals whose names will be perpetuated at the museum." Cleland then replied to Hamilton, writing that "your letter has forced our hands to some extent" and informing him that organizers of the centennial would hold a "Cartwright Day" as part of the celebrations and that a plaque in his memory would be unveiled.[21]

This was a major concession based on the limited evidence provided by Bruce Cartwright, who insisted that his grandfather had told him about the origins of the game. Cleland was busy promoting a dream based on Abner Graves's story and, rather than risk everything at such a late date, he and Frick were prepared to throw a bone to the Cartwright family. As Alexander Cartwright's biographer Monica Nucciarone has put it, a compelling reason to play up Cartwright's accomplishments "was to appease critics of Doubleday ... but it was also done to appease the descendants of Alexander Cartwright and the city of Honolulu [which had just named a baseball park after him].

Celebrating Alexander Cartwright on a special day was a diversion the organizers of the museum felt was needed to draw attention away from the doubt being shed on Doubleday's connection with baseball."[22]

Cartwright was inducted into the Hall of Fame in August 1939, five months after Bruce Cartwright died at his home in Hawaii. Alexander Cartwright's plaque in Cooperstown reads: "Alexander Joy Cartwright Jr. 'Father of Modern Baseball.' Set bases 90 feet apart. Established 9 innings as game and 9 players as team. Organized the Knickerbocker Baseball Club of N.Y. in 1845. Carried baseball to Pacific coast and Hawaii in pioneer days." The haste to recognize Cartwright was reflected in the overstating of his accomplishments with precious little corroboration. If the idea was to satisfy critics, it worked. Interestingly, in 1938, the same year that Cartwright was voted for inclusion into the hall of fame, Henry Chadwick was enshrined. During his life, Chadwick was sometimes called the "Father of Baseball" because of his extensive writing about it, his editorship of *Spalding's Base Ball Guide,* his development of the box score and other contributions. But Cartwright's plaque described the old Knickerbocker as a "father" of the game, while Cooperstown was dedicated to the father-inventor of the game, Doubleday. So, rather than confuse visitors about too many daddies, Chadwick's plaque was worded this way: "Henry Chadwick. Baseball's preeminent pioneer writer for half a century. Inventor of the box score. Author of the first rule-book in 1858. Chairman of the rules committee in first nation-wide baseball organization." Writer, inventor, author and chairman, but not a father.

The baseball centennial was barely underway when two more broadsides were fired at the Doubleday story that caused an even greater headache for Cleland, the centennial committee, the village, and the baseball establishment. A sportswriter named Frank G. Menke published an article in the new and little-known magazine *Ken* in 1938 in which he attacked the Cooperstown-Doubleday story, arguing that Doubleday was a student at West Point and couldn't have been in Cooperstown as Graves insisted. He also asserted that baseball was derived from cricket. Menke was critical of the Mills Commission and claimed that it was Alexander Cartwright who invented the game, not in 1845, but in 1839.[23]

Likely because of Menke's obscure platform for his claims, little heed was paid to them, despite his growing reputation as one of the best sportswriters of his day. But Menke was back in February 1939, when his book, *Encyclopedia of Sports,* was published. He reiterated his belief that baseball's origin lay in cricket, and that Cartwright had devised the first modern game of baseball. This time, Menke claimed that Cartwright had drawn up the game in 1845 or 1846. He dismissed A.G. Mills as "a doddering old man" whose final commission report was self-contradictory, illogical and expressed dismay that it had misled "the present ruling powers in the sport."[24] The sportswriter reprinted the Mills Commission report and then picked it to pieces.

Menke noted that Doubleday was neither a schoolboy nor an "embryo" West Pointer in 1839 because he began his studies there the previous year and would have been a sophomore aged twenty. Menke also pointed out that Doubleday had not eliminated the practice of plugging, an innovation he credited to the Knickerbockers in 1848. Menke observed that Mills had referred to a drawing made by Doubleday, but that no such thing had been found. He observed that Mills had known Doubleday for 25 years yet had been oblivious to the major general's involvement with baseball until the emergence of the letter from Graves years later. Menke declared that Doubleday never breathed a word to anyone about inventing the game or ever mentioned it in his public speeches or his many writings. The connection between baseball and Doubleday, he concluded, was based on the evidence of a man "who remains forever unknown." This comment arose from the fact that Mills hadn't named Graves in his report and neither had Spalding in *America's National Game.*

Bob Considine, a reporter with the *New York Daily Mirror*, helped to publicize the views of Menke, whom he described as "the great sports historian." Considine characterized Menke's encyclopedia entry as "an embarrassing revelation" just as Doubleday was about to be honored in Cooperstown. The *Sporting News* also carried an article about Menke and his evidence, which "completely upsets the base on which the anniversary rests." It conceded that there was a dearth of reliable and credible information about baseball's past and that the National Baseball Centennial Commission would have to dig deeply to refute Menke.[25]

The timing of Menke's attack couldn't have been worse for tiny Cooperstown as it prepared to welcome ball fans and the media. But there was more to come. For several years, Robert W. Henderson, a librarian at the New York Public Library and a curator at the New York Racquet and Tennis Club, had been doing research in the vast collection of materials possessed by his two employers. He believed in solid research and was disinclined to accept anything at face value. He brought a scholarly approach to his work as he probed the origins of baseball. In April 1939, the product of his labors was published in the *Bulletin of the New York Public Library*. In a detailed critique, Henderson demolished the story of Cooperstown and Doubleday. Relying on source documents, he showed that there had been a description of baseball and a drawing of its field in the mid–1830s and he found that the same rules of the game dated back to 1828 for a game called "rounders." Henderson's work was so well documented that few writers could find fault. But Cooperstown was so committed to the Graves story by then that there was no way to turn back. So Cooperstown, Major League Baseball and even the big newspapers did their best to downplay this damning new evidence. Even a columnist in the vaunted *New York Times* joined the fray to denounce the unwelcomed revelations:

Never mind Europe. Consider what's happening in this country. Baseball officials have been going around making plans for the first hundred years of the national pastime.... Now Mr. Robert W. Henderson of the New York Public Library staff has dropped a regular bomb on the big baseball program.... His researches have led him to the clammy conclusion that baseball was played before 1839, and at other places than Cooperstown.... The Cooperstown origin and the date of 1839 have been accepted for centennial celebration by common agreement among peace loving citizens, and disturbance of that peace should be placed in restraint until the big parade at Cooperstown has passed its given point.[26]

Cooperstown and the baseball establishment held firm and withstood the latest barrage. No one was willing to let it rain on Cooperstown's parade.

Some good news had arrived in February 1939, with recognition from Postmaster General James A. Farley. He announced that a stamp would be issued to mark baseball's centenary in a speech at the annual dinner of the New York Chapter of the Baseball Writers' Association. The first-day sale, he revealed, would be in June in Cooperstown to coincide with the formal opening of the hall of fame. Farley added that the Post Office was open to suggestions for the image to appear on the stamp, although he noted a policy against depicting living persons.

Further recognition for Doubleday and Cooperstown came at the same banquet in a letter read to attendees from President Franklin Roosevelt. The president declared that Americans should be thankful to Doubleday for devising a game that "remains today the great American sport." He saluted the general's military exploits in Mexico and in the Civil War before noting that by devising baseball Doubleday had proved that peace can produce victories no less important than those in war.[27]

Roosevelt had further contributions to make in his effort to support Cooperstown's claim to baseball. Opening day for the professional game across America on April 18, 1939, featured a variety of centennial-themed activities. Roosevelt was scheduled to throw out the first pitch in the Washington contest pitting the Senators against the New York Yankees, but poor weather forced cancellation of many opening day games and ceremonies, including Roosevelt's pitch. The president made up for it the following day when he sent a letter to the Baseball Hall of Fame and Museum in which he stated that, aside from being America's game, baseball was "also the symbol of America as the melting pot," acknowledging the many offspring of immigrants who had joined the ranks of elite players. He continued that he found it "most fitting that the history of our perennially popular sport should be immortalized ... where the game originated and where the first diamond was devised a hundred years ago." Given the noise from naysayers, the ringing endorsement from the president himself came as great comfort to Cooperstown interests and to baseball. Menke and Henderson and their troublesome facts had been trumped by a president. The president's letter was framed and placed on a prominent wall in the museum.[28]

As events were being planned to celebrate baseball's centennial, it seemed appropriate to include relatives of the childless Abner Doubleday. Alexander Cleland heard from a man named Robert S. Doubleday, of Tacoma, Washington, who claimed to be a direct descendant of baseball's purported inventor. The Tacoma resident also wrote to Walter Littell, editor of the *Otsego Farmer*, explaining that he was a nephew of the old general. He described himself as the closest living relative of Abner Doubleday and stated that he had already received a letter from Ford Frick inviting him to take part in centennial events. Most importantly for Cleland and Littell, Doubleday claimed that in the last visit his uncle made to his childhood home in New York, the old general shared "the story of the beginnings of baseball."[29] Here was more evidence of the link between Doubleday and baseball. Cleland and Littell felt it could be used to counter critics who maintained that Cooperstown was built on a myth.

Another Doubleday, Robert F. Doubleday of Johnstown, New York, had met Stephen Clark and was able to supply some of the educational and military record for the major general, but nothing connecting him to baseball. This Doubleday seemed to have a better grip on his family history and after contacting the Tacoma Doubleday, he declared that the Washington man had no connection to the family. The Doubleday of Johnstown warned Cleland and the others to proceed with caution if they were planning to rely on the Tacoma Doubleday in any way.

Cooperstown officials decided that the best time to salute Abner Doubleday would be Memorial Day, when they would unveil a portrait and plaque dedicated to him. On that day, the military connection was addressed with an invitation to Lieutenant Daniel G. Doubleday, a 1929 graduate of West Point. A brother of Robert F. Doubleday of Johnstown, he was posted to the Army Air Corps in Dayton, Ohio. Aside from him, 23 other members of the Doubleday family attended the Memorial Day salute to Abner, coming from the village itself and from surrounding communities, as well as places farther afield such as Johnstown, Binghamton, Long Island, Scarsdale, New York City and Kalamazoo, Michigan. Robert F. Doubleday delivered a speech in which he said that his famous ancestor had invented the game quietly and had been subject to some criticism for not being more public about it. He saluted Cooperstown for the recognition by its centennial commission and everyone proceeded to Doubleday Field to unveil the bronze plaque to the field's namesake.[30] On June 12, for the hall of fame dedication, the Doubleday family contingent swelled to 35 as pictures of the old general filled store windows all along Main Street.

The Cavalcade of Baseball events, the induction of Babe Ruth, Ty Cobb and the others drew thousands of visitors and 10,000 crammed into Doubleday Field for a game of town ball with schoolchildren, then soldiers played on teams to represent the Knickerbockers and Excelsiors, followed by a "choose-up" game featuring current major league players. The U.S. Post Office issued its three-cent stamp saluting baseball's centennial, which depicted young boys playing on a field that could easily have been Elihu Phinney's. And, as promised, a Cartwright Day was held later in the summer, attracting some of his family. Overall, the centennial celebration was a big success, drawing coverage from major newspapers across the country. More than 75,000 visitors streamed into the village that summer and paid attendance at the hall of fame and museum exceeded 30,000. While not all events had been financial successes, Cooperstown was firmly planted on the baseball map. Annual inductions of Hall of Famers ensured its ongoing success after a few lean years during the Second World War. On June 29, 1956, the hall recorded its one millionth visitor, John H. Morrissey of Bronxville, New York. The five millionth was recognized on October 21, 1977, the ten millionth on August 9, 1995, and the fifteen millionth on May 13, 2011. Ironically, the latter record-setting visitor to America's baseball shrine was a Canadian, Ken Gallinger of Ormstown, Quebec, on his annual pilgrimage.[31]

Critics continued to hammer away at the myth upon which Cooperstown was founded, but the shrine continues to flourish. The "Doubleday Baseball" is still on display and the initial claims about it have been put to rest. Today, this text appears alongside it:

> Inventing Abner Doubleday.
> In 1905, the United States was taking its place on the world stage, eager to establish its distinct heritage. In that spirit, sporting goods magnate Albert Spalding handpicked a special commission to prove the national game's American roots. The eventual verdict? Civil War hero Abner Doubleday created baseball in Cooperstown in 1839.
> In fact, baseball was played decades earlier, evolving from similar bat and ball games. Doubleday *didn't* invent baseball ... baseball "invented" Doubleday, a thriving legend that reflects Americans' desire to make the game our own.

Even Stephen Clark, the tireless booster of Cooperstown who sank so much of his own money into the field and museum, confessed that he had little faith in the tale spun by Abner Graves. Shortly before his death in 1960, Clark was quoted as saying: "Nobody invented baseball ... it grew out of town ball and rounders and things of that sort."[32]

Other Cooperstown interests readily acknowledge that the National Hall of Fame is founded on a myth. They include the James Fenimore Cooper Society, which keeps alive the memory of the pioneering hometown novelist and takes comfort in arguing that at least the village is the scene of the first "literary" baseball game. The society notes that Cooper often used Cooperstown as the basis for the town he called Templeton and that his family home of Otsego Hall and its grounds for the mansion appears in several of his novels. The society also points out that an 1816 order by Cooperstown village trustees decrees that "no person shall play at ball in Second, or West street, in this village, under penalty of one dollar, for each and every offence."[33] Second Street became Main Street and West Street was renamed Pioneer Street. That puts the site very close to Doubleday Field and the National Baseball Hall of Fame and Museum. The order by the village trustees was referred to in one of Cooper's novels.

The society also notes that in his 1838 novel *Home as Found*, Cooper wrote about a game of ball played on the grounds of a mansion in "Templeton" that irked its owner, John Effingham, who had just returned from 14 years in Europe. He learned that his property had become popular with ballplayers in his absence. A passage in the book captures the discovery that prompted Effingham to order his estate manager, Aristabulus Bragg, to send the players packing:

Known as the "Doubleday Baseball" and once touted as having been used in the first game in Cooperstown, the National Baseball Hall of Fame and Museum makes no such claim today. The Hall now explains that its discovery in 1934 helped promoters raise funds to build the shrine to baseball at a critical time. The ball was found in a trunk in a home purportedly once owned by Abner Graves. Author's collection.

As they [the Effinghams] came in front of the hall windows, a party of apprentice-boys were seen coolly making their arrangements to amuse themselves with a game of ball, on the lawn directly in front of the house....

In passing the ball-players, he [Bragg] called out in a wheedling tone to their ringleader, a notorious street brawler—"A fine time for sport, Dickey; don't you think there would be more room in the broad street than on this crowded lawn, where you lose your ball so often in the shrubbery?"

"This place will do, on a pinch," bawled Dickey—"though it might be better. If it warn't for that plagued house, we couldn't ask for a better ball-ground."

"I don't see," put in another, "what folks built a house just in that spot for; it has spoilt the very best play-ground in the village."

The tale continues with Bragg continuing to argue with the ballplayers to get them off the lawn. Using some psychology, he noted the order of village trustees banning play in the street and appealed to the defiant young men:

"There are so many fences hereabouts," continued Aristabulus [Bragg], with an air of indifference; "it's true the village trustees say there *shall be no ball-playing in the street,* but I conclude you don't much mind what *they* think or threaten."

"Let them sue for that, if they like," bawled a particularly amiable blackguard, called Peter, who struck his ball as he spoke, quite into the principal street of the village. "Who's a trustee, that he should tell gentlemen where they are to play ball!"

Moments later, Bragg returns to Effingham and announces "that the ball players have adjourned...."[34]

The James Fenimore Cooper Society draws attention to the passage from *Home as Found* as representing the first account of baseball, albeit in a novel. It concludes:

In all probability this incident in Cooper's novel reflects a real event when James Fenimore Cooper, having bought back and remodeled Otsego Hall in Cooperstown (which, with its grounds, had lain vacant since 1817), moved in about 1835. It thus comes *before* the supposed 1839 date of Abner Doubleday's "invention."[35]

For its part, the Hall of Fame, which never inducted Doubleday, has insisted over the years that Cooperstown is merely representative of the place or places where baseball likely originated. Today it explains the connection this way:

Cooperstown. It's a place that's pure Americana, a one-stoplight town nestled between the Adirondacks and the Catskills in Central New York, with its name drawn from the family of James Fenimore Cooper, whose works of literature have become American Standards.

So it's fitting that Cooperstown has become synonymous with another American standard—baseball—thanks to a story about a Civil War general and the country's enduring love for a timeless game.

...The Doubleday Myth has since been exposed. Doubleday was at West Point in 1839, yet "The Myth" has grown so strong that the facts will never deter the spirit of Cooperstown."[36]

Interestingly, Bud Selig was appointed to the board of directors of the National Baseball Hall of Fame and Museum in 1976. Yet even after becoming commissioner of Major League Baseball, he clung to the belief that Doubleday invented the game.

Despite the measured words from the Hall of Fame, nearby Doubleday Field has a sign that touts itself as the "birthplace of baseball." A plaque on the structure states that this was the place "where Abner Doubleday invented the game of baseball in 1839." Perhaps that is what Selig recalled.

Doubleday Field is owned and operated by the village of Cooperstown, which has found keeping the myth alive to be very profitable for local merchants and village coffers. Tens of millions of dollars are generated annually

Aside from profiting from the bogus claim that it is the birthplace of baseball, Cooperstown is also home to the Cardiff Giant, America's greatest hoax. The ten-foot-long giant, supposedly a petrified man, was "discovered" about eighty miles west of Cooperstown in 1869. It created a sensation and prompted circus impresario P.T. Barnum to make an unauthorized copy so he could cash in, too. In the late 1940s, the original fake found a home at the Farmers' Museum in the village. Author's collection.

by 300,000 Hall of Fame visitors, so there is a compelling reason to promote the birth of the national pastime. Merchants on Main Street sell souvenirs that tout the myth. One vendor of baseball bats calls itself the Where It All Began Baseball Bat Company, for instance. Having traveled from all over to see the Mecca of baseball, pilgrims expect to see some evidence that their trek was not in vain.

As a fascinating aside, the village that has profited so handsomely from the myth it was so slow to embrace, is also home to a hoax. The Cardiff Giant, a ten-foot-long image of a man carved from gypsum, found a resting place at the Farmers' Museum in the late 1940s. Known as "America's Greatest Hoax," the figure was touted as a petrified man when it was found in 1869 near Cardiff, New York, about eighty miles west of Cooperstown. The father of the giant was Binghamton cigar-maker George Hull, an atheist who became embroiled in an argument with a revivalist minister about a passage in Genesis indicating that giants once lived on earth. Hull found a five-ton block of gypsum in Iowa and convinced a stonecutter in Chicago to carve it into the figure of a naked man. The mischief-maker then hired a crew to secretly bury the giant on his cousin's farm near Cardiff and later hired a well-digging crew which conveniently "discovered" the giant, creating great public excitement. Hull charged admission to see the "petrified" man and earned tens of thousands of dollars in the ensuing months as he exploited the gullibility of his customers, many of them caught up in the religious fervor of the time. Controversy raged about whether it was a petrified fossil or a statue created by some ancient race. Academics weighed in with their opinions. Circus impresario P.T. Barnum tried to buy the giant and, when Hull refused, simply made a copy which he exhibited, passing it off as the "real" giant.

Both giants proved to be prodigious earners for their creators. Eventually, shortly after both were displayed in New York City, the hoax was revealed. Barnum's copy now lives in Michigan, but the "real" giant calls Cooperstown home. A local baseball team in Cooperstown has called itself the Cardiff Giants. In a village of not much more than 2,000, America's greatest myth and its greatest hoax are neighbors, an intriguing situation that caught the attention of the late paleontologist and writer Steven Jay Gould. In wondering why we prefer to embrace creation myths rather than evolutionary tales, Gould took note of the proximity of two great ones in Cooperstown: "What could be more fitting than the spatial conjunction of two great American origin myths—the Cardiff Giant and the Doubleday Fable?"[37]

The baseball myth, of course, is far more potent than that of the gypsum giant. It endures because the story told by Abner Graves many years ago remains so compelling. It has resisted thorough and repeated debunking. Americans like their myths, as another historian James A. Vlasich ably puts it, because they "love simple answers to complex questions." He goes on:

> In the process of establishing apparent truths, we often create half-truths or untruths. How much this affects us depends on the consequences of the story. Does it really matter if Washington didn't cut down the cherry tree or Babe Ruth didn't point to the area where he hit his famous home run?[38]

Vlasich suggests that the Cooperstown tale is "harmless fantasy" and reflects the romance of the game. Certainly the fantasy that sprang from the mind of mining engineer Abner Graves has had a huge impact on the game and on America. It captured the imagination not only of children and fans of the game but of baseball commissioners and presidents. Whatever else is said or written about Graves, that's quite an accomplishment.

# Eleven

## *Remembering the Storytellers*

The death of Abner Graves did not mark the passing of his story. Far from it. It grew to be accepted as truth as the years went by and as Cooperstown slowly began to capitalize on it.

His son Nelson moved his wife, Edith Pearl, and young daughter, Claire, into the large home at 1535 Logan St. where Abner had shot Minnie. The Graves family took in boarders in the large house to supplement Nelson's income from the McMurtry Paint Company. By the time the Great Depression gripped Denver, they had as many as five others in the house for whom Edith cleaned and changed bedding. In about 1935, however, they lost the home to foreclosure and the family was forced to move into an apartment on the same street. In 1939, the year of baseball's centennial in Cooperstown based on her grandfather's story, Claire graduated from East High School. She learned secretarial skills and found a position in a real estate agency, entering the same business as her father and grandfather before her. At age 19, Claire met Sumner ("Bud") Strashun, 24, on a blind date, and they married in 1943. Strashun had an interest in agriculture and science and after living in Denver for a year the young couple moved to California where Bud attended the University of Southern California, obtaining a master's degree in science in 1948.

Bud soon found a position with the United States Department of Agriculture at its research laboratory and he and Claire settled in the San Francisco suburb of El Cerrito. Children followed, starting with Edith Anne in 1948, Nelson Chandler in 1950, and Barbara Jane in 1954. Shortly before their third child was born, Bud became chief chemist for Vacu-dry Company and later its director of research. The firm, located in the Sonoma County town of Sebastopol, an area then famous for its apples, specialized in producing low-moisture fruits, primarily apples, but also apricots, dates, peaches and prunes. As the family fortunes improved, the Strashuns moved to a larger house, which proved helpful when Claire's aging parents, Nelson and Edith Pearl, moved in. The extended family was an active one and Barbara later recalled that life in the 1960s was much like the "Leave It to Beaver" family of television fame with "good values and wholesome living."

In 1965, Bud was lured to the small Washington city of Wenatchee, known as the apple capital of the world. There, he designed and managed a plant that dehydrated apples and other fruit, the same sort of operation as at Vacu-dry. The family found moving from the San Francisco area to Wenatchee to be a big adjustment. Not long afterward, Nelson's wife, whom he preferred to call Pearl, suffered a stroke that affected her speech and ability to walk and had to move into an extended care facility. Claire recalled her father saying that the move to a smaller place could have been far worse if it had been to a community of 200, a comment she took as a reference to Dow City, Iowa. Nelson, a gentle man who never complained or raised his voice, enjoyed his twilight years in his big chair, smoking a pipe and reading the newspapers. His granddaughter Barb remembered that when Claire took a job as a stenographer, the task of preparing dinners on weekdays fell to her. "This became a joint effort between me and Grandpa," Barb recalled. "He taught me how to cook roasts, chops and other cuts of meat. Nelson loved to explore the backroads and countryside, so even when it was harder for him to walk, Dad would take him on various drives." Nelson's experience in the kitchen and a passion for outdoor discoveries were likely forged during his time in Mexico when his father placed him in charge of mine operations and left him to fend for himself. Three years after his beloved Pearl died, Nelson passed away in 1972 at the age of 89. His longevity was shared with his father and, quite possibly, his genes. But Nelson had been adopted, the family was told. Claire wasn't so certain about that. In her heart, she believed that her father was actually the biological son of Abner, despite the adoption story. She had no idea as to the identity of his birth mother back in Iowa. Claire always remarked on how very close Abner was to the boy he and Alma had adopted as an infant.

In 1975, the business Bud Strashun had worked so hard to establish and operate ran into financial troubles and he suddenly found himself without a job. His specialized skills were in demand, fortunately, and he found work in Yakima as a consultant for clients interested in building food processing plants or needing analysis of the quality of food processing efforts. He and Claire, now empty-nesters, kept their home in Wenatchee and Bud commuted home on weekends. Bud's expertise saw him called upon by foreign governments for advice and he began to travel widely. Government programs underwrote the costs and he often was able to take Claire with him. The countries they visited included India, China, Honduras, Guatemala, Indonesia, the Philippines, the Solomon Islands, Bulgaria and Ghana.

In 1997, shortly before his 82nd birthday, Bud Strashun succumbed to lymphoma. Widowed after nearly 54 years of marriage, Claire stayed in Wenatchee for seven more years before moving in with family on Bainbridge Island, a short ferry ride from Seattle. She joined the household of daughter, Barb, and her husband, Tom Hemphill. Some time later, older daughter Edy also moved to the island, while her son, Nelson, lived in nearby in Seattle.[1]

Reflecting back, Claire remembered her father telling stories about Abner Graves, and she and her family believed that he played in the first game of baseball. For some time, Claire talked about wanting to do something special to recognize her grandfather's life and thought something like a book would be the best way. When she saw one that was produced by Margalyn (Maggie) Hemphill, the wife of her grandson Luke, documenting the life of one of Maggie's relatives, Claire was determined to do the same. And while she was at it, she decided to do another one about her late husband. Barb recalled later: "Claire was intent on saving the legacy of these important men in her life in the hopes that the next generation could appreciate what wonderful men that they were, and learn about their unique contributions." Claire teamed up with Maggie to produce books about Abner and Bud. In 2008, the year she turned 87, *A History of Abner Graves* was published privately by Preserving Heritage, a small memory-book company established by Maggie Hemphill and her mother, Anna DuPen. The attractive 72-page hard-bound effort was richly illustrated with photographs and mementos that Claire had saved from Abner's long life. Included were documents, maps, mining and Masonic documents, his typewritten will, a copy of the letter he sent to the Mills Commission, and newspaper clippings, including those about the shooting of Minnie and other items about his long and colorful life.

In a section about the Cooperstown story, titled "The Baseball Controversy," Claire and Maggie handled the issue this way:

> The controversy started with A. G. Spalding, one of baseball's pioneers, who believed that baseball was entirely an American invention. This led to the formation of the Mills Commission in 1905, which was established to find the origins of Baseball. On a business trip to Ohio, Abner stayed at the Thuma Hotel and picked up the local newspaper. He read an article in the *Beacon Journal* calling for anyone with knowledge of the beginnings of baseball to come forward. Abner then composed a letter on April 3, 1905 to the editor of the *Beacon Journal*. Following the letter there was a flood of newspaper articles of which Abner was featured in and interviewed. Two years later the Mills Commission released its final report stating "the first scheme for playing baseball, according to the best evidence obtainable to date, was devised by Abner Doubleday at Cooperstown, N.Y. in 1839." These findings were largely influenced by Abner's letter. Since then, the National Baseball Hall of Fame and Museum along with the Society for American Baseball Research, have found Abner's claims to have been largely false, based on several dates not adding up right as well as many researchers who believe baseball to have been developed from other bat-and-ball games of the early nineteenth century. However, there is still one of Abner Graves's old baseballs in the Museum in Cooperstown, N.Y.[2]

Family pride in Graves's life is completely understandable. His was a full, productive and long life. It is not surprising that his granddaughter would want to chronicle it—warts and all—in a book. To the family's credit, they acknowledged problems with the Cooperstown tale. They made no attempt to hide the shooting of Minnie, including the newspaper clippings about it and the painful headlines. There was no effort to sanitize or excuse it. A copy of the book was provided to the National Baseball Hall of Fame and Museum. In all, only about 10 copies were produced.

Toward the end of the handsome volume can be found photographs of Claire and Barb and their family visiting the Dow House historic site in Dow City in 1993. This is the former home of Dow City founder Simeon Dow, father-in-law and business partner of Abner. Another image shows Claire posing with the headstone of Abner and Alma Graves, almost seventy years after Abner died. Despite what her family described as some "health challenges," Claire was still sharp and her memory was good in mid–2011, at age ninety, when she entertained questions from the author sent in written form and which she answered in the same way. Claire was helped by daughter Barb. The exchange is dated August 1, 2011:

Q: Your grandfather, Abner Graves, died when you were very young, so you would not know directly what your grandfather might have said about his friends or about baseball. But do you recall your father talking about his father's life and accomplishments? Was baseball one of them?

A: Nelson talked about Abner going around the horn [Cape Horn at the tip of South America] to the gold fields. Abner took care of a passenger who was very ill (TB?). There is a record of him sailing on the trip. I have a drawing of the first baseball game that Abner drew (to present to the Mills Commission). My father, Nelson, mentioned several times to me as I was growing up that his dad, Abner, played in the first baseball game. He used the term FIRST in describing the game.

Q: Did your father ever mention a medical doctor, a man named Adam Ford, as a friend of your grandfather, or even as his doctor?

A: No.

Q: Did your father ever mention anything about his father's story about baseball, Cooperstown and Abner Doubleday? What, if anything, did your dad say about it?

A: My dad, Nelson, could tell the story of his dad playing in that game. It was a story he liked to tell when he was "shooting the breeze" (casually visiting) with his friends. He also liked to tell people that his dad rode for the pony express. My father also talked about an old hand-made (hand-stitched) baseball before it was found in Abner's trunk in the attic or doorway of the second floor. The trunk was left behind in the house in which Graves lived in Cooperstown. I never had an address for their house, but I'm sure people there knew where the house was. The baseball can now be seen in the Baseball Hall of Fame in Cooperstown.

Q: Was there any sort of family pride about your grandfather's connection to baseball and the story of its origins?

A: Yes. Dad kept the story alive and well.

Q: I am told American schoolchildren were taught about Abner Doubleday and the first game of baseball at Cooperstown. Were you? If so, did you tell others in class, or elsewhere, about your grandfather and his story?

A: I wasn't told at school—just at home. I told a few friends at school about the story.

Q: I know you put together a book about the history of Abner Graves. Why? What is your feeling today about your grandfather?

A: a) I did a book because I thought it was an interesting story about his life, and I had a lot of information. I wanted to make sure it was recorded before I die; b) I feel that he wanted to be remembered for his life and accomplishments.

Q: What is your feeling today about all the interest—including mine—that your grandfather created in himself and his story?

A: I think it's astounding. I think Abner would be pleased. He sure worked hard for it (recognition). He worked hard all his life to make a living.

Q: Do you have any theory as to why your grandfather, at age 71, told the story he did about something he said happened when he was five years old in his hometown of Cooperstown?

A: The commission was asking for information on baseball history, and Abner supplied what he knew.

Q: What, if anything, do you want historians to know about Abner Graves and the kind of man he was?

A: He was always very dignified (Aunt Helen said that). Abner was always looking for opportunities for business ventures. He was able to move from business to business as opportunities arose. (Note from Barb here: Aunt Helen is a fifth cousin of Claire's mother, Edith Pearl Graves.)

Q: Is there anything else you would like me to know about your grandfather?

A: I didn't know him that well. He died when I was four or five years old. I don't like him to be remembered for shooting his wife. People used to keep these "skeletons" in the closet. But I guess it's part of his history. Abner had a colorful life. He got to travel around the country. Nelson, his son, was adopted. I believe Nelson is Abner's son. Abner brought Nelson home as a baby as a surprise! Abner ADORED Nelson.

Note from Claire's daughter, Barb: I remember Grandpa (Nelson) Graves telling me of the time when he found out he was adopted. He said he was in his thirties and was standing on the corner of the street. He happened to run into an old friend of his father's who recognized him and said as if his memory was jogged, "Oh, you're the adopted son of Abner...." That shocked Nelson, because it was the first he heard of it (Claire verified the story).

Note from Claire's daughter, Edy: Mom says there were two Abner Doubledays. One was "General Abner Doubleday," the other was Abner Grave's [sic] cousin, Abner Doubleday. Cousin Abner Doubleday is the one Abner Graves played baseball with. Abner Graves called the other Abner Doubleday "General" to distinguish between the two Abner Doubledays.[3]

The pride of a granddaughter is evident—and entirely understandable. Claire's answer as to why Abner Graves told the story he did is perfunctory: the Mills Commission was looking for information and Abner merely supplied what he knew. Her description of Abner always working hard for recognition is interesting and helps explain his frequent interactions with the press. But the clarification provided by Edy doesn't really clarify much. In his original letter, Graves very specifically referred to Abner Doubleday, the Civil War hero of Gettysburg, as the Doubleday who invented baseball.

In follow-up exchanges, Barb Hemphill shared further information gleaned from her mother: "Claire would like to put to rest about Abner having been in mental institutions while in Iowa. She was emphatic about the fact that Abner's only time in an institution was in Pueblo, Colorado."[4] The assertion was in reference to a claim by a historian (later picked up by another writer) that Abner Graves had spent time in an institution during his Iowa days. This suggested that his mental problems pre-dated his letter to the Mills Commission and that the letter should be considered in that context. Claire was asked about any stories she could remember about her grandfather meeting Mark Twain in the days the two were in Virginia City. In a letter she had sent to Barb and her husband Tom in 1976, Claire stated: "When he was at the Comstock Lode (Virginia City), he met Mark Twain ... I have the whiskey flask he [Abner] carried with him in those days and down in old Mexico."[5] But she drew a blank about further details. "Claire doesn't remember any more about Abner meeting Mark Twain," Barb said after questioning her mother. "It was a story that Nelson passed down to her."[6]

Hugh MacDougall, the official historian for the village of Cooperstown, also decided to look into the life of Cooperstown's "other" famous son. With access to local newspapers and their files, MacDougall was able to shed more light on Graves, focusing on his early years. He also traced Graves's movements up to the time he made his claim about the first game of baseball and then on to the killing of his second wife, effectively using the Internet and other resources to uncover information not known to Graves's family, whom he located and consulted. MacDougall's tenacious research occupied many months, work which resulted in a lecture he delivered to the Center for Continuing Adult Learning in nearby Oneonta in 2010. He summarized his findings in a well-documented paper titled "Abner Graves: The Man Who Brought Baseball to Cooperstown." MacDougall generously shared his paper with the author of this book. In his paper, he explained the existence of two Abner Doubledays and clarified the confusion that Graves had sown about the schools in Cooperstown at the time of his youth.

MacDougall drew some conclusions from his painstaking research which are worth sharing:

I believe Abner Graves was honest when he wrote his famous letters in 1905, which launched General Abner Doubleday on a fictitious road to fame. I strongly suspect that his childhood memories had been reinforced, or even altered, by his later contacts with Cooperstown-born relatives. I think he was speaking the truth as he then saw it, though we have seen his exuberant personality and tendency to exaggerate in other aspects of his long life. His later and virtually impossible claims to have been personally involved in the early games he described may be attributed to an aging memory preyed upon by reporters seeking a good story.

I also believe that Graves made a false but reasonable assumption that the Abner Demas Doubleday he had known in Cooperstown about 1840 was the same Doubleday who grew up to be a famous Civil War General, an assumption that others were all too willing to accept.[7]

MacDougall concluded that Abner Graves was "an unusual, talented, and extraordinarily versatile man well worth knowing about." He noted that Graves had taken part in the California Gold Rush and went on to careers as a businessman, engineer and miner. "Just as General Abner Doubleday has been virtually smothered by

Claire Strashun, the only granddaughter of Abner Graves. She was a youngster when the baseball storyteller died, but remembers visiting him in a mental hospital. She keeps alive the story of Abner Graves. Strashun shared photographs with the author and was interviewed for this book. Courtesy Margalyn Hemphill.

baseball, so too has Abner Graves," he observed rather eloquently.

\* \* \*

While Abner Graves was survived by family members who heard his stories, cherished his memory and preserved his photographs and documents, the same could not be said for Adam Ford, the other teller of a compelling baseball story. None of Ford's three children, Julia, Arthur or Leon, ever married, so that branch of the Ford family tree came to an abrupt end. And because his story about Beachville had so little impact and was soon forgotten, there would have been little incentive for anyone to preserve his memory. Luckily, a neighbor of the Ford and Cruttenden families stepped forward.

Burnie Lancaster McLay was born in 1909 in St. Marys, Ontario, and was raised in the west ward of the town. She lived next door to the Cruttenden family, whose patriarch Lauriston had been a town pioneer and the father-in-law of Adam Ford and Leon Clench, the town solicitor. McLay was quite familiar with the nearby white hillside cottage of the Ford family, where the reclusive Julia Ford tended to her ailing mother Jane until the latter's death in 1914 and then later to her aunt, Alice Stoddart. As a child, McLay heard many stories about the Cruttendens, the Clenches and the Fords. McLay was particularly interested in the stories she heard about Nora Clench, Leon's daughter and a cousin of Julia Ford. Clench was a violinist who studied music in Leipzig, Germany, and in 1883 gave a command performance for Queen Victoria. While in England, she also premiered works by Debussy, Wolf and Reger. She married Australian landscape painter Arthur Streeton and moved with him to Melbourne. Meanwhile, McLay married a banker and became active in local theatre as she moved about Ontario. She produced plays and acted in them, reflecting her fascination with interesting characters. In later life, when she returned to St. Marys, McLay's interest in history and her friendship with the families allowed her to put together a brief history of the clans she felt she knew. In so doing, she spent countless hours poring over old newspapers on microfilm upstairs at the *St. Marys Journal-Argus* weekly newspaper. She had to content herself with files from the *Argus* as those from its rival, the *Journal*, had not survived. Despite the absence of any indices to guide her, her avid digging enabled her to find the stories about Ford being charged in the poisoning of Robert Guest and the scandal that subsequently rocked the town.

Help was on its way for McLay. When Julia Ford needed to move into a nursing home in her twilight years, a friend, Edward Kinsman, a banker, antiques collector and dealer, purchased her home for $500. This provided the funds she needed to obtain suitable care. When she passed away in 1948, Julia left everything to Kinsman. He stored everything in his house on Thomas Street and then carted it all with him when he moved to a large Victorian mansion on Church Street, located next door to a fine stone home that had become the St. Marys Museum. He stored the boxes of Julia's materials in his attic. When Kinsman died in 1976, his home and its contents were left to a nephew, Gary Jackson. For his part, Jackson realized that the boxes contained items of potential historical interest so he contacted Larry Pfaff, a town resident with an interest in history who had worked for years as a student assistant at the town library. Pfaff had just taken a post as a research librarian at the Art Gallery of Ontario in Toronto, but continued to live in St. Marys and retained a strong interest in local history. Upon opening the boxes, Pfaff instantly recognized that they contained invaluable material about the pioneering Cruttenden, Clench and Ford families. One of the items that excited Pfaff was an ambrotype (an image on a fragile glass plate) of downtown St. Marys from about 1857, the earliest known photograph of the community. Perched on a hill in the distance was Adam Ford's new white home overlooking the business section below. Pfaff borrowed the treasure trove to copy and returned the documents to Jackson, who moved from the mansion in 1989 and ultimately donated all the original materials to the local museum.

Soon after connecting with Jackson, Pfaff learned that McLay had assembled a short history of the Fords, Clenches and Cruttendens. He shared news of his find with her that same year, 1976. She was delighted and the pair became collaborators, studying the photographs, documents, letters and other materials Pfaff had located. McLay began to rework and expand her history.

While working in Toronto during the week, Pfaff was able to conduct detailed research into members of the three families at the Archives of Ontario and through Canada Census records. He found deeds, obituaries and Ford's accounts of his curling exploits. Pfaff searched farther afield and wrote to obtain copies of newspaper accounts from Denver concerning the death of Adam Ford. He tracked down members of the Clench-Streeton family in Australia, who shared with the museum copies of many photographs in their possession.[8]

McLay, meanwhile, sorted the materials, expanded her research and assembled a longer history with the significant help of her new collaborator. The result was a typewritten manuscript with the descriptive but rather inelegant title "The Whole Truth and Nothing But: A Century of Actual Happenings in One Man's Family." She died of cancer in 1979 and gave her work to Pfaff, who donated it to the St. Marys Museum. McLay's manuscript and the associated Ford/Cruttenden/Clench files are preserved at the museum and provide an interesting glimpse into the three prominent town families linked by marriage. They include items such as Arthur's letter to his sister describing the final hours and death of their father, Adam's notes to Julia enclosing money and apologizing that he didn't have more, and Leon's letters about his latest mining project and next surefire success. In her work, McLay carefully transcribed the newspaper accounts about Adam Ford and the poisoning case and those describing his death in Denver. She also told the stories of all of Jane (Cruttenden) Ford's six brothers and sisters. McLay came to know the families so intimately that it was almost as if she adopted the Fords, the Clenches and the Cruttendens.

She had great sympathy for the older ladies who lived in the Ford home and whom, as a young girl, she found to be mysterious and intriguing. McLay's writing had a distinctly melodramatic quality to it:

> In any story there must be a heroine, and Julia Ford played that role well. She carried the entire burden at home, patiently caring for her asthmatic mother— holding her head high in spite of frequent humiliations—pretending that all was well, when indeed their financial position was so desperate that tradesmen refused her credit. She was forced to beg loans from relatives to meet some cri-

sis like buying winter fuel when last year's bill was still unpaid. Taxes were in arrears—there was forever a mortgage and nothing at all left for clothes, even if she could have found money for the dressmaker.[9]

Toward the end of her life, Julia was a mere shell of a woman, eking out a precarious existence in her crumbling home. McLay wrote that the house on the hill was falling into disrepair, "with cardboard utilized to fill up holes made by falling plaster. The original electric wiring still had a single cord from the ceiling and a dingy light bulb to save electricity." For 17 years, Julia looked after her aunt Alice, who, like Julia's mother before her, became an invalid and a recluse. McLay wrote, "Alone, weak and feeble, totally dependent on the compassion of friends and neighbors, Julia suffered much privation." She had similar observations about the wife Adam Ford left behind:

One feels overwhelming pity for the Ford family. Here was Elsie Jane separated and widowed for a period of 34 years, spending much of that time behind the fence in her own backyard, suffering uncertain health, which in all probability would have greatly improved if her husband had prospered to the extent that they could have resumed a normal marriage.[10]

McLay's work is a remarkable account of a family that had its rascals and heroes, winners and losers. She seemed to be particularly captivated by the story of Adam and Jane Ford and their children. McLay concluded her detailed and highly sympathetic account of the family this way: "How very sad that a family with such brilliant potential should end so pitifully. Fate truly dealt the Fords a mean, unlucky hand."[11]

The museum in St. Marys, the town where Adam Ford practiced medicine, married a pioneer's daughter, was elected mayor, and poisoned a young man, is the home for the vast majority of historical material about him. A much smaller museum at Beachville, about 30 miles to the southeast, contains copies of materials related to Ford's story about the 1838 game he said was played there. A locally authorized historic plaque near the museum notes the community's claim as the site of the first recorded game of baseball in Canada on Militia Day in 1838.

Larry Pfaff lauded the work of his one-time collaborator McLay as having provided a revealing glimpse into the early days of their community "which you'd never find in a history book—the interrelationship of families, the importance of sports and how one event can ruin a family's reputation." He added: "none of this is unique, but the photographs and obituaries give evidence that would be lost if the documentation had not been preserved and written about." He noted that his work and that of his collaborator also revealed that "certain newspapers" could be unreliable and sensational at times.[12]

Despite her digging and that of her friend Pfaff, when McLay died she knew nothing about Adam Ford telling a story about baseball in his childhood

Historical marker near Beachville Museum, Beachville, Ontario. In Denver, Adam Ford wrote to *Sporting Life* about witnessing a game here as a boy in 1838. Researchers have tested his story and concluded that it appears valid. After completing medical school, Ford moved to St. Marys and began raising a family. Author's collection.

home in Beachville. There were no clues and no mentions of baseball, other than in his last letter sent home a few days before his death, in which Ford seemed happy that the 1906 baseball season was underway.

"How she would have delighted in that," Pfaff reflected many, many years after McLay's death. It was a discovery yet to be made and a chapter yet to be written. Those tasks would fall to others.

# Twelve

## *Testing a Tale*

It took an outsider to persuade Cooperstown that it was the birthplace of baseball. And it was an American who told Canada that its first recorded game predated Cooperstown. The same pattern of migration that brought games that became baseball from England to the American northeast and into Britain's adjacent colonies also brought a New Englander with a passion for baseball to the Canadian province of Ontario. This diehard fan of the Boston Red Sox set for himself a daunting task: to consider a claim made a century earlier about a game played in his new backyard another half century before that.

Robert Knight Barney had been born in Winthrop, Massachusetts, in 1932, with his twin, David Ellsworth Barney. A younger brother, Peter Bruce, followed. Their father was Robert S. Barney, a colonel in the United States Air Force (then known as the U.S. Army Air Service) who in 1931 had graduated from Norwich University, America's oldest private military college. He became commandant of the Michigan Military Academy in upstate Michigan, but when that venture failed, he returned to his native Massachusetts where he painted fences and cleaned windows. Upon the establishment of make-work programs during the Great Depression, Robert S. Barney became a second lieutenant in the Civilian Conservation Corps and supervised dam-building projects in Vermont. Upon America entering the Second World War, he was activated for service and became an intelligence officer, rising to the rank of colonel by the time he retired in 1962.

Robert Knight Barney's mother was Blanche Barney, a noted professional pianist, trumpet and cornet player, who could trace her lineage to the arrival of the Mayflower in America in 1620. When she passed away in 2011, at the age of 103, her obituary noted her musical accomplishments and how, after settling down to raise a family, she taught piano to hundreds of students: "Her only disappointment in this regard was with her twin sons, who were much more interested in baseball than mastering octaves."[1]

As a young boy during the Great Depression, Bob Barney listened to afternoon radio broadcasts from Fenway Park as play-by-play announcer Jim

Britt described games of the Boston Red Sox. His first hero was Jimmie Foxx, but as luck would have it, Barney never saw him play. When his father found a job in 1941, after a jobless stretch, he celebrated his first paycheck by taking his boys to their first Red Sox game:

> In ensuing years Fenway became my cathedral, Ted Williams and Dom DiMaggio my bishops. Beyond my immediate family, I came to worship baseball most. From the start, I had visions of someday becoming a major-leaguer. I lived baseball, breathed it, immersed myself in its every facet. And there were millions of American boys just like me: we were all preoccupied with baseball.[2]

Bob Barney never made it to the major leagues. He excelled at his studies, however, particularly in physical education and history. He followed in his father's footsteps into the United States Air Force, where he became an atomic armorer in the U.S. nuclear bomb testing program in the southwest. Leaving the service, he enrolled at the University of New Mexico, where he became a scholarship athlete in baseball and swimming. He obtained his bachelor of science degree in physical education in 1959, followed by his master's degree and then a doctorate in both physical education and American history.

After short stints as an associate professor at the State University of California at Sacramento, at River College, in Nashua, New Hampshire, and at Boston State College, in 1972 he took a position as associate professor of physical education and director of intercollegiate athletics at the University of Western Ontario, in London, Ontario. A visit to the 1984 Summer Olympic Games in Los Angeles inspired Barney to establish a research center to provide serious scholarship into the games. The Centre for Olympic Studies was created at the university and to this day remains the only independent research facility in the world focused solely on the Olympics. It has been a hub of activity for graduate students from around the world conducting research into issues surrounding the Olympics games and the Olympic movement. The center, for which Barney served as director from 1989 to 1999, has led to the publication of a wide range of papers on ethical and other issues surrounding the games. Barney himself has written and edited more than 130 journal articles, books, book chapters and scholarly reviews on topics related to the Olympics. In 2010, he received the Pierre de Coubertin Award of the International Society of Olympic Historians for "lifelong and dedicated historical work on behalf of the Olympic Movement." In 2003, a book he wrote with Stephen R. Wenn and Scott G. Martyn, *Selling the Five Rings: The International Olympic Committee and the Rise of Olympic Commercialism,* was deemed the best scholarly work on sport published anywhere in the world by the North American Society for Sport History. The same year, Barney received the society's Lifetime Achievement Award for contributions to the discipline of sport history.

In 1991, he was elected president of the North American Society for Sport

History (of which he was a charter member in 1972). He was also able to pursue his interests in baseball and history. For seventeen years, he was an editorial review board member of *NINE: A Journal of Baseball History and Social Policy Perspectives.* He became a member of the board of governors of the Canadian Baseball Hall of Fame and Museum and from 1998 to 2002 chaired the hall's selection committee. Barney has published abstracts, refereed journal articles, or written book chapters on baseball topics eighteen times.[3]

For a Massachusetts kid who never learned his octaves or made it to the major leagues, Bob Barney did pretty well. But he wasn't the kind of person to sit on his laurels.

About the same time that he was spearheading the creation of the Centre for Olympic Studies, Barney began looking into a sport history topic much closer to his adopted home in southwestern Ontario. Having recently published a scholarly article about the Cincinnati Red Stockings, which in 1869 became one of the first all-professional baseball teams, Barney had turned his mind to the beginnings of the professional game in Canada. He was aware of the great rivalry between two Ontario teams packed with professionals by the 1870s, the London Tecumsehs and Guelph Maple Leafs, when he learned that a former graduate student of his, Nancy Bouchier, was looking into the history of sport in small Ontario communities. Just as they were considering their research and potentially meshing their efforts, they came upon a brief reference to Adam Ford and the Beachville game in a then-recent book by Canadian baseball historian Bill Humber. Humber's *Cheering for the Home Team* mentioned an account about it that had appeared in a weekly newspaper in a town near Beachville.[4] Barney tracked down the original—and complete—1886 account in *Sporting Life.* Upon studying it, he and Bouchier decided to see if Ford's tale could withstand rigorous academic scrutiny.

"Ford's reminiscence was a most remarkable document," Barney wrote several years later. "If true, it reflected the most detailed, documented account of baseball in its entire history before 1840."[5] So he and Bouchier set out to test the tale. They read everything they could find about early baseball and predecessors to the modern game. They dug into primary sources such as nineteenth-century maps of Beachville and genealogical and family records of its residents. Barney and Bouchier studied headstones, looked up land ownership documents and checked property tax records and obituaries. In the course of their research, Barney learned much about the migration of New Yorkers and New Englanders such as himself into Ontario 150 years earlier. He complemented his knowledge of American history with digging into that of British North America. He discovered that by the outbreak of the War of 1812, when the new republic initiated hostilities with Britain and boasted about conquering its colonies, Upper Canada (later Ontario) had welcomed about 60,000 immigrants from neighboring states. Some were motivated by a desire to remain subjects of the British Crown, some were attracted by the prospect of cheaper farmland and others merely decided to abandon their shortcut through the sparsely settled colony while on their way to the territories of Michigan, Illinois and Wisconsin. These newcomers accounted for three-quarters of the population of the colony. After the back-and-forth battles that accomplished little during the two-and-a-half years of the war, boundaries reverted to what they had been beforehand. American immigration continued in the thousands, but the British government countered with a special push to populate the colony with loyal Brits, Scots and the Irish in an effort to dilute the presence of the more free-thinking Americans.[6]

American settlers brought with them a strong work ethic and knowledge of farming, both of which were essential to transform the heavily forested colony bordered by three of the five Great Lakes. They also brought their customs and games with them. Those games included early bat-and-ball games resembling baseball, Barney and Bouchier found. The researchers also learned that as far back as the 1820s, the Oxford County Militiamen gathered annually to mark the birthday of the king, who until 1830 was George IV. Known as Militia Muster Days, these events included an inspection, perfunctory drills and marching, followed by social activities and games, including sack races, horseshoes, wheelbarrow races, footraces, catching greased pigs and the climbing of greased poles.[7]

Aside from their skills and their games, American settlers also brought with them some political thinking that governors of Upper Canada and its sister, Lower Canada (Quebec), found troubling. The colonial elite faced new-fangled notions of liberty and freedom that clashed with the paternalistic "family compact" that held all positions of authority. Rebellions by inhabitants seeking greater freedoms were put down by the authorities in both colonies in 1837.[8] The administrators had relied on local militia to quell the rebels, so by Militia Day 1838, memories of the previous year and an understanding of the need for proper training for the militia were still fresh in the minds of colonists. At the time, repercussions were still being taken against the rebels, dubbed as traitors, who were tried and hung or deported to exile in Van Diemen's Land (now Tasmania). Despite the lingering after-effects of the uprisings, participants in Militia Day at Beachville that year still found time for the customary games, including the one described so many years later by Adam Ford. This Militia Day, in early June, marked the birthday of Queen Victoria, who was just completing the first year of what would be a long reign:

> It was into this atmosphere of American cultural manifestation and the hostility that it all too soon raised between Yankee settlers and British subjects, that one Adam Enoch Ford was born in Oxford County, Ontario in 1831. During his youth he witnessed baseball games played by older youths and adults, later he played the game himself.[9]

As Barney and Bouchier embarked on their bid to assess Ford's story a century after it was published, they observed that "historians have neither subjected Ford's reminiscence to detailed critical examination, nor have they analyzed Ford's authority in the matter. The letter's contents have nevertheless been accepted by some at face value."[10] That sounds very much like the initial reception for another letter, written at another time, for another purpose, by another man, who, like Ford, was living in Denver.

In the case of Ford, his letter to *Sporting Life* was published in part in the *Ingersoll Chronicle*, a newspaper in a town near Beachville, but it received scant attention beyond that. Much later, Beachville used Ford's account in a bid to persuade the Ontario Historic Sites and Monuments Board to declare the site of that first game historic. No such designation has yet been granted, however, so local authorities erected their own plaque. Other than that unsuccessful effort, little use was made of it.

Collaborators Barney and Bouchier were struck by how much of what Ford described from a time when he was a lad about to turn seven, they were able to confirm. "Drawn from his memory, which sources suggest was keen until the day he died, Ford's reminiscence provides much information which our own research verifies," they wrote. To buttress their view, they cited the praise bestowed upon Ford by the editors of the Ontario Curling Association annual reports to which he contributed. Upon his passing, the 1906–1907 annual report noted that Ford "had a combination of talents granted to but a few—and carried them all, bright and alert, to a green old age."[11] Barney and Bouchier added that "superimposing Ford's reminiscence on known events in the history of Oxford County, and further, on baseball history itself, there can be little doubt regarding the validity of the circumstances described by him."

About the only fault they could find in Ford's account was his reference to the birthday being celebrated that Militia Day in 1838. In his letter, Ford said the birthday of George IV was being celebrated, when in fact it was that of Queen Victoria. George IV was king from 1815 to 1830, followed by William IV from 1830 to 1837, when Victoria assumed the throne. Inexplicably, Ford also misspelled Beachville as "Beechville." The community had never used the latter spelling. Barney and Bouchier found nineteenth-century maps of Beachville depicting the shop of Enoch Burdick, mentioned by Ford as being near the field of play. They concluded that spectators of the game described by Ford as "Scotch volunteers from Zorra" were likely members of the Third Oxford Regiment under the command of Colonel J. Barwick, then taking part in regimental movements in the area while dealing with remnants of rebel threats in the southeast corner of the county.

Genealogical and headstone evidence told the researchers that many participants in the game described by Ford were between the ages of 15 and 24. The Beachville cemetery proved to be an invaluable source of information, as were Oxford County assessment rolls, the *Oxford Gazetteer* of 1852 and an unpublished history of the Karn family found at the Oxford County Library

The field in Beachville, Ontario, where Adam Ford reported that the 1838 game of baseball was played. Today it is covered with small homes. This view is from the lawn of the Royal Canadian Legion across Zorra Street. Author's collection.

in Woodstock. Four members of the Karn family, with branches in Beachville and Zorra Township, were mentioned as participants in the game: Adam, Peter and Harry, all 16, and Daniel, 18. The headstone of Reuben Martin was found in the cemetery but it contained no dates. Nathaniel McNames, 24, and George Burdick, likely a relative of blacksmith Enoch Burdick, were identified from assessment rolls. Also present for the game, Ford believed, was William Ford, 13, one of Adam's older brothers. (William Dodge, another participant, was most likely a member of the pioneer Dodge family, whose members included the wife of merchant Lauriston Cruttenden, later to become Adam Ford's father-in-law.) "These findings validate Ford's reminiscence on the point relating to the players involved in the June 4th contest," the baseball sleuths concluded.

In his account of the Cooperstown game, Graves also took it upon himself to name players. They were Elihu Phinney, John C. Graves, Nels C. Brewer, Joseph Chaffee, John Starkweather, John Doubleday and Tom Bingham. But because his story fell apart with the discovery that Abner Doubleday couldn't have been present, no corresponding research was conducted to determine more about these individuals.

Barney and Bouchier then turned their attention to Ford's description of the playing field in the Beachville game. Ford had described the infield as "a square, the base lines of which were twenty-one yards long, on which were placed five bags." He drew a diagram showing "first bye" through fourth and a home "bye." First and home were separated by six yards. This configuration, the researchers noted, "appears quite similar" to the square layout of the New York and Massachusetts games of 1842 and 1845. On closer scrutiny, however, they concluded that it was also similar to the 1845–46 infield of Alexander Cartwright and the Knickerbockers. Both of these layouts included territory for fair and foul struck balls (Ford called them "fair hit" and "no hit" balls) that distinguished them from the New York and Massachusetts versions of the game. This innovation, they noted, also distanced baseball from cricket. Ford and Cartwright's games also featured a common "striker's stone" and home base.[12]

Comparing the game as described by Ford to records of the Massachusetts Game, the New York Game and the version played by Cartwright's Knicker-bockers, they indicated similar positions for players: "All had strikers or knock-ers (batters), catchers, throwers or tossers (pitchers), fielders, base lines and byes (bases). As in the Massachusetts and early New York games, a runner in Ford's game had an easy time getting to first bye [it was only six yards]."

Ford's field placed bases a bit more than 60 feet apart, similar to softball diamonds of today, but the distance from fourth bye to home was 45 feet because it fell 18 feet short of the striker's position. The 1842 New York game stipulated forty-eight feet from the striker's base to first, sixty feet to second, and seventy-two feet to third and home. The 1845 Massachusetts game was thirty feet to first, then sixty feet to second, third and home.[13] No dimensions were given by Graves other than a description of a six-foot ring within which the pitcher had to stand.

In Graves's Cooperstown game, by comparison, there were four bases and eleven players, four outfielders, three basemen, a pitcher, catcher and infielders placed between first and second and second and third bases respectively.

Similarities existed in the rules described by Ford and Cartwright, the researchers found. The retiring of a side with "three hands out," the acceptance of first-bounce catches to make outs and limiting the duration of the game were shared traits. On the latter count, both the Ford and Cartwright games were limited by a specific number of innings or runs. Ford's games were gen-erally six to nine innings or 21 runs while Cartwright's called for 21 "counts."[14] In both the Ford and Cartwright games, a foul hit meant that neither the batter nor runners could advance.

The practice of "soaking, burning, or plugging," the act of striking a base runner with the game ball to record an out, and the runner dodging the ball to avoid being put out, was shared in all games, except in Cartwright's. He introduced the tag. The account of Abner Graves also involved "soaking" run-ners, despite the later and significant revision eliminating it by A.G. Mills. In Ford's letter, Barney and Bouchier noted, he commented on the incursion of the New York game into the area when he returned home from university, likely no earlier than 1849 (when Ford would have been eighteen). Ford noted that India rubber was being used in balls in that game, a move that transformed the game he'd played with a stick and ball wound from yarn. This made for a much more lively game, Ford wrote: "You could knock it so far that the fielders would be chasing it yet, like dogs hunting sheep, after you had gone clear around and scored your tally." He reported that he and a number of locals decided to play with the new ball and "the next day we felt as if we had been on an overland trip to the moon."[15] Ford and his fellow players were apparently "dog" tired from chasing the lively new ball that transformed the more sedate game they knew. The researchers noted that the game with the imported ball would have had a "quickened pace" from the 1838 game and it led to other changes: "The changing technology of ball manufacture, in time, demanded better groomed playing fields and more deceptive pitching techniques if fielders were to cope with the edge given to batters."[16]

Despite the growing acceptance of the New York Game, people in places like Oxford County clung to their local variation for several more years. Barney and Bouchier found that in 1860 games between Beachville's neighbors Woodstock and Ingersoll saw eleven players still employed on each team and the use of four, rather than three bases. The *New York Clipper* took note of the differences in the "Canadian Game" played in centers like Woodstock, based on older rules than those then in vogue in New York.[17]

The relative isolation of communities like Beachville, Woodstock and Ingersoll ended with the arrival of the railroad in the mid–1850s. Combined with the telegraph, the steel rail began to shrink their world and standardized rules were needed. The rules as developed by Cartwright and the Knickerbockers were adopted in most quarters, putting an end to regional variations. Games were played against teams who traveled greater distances and cross-border matches involving New York teams were not uncommon. By 1861, a game played by the Woodstock Young Canadian Club was noted by the *New York Clipper* as the first played in Woodstock using the New York rules.[18] A similar change had been made by teams in Toronto and Hamilton to the east.

Having dug as deeply as they could into Ford's account, researchers Barney and Bouchier found many aspects of it stood up to scrutiny. After reviewing what they found, it was time for the collaborators to draw some conclusions:

The question remains: How credible is Adam Ford's letter relative to the early history of baseball? A thorough investigation of Ford himself, his sport involvement, and the context of his times, all suggest that his reminiscence is valuable. Ford was fifty-five years when he penned his letter to *Sporting Life* in April 1886. Two decades later he continued to provide reminiscences of this nature, especially on the sport of curling. In many ways Ford typified an active breed of middle class nineteenth century sportsmen in Ontario. He was an avid, dedicated, and versatile sport participant and promoter. He helped to organize, administer and popularize sport clubs and teams in a period when few existed in small Ontario communities. Well after his own playing career, he fondly remembered the games of his youth.

Ford's letter leaves strong implications for our broader understanding of the process of sport change, especially as it occurred in the nineteenth century. It clearly demonstrates the existence of long-lived local, communal tradition of baseball played in one small Ontario community. It further reflects the nature of change to that baseball tradition, and emphasizes the continuity in the context of change. Few reminiscences thoughtfully consider this matter. Baseball played in Ford's youth obviously drew from a tradition existing long before his own time. To that tradition, mutually accepted changes were made which resulted in a modified form of contest. Baseball continues to change to this day; but always within the context of that which has come before. For this reason, the significance of Adam E. Ford's reminiscence extends far beyond a mere baseball game played in Ontario on a June day in 1838.[19]

In their assessment, Barney and Bouchier placed much emphasis on the high quality and detailed accounts Ford produced in his twilight years about the sport of curling. As to his ability at age 55 to recall the Beachville baseball game he witnessed the summer he turned seven, they looked inward: "Our own powers of recollection regarding memorable events that occurred when we were so young inclines us to believe Ford."[20] In a later publication, Barney wrote: "We found Ford's recall, indeed his reconstruction of events, to be almost without challenge."[21]

Their pioneering research into Adam Ford and his story was shared at the fifteenth annual convention of the North American Society of Sport History in Columbus, Ohio, in May of 1987 and later published in the spring 1988 edition of the *Journal of Sport History*. They even traveled to Cooperstown to present it to an audience there. Their work attracted media attention, citations in academic journals and baseball books, and many invitations to scholarly meetings and symposia. A documentary film was produced. Canada Post issued a stamp in 1988 commemorating the Beachville game and 150 years of baseball history in Canada. Players in the Beachville game named by Ford were inducted into the Canadian Baseball Hall of Fame that same year. All this wasn't particularly well received south of the border. A Canadian claim that a game of baseball predated Cooperstown by a year was hard to accept in the land that had embraced baseball's creation myth. John Thorn, co-editor of *Total Baseball*, who years later would be named the official historian of Major League Baseball, was gracious when asked about the Beachville game in a 1988 interview published in Canada:

> I think the average fan in the States would not realize that Canada has such a long history in baseball with professional teams dating back to the 1870s in places like London and Guelph. A lot of people think that Canada is a Johnny-

Roadside sign in Beachville, Ontario, stating the village's claim about baseball. The community, near which Adam Ford was born, is too tiny to host the Canadian Baseball Hall of Fame, which is located not far away in St. Marys. Author's collection.

come-lately in baseball because it got its first major league team in 1969 [the Montreal Expos]. What the Beachville game does is focus on the inter-America and international aspect of the game.[22]

Thorn found the research of Barney and Bouchier to be excellent, but quickly added: "Anyone thinking that June 4, 1838, is a central event in the history of baseball, that this was a beginning, is on the wrong path." No claim had been made that the Beachville game marked the birth of the game, however. In his comprehensive *Baseball in the Garden of Eden* in 2011, Thorn made no mention of the Beachville game or Adam Ford. And at conferences they both attended in later years, Thorn admitted good-naturedly to Barney that he had given "the back of my hand" to the latter's probe into the game described by Ford. For his part, Barney good-naturedly put it down to the prevailing attitude in his homeland that if something didn't happen in America, it wasn't important. Especially in baseball.

Thorn wasn't the only baseball historian to be dismissive of the Beachville game. In his *Baseball Before We Knew It*, David Block lamented:

Whatever the true story, the authorities of Canadian baseball have inexplicably chosen to commit themselves to the same type of dubious fable about a "first" game that the collapse of the Doubleday story should have warned them against. National pride has always been a powerful motivator, and perhaps the allure of preempting their American neighbor as the earliest country to host a baseball contest has blinded some Canadians to the precarious value of Ford's narrative. While we can hope that the tale of baseball at Beachville in 1838 stands on firmer ground than the North Woods legend of Paul Bunyan and Babe his blue ox, in the end it may be that both are equally apocryphal.[23]

Interestingly, the most avid promoter of the legitimacy of the Beachville game was Barney, a New Englander. It's a stretch to paint him as some sort of rabid, chest-thumping Canadian nationalist. Here was another "backhand."

Despite criticism by some outsiders, the story of the Beachville game has played an important role in the re-establishment of the Canadian Baseball Hall of Fame and Museum. In late 1982, five years after the Toronto Blue Jays joined the American League, a group of baseball devotees and businessmen announced the creation of the Canadian Baseball Hall of Fame in Toronto. The hall was provided temporary quarters in the Canadian Sports Hall of Fame, near Exhibition Stadium, original home of the Blue Jays. Officials expressed hope that they would be able to find permanent quarters within a year. At the time, it was noted that 143 Canadians had made it to the major leagues and that there was a need for some place to tell their stories. Hall of Fame president Bruce Prentice continued to scout locations for a permanent home and by 1984 tiny Beachville was included in his search. "At this point," Prentice told the *London Free Press*, "we're investigating all possibilities as to where to permanently house the hall of fame. We're looking at all the different possibilities and Beachville was mentioned some time ago, so we thought we'd go and have a look to see what's there and what's not there."[24]

By then, the Hall had already moved from the Sports Hall of Fame to premises on Front Street in Toronto, but its promoters still wanted something more permanent. In Beachville, they would have found a small community bisected by railroad tracks and the Thames River. The field where Ford claimed that the 1838 game was played long ago had been covered with modest homes. To the west, and dominating the community, was an open-pit limestone operation which deposited white lime dust on its surroundings when the wind was strong. An idyllic venue like Cooperstown it was not.

The Canadian Hall of Fame continued its search for a home. There was some talk that it might find room in SkyDome, the new $300 million home field for the Blue Jays that opened in 1989. The Hall had moved into quarters at Ontario Place, not far from Exhibition Place on the Lake Ontario waterfront. But high rent caused it to close in 1988 and all its memorabilia had been tucked away in a suburban warehouse by the time SkyDome opened.

World Series wins by the Blue Jays in 1992 and 1993 inspired newfound pride in Canada's long connection to baseball and Prentice was back, heading a group looking for a community to host a resuscitated Hall of Fame. The city of Guelph, Ontario, was keenly interested. In the 1870s, the professional Guelph Maple Leafs were Canadian champions and had played and defeated some of the top American teams of their day. Also interested was the Niagara peninsula city of St. Catharines along with a handful of smaller Ontario communities, including Collingwood and Simcoe. The winner, however, was St. Marys. Its proximity to Beachville and to a major superhighway were factors, but it didn't hurt that it had been the home of Adam Ford, whose story about the 1838 game had been so widely celebrated. Ford had migrated from Beachville to St. Marys, so a shrine to his game could follow a similar path, it was argued. An important additional consideration was that the St. Marys bid included a property of about 30 acres on the west side of town that had been donated for the purpose by the St. Marys Cement Company. The site already had tennis courts, playing fields and an attractive water-filled former limestone quarry billed as Canada's largest natural swimming pool.

The announcement that St. Marys had won came in mid–1994 and an $8.75 million fund-raising goal was soon established for creation of a museum, library, baseball gardens, and ball diamonds large and small. From the outset, however, locals expressed little interest in emulating Cooperstown. With a population of 5,400, St. Marys was more than twice the size of its American counterpart. Both are picturesque communities. Leafy Cooperstown has Otsego Lake, while St. Marys has a small waterfall, its riverforks and widespread use of native limestone in its busy commercial heart and on its stately older homes.

Dick McPherson, a former mayor and spokesperson for the local committee that won the hall for the Stonetown, expressed modest expectations in 1994. "Of course we want economic benefits for the town but we're going to be careful about promotion so the town isn't overrun," he said. Even the town's tourism coordinator, Gord Soutter, was quoted as saying: "I think the greatest fear is that it will turn the town into some sort of commercial hub. But St. Marys itself doesn't want that to happen." He declared that there was general community support for "guarded growth." The downtown, he added, was still dominated by small, independent retailers and no one in St. Marys was interested in living in a "chintzy" tourist town.[25]

Despite its status as Canada's baseball town, little has changed in St. Marys because of slow fundraising and plans that remain in the concept stage. The town still retains its historic charm and healthy core—agriculture, commerce and small industry keep it humming along. Up the hill on Queen Street, Adam Ford's home, built in 1857, still stands like a sentry, its view of the community now obstructed by newer homes. Annual inductions into the Hall of Fame are held in conjunction with a fundraising breakfast and other activities in the nearby large city of London. A softball game and golf tournament also help to pay the bills. Ball diamonds now occupy the sprawling site but the Hall of Fame itself remains largely notional rather than structural, and the museum is an old quarried stone farmhouse crammed to overflowing with baseball memorabilia. Because of cramped quarters, only about one-third of the thousands of artifacts can be displayed. Larger premises such as a fine old vacant schoolhouse nearby have been considered as acquisitions; so too has been construction of dormitories to house participants in summer baseball camps. But finances have left many of the dreams unfulfilled to date. More recent plans called for a $2-million fundraising campaign to build a 10,000-square-foot building to replace the old farmhouse. The millions needed to create a suitable place for priceless artifacts and to showcase Canadian players have been hard to find. A benefactor like Stephen Clark does not exist in the community. St. Marys has not been transformed, far from it.

Bob Barney found it worth noting that the announcement of a new home for the Canadian Baseball Hall of Fame and Museum came during the 1994 season of Major League Baseball—when many observers predicted another Canadian team, the red-hot Montreal Expos had a good chance of reaching, perhaps winning, the World Series. However, a strike by players caused the season to be scrapped, with no World Series played. It was little consolation, but Canadians that year were able to watch the televised announcement that St. Marys had won the competition to become the new home base of Canadian baseball history:

> Who among the viewers had ever heard of St. Marys? But, then again, who, among millions of American baseball fans had ever heard of Cooperstown at the time of the National Baseball Hall of Fame and Museum's opening there in 1939, one hundred years after Abner Doubleday did not "immaculately conceive" baseball? The events linking Adam Enoch Ford to the site of the "new" Canadian Hall are certainly not "immaculate." In effect, they demonstrate a triumph of real historical substance over that which represents something quite less.[26]

When a visitor drives through small-town southern Ontario he is struck by the prevalence of baseball diamonds in even the smallest of places. Villages and towns dotting farm country might not have an arena, in a country that worships ice hockey, but they invariably have a ballpark of some description. Games on warm summer evenings are often community events, a time for bonding, just as they are south of the border. Baseball has been played in Ontario for 175 years, far longer than ice hockey, a fact that would surprise Canadians and Americans alike. And four or five times as many Canadians have played baseball, in all its forms, including softball, slo-pitch, T-ball and three-pitch, as have played hockey, another fact that would surprise. As the *Globe and Mail*, which bills itself as Canada's National Newspaper, observed in 1995 as St. Marys formulated its plans to salute the game: "baseball is organically of this country."[27]

And it is perhaps fitting that in a country not known for beating its breast about its connection to baseball, the low-key shrine to the game that has emerged in St. Marys seems just about right. It's not Cooperstown, but it never aspired to be. And there is something organically Canadian in that.

# Thirteen

## *Grand Theft, Baseball?*

Fundamental and intriguing questions remain about Abner Graves. The hard-working, resilient and opportunistic entrepreneur, cattleman, banker, mining engineer and real estate salesman had a long and productive life. But many men can claim long and productive lives. The thing that sets Graves apart is a story he put on paper more than a hundred years ago, a story that still resonates with many Americans.

Delving into his life provides some answers about his character. One persistent trait was his ongoing willingness to revise and improve his story. As time wore on, Graves embellished his role in the game he claimed had been played in Cooperstown. He graduated from a five-year-old onlooker to an active participant in the game with older boys, some of whom would have been as old as 18 or 19, such as Abner Doubleday. It's apparent that he enjoyed his fame and that he received a free pass from reporters who ate up his stories and failed to apply any common sense or reality test to them.

Was Graves simply mistaken in his recollection? Some have claimed that his sanity may have been a factor, but the mental issues that prompted him to kill his spouse came nearly two decades after he wrote to the Mills Commission and were likely connected to senility. There is no evidence of mental impairment before he sent the letter, despite the uncorroborated suggestions of historians anxious to dismiss him with an easy explanation. If Graves was suffering from some form of mental illness in 1905, as alleged, it was certainly not reflected in his performance in society. His services were in demand to assess mining prospects in the west and he was trying to exploit his operation in Mexico with the help of his son, Nelson. Was Graves merely confused in some of his details? Some observers point to the existence of two Abner Doubledays in Cooperstown at the time Graves was growing up in the area. The first was the hero of Gettysburg, specifically identified in the letter by Graves. This Abner Doubleday was born in Balston Spa, north of Albany and as a boy moved with his family to Auburn, east of Syracuse. He had relatives in Cooperstown and likely visited them, including Abner Demas Doubleday, a younger cousin and lesser army officer who was disabled by sunstroke during the Civil

War and later moved to Kalamazoo, Michigan.[1] Graves was clear that it was the Civil War hero to whom he was referring, however. And we know that over the years Graves returned to Cooperstown, where friends likely would have kept him abreast of the whereabouts and exploits of boyhood acquaintances like the Doubledays. He may have legitimately mixed them up.

Was Graves guilty of writing pure fiction? And if so, what motivation would he have for that? That question goes back to his character. As we have seen, Graves often filed glowing reports about mining prospects. Several newspaper accounts attest to his excessive enthusiasm and occasional bouts of hyperbole. It may well be that his natural exuberance and willingness to express it landed him assessment work from mining companies. In any case, he seemed to have no shortage of work and was never at a loss for words when a newspaper reporter was around.[2] Further research comparing his glowing assessment reports to the subsequent success or failure of various mining ventures would shed more light on the quality of his work and his credibility in his chosen field.

We know that Graves was prone to wishful thinking. Witness his claim as he approached the age of 80 that he was expecting to play shortstop in an exhibition game between Denver's chamber of commerce and the real estate exchange.[3] Likewise, as he touted his Mexican mine, he maintained that the area is "the greatest mining country of the south and has a future before it second to no district in the world."[4] But the letter sent to the Mills Commission is far more than embroidery—no substantial story existed for him to improve upon. Or was there in the account of another game in another country? Graves's tale of Cooperstown had never been heard before, but was it a case of retelling the bare bones of another story with only the names and dates changed?

So it comes back to the question of whether Graves made it up. And if so, why? As a Mason and then a Shriner, he was expected to live his life according to the beliefs of the fraternal organization. One of those fundamental tenets is truthfulness. Had he not been truthful in his dealings with others, he would have been subject to repercussions, such as expulsion. He never would have reached the level of a Shriner in the fraternity. One would be hard-pressed to say no Mason or Shriner has ever lied, of course, but given his lengthy involvement in Freemasonry, a connection he valued, Graves would have been aware that his behavior would be scrutinized by others in the organization.

His granddaughter and family maintain that Graves, a man who sought recognition, was simply responding to a request for information and that he provided what he knew to Spalding's commission. They claim that the reason his story didn't add up when subjected to historical scrutiny was attributable to a mixup of dates. A family so proud of the accomplishments of Abner Graves as to publish a book about him would not want him remembered as a fabricator or plagiarist. Understandably so. Graves had an inventive mind and an ability to spot an opportunity to draw attention to himself and his boyhood home when one presented itself. That may help address "why" he did what he did. Albert Goodwill Spalding was determined to find evidence that proved baseball was American in origin. Graves delivered a story that provided enough evidence to suit the purposes of the iconic sporting goods entrepreneur. Spalding, then America, ran with the tale Graves told because it was so compelling—it included an American hero, an idyllic American setting and simple facts. The story then developed legs that likely surprised even its teller. And once it was out there, Graves reveled in its retelling and enhancement, never once correcting the change made by A.G. Mills to eliminate "plunking." He wasn't going to mess with the powers that had propelled him and his story to center stage.

For years, Graves has been dismissed in some circles as a crank, a mental case, an oddball or even a practical joker.[5] Concerted probing, however, suggests that his mythical creation was inspired by another lesser-known tale that he may have seen in print or, more likely, heard first-hand on many occasions.

Adam Ford and Abner Graves were similar in many respects and so too were their stories. Three years apart in age, they had played baseball for as long as they could remember. They had coached and promoted the game. They married daughters of pioneers in the communities to which they moved from their hometowns. Graves and Ford were both involved in local government, Graves as a municipal treasurer, Ford as a councilor and mayor. Both left wives back east as they opted to start again in Denver, setting up shop downtown. Both enjoyed alcohol and baseball games and they must have shared friends through the Masons. Graves and Ford were self-promoters, the former through newspaper reporters mostly, while the latter penned his own accounts and delivered speeches in which he was the central figure. Both men also felt compelled to promote their hometowns as special places in the history of baseball. The era in which they lived was one of widespread interest in manly sports inspired by an athletic president who exerted not only his own muscles, but those of America as it took its place on the world stage. Teddy Roosevelt set the tone for his time. In Denver, ego, bravado, alcohol and interest in sport brought many residents together in the early days of the twentieth century. The saloon, as has been noted, was the ideal venue for swapping tall tales. So was the ballpark.

Adam Ford shared his story with *Sporting Life* in 1886, his immediate reason unknown. Perhaps he was responding to reports in previous issues that Spalding was wooing Toronto to consider a National League baseball franchise and Ford wanted readers to know about the longstanding baseball tradition on his home turf of tiny Beachville, about 150 miles west of the Ontario city. Or, he may have been motivated by ongoing stories in the publication about games from long ago and how rules and playing techniques had changed over time. At the time of his letter, Ford was acutely interested in the major professional leagues and following *Sporting Life* closely because his son Arthur was involved with the Cincinnati team that spring. Unlike Abner Graves, however, Ford

The National Baseball Hall of Fame and Museum in Cooperstown, New York, has attracted more than fifteen million visitors since it opened in 1939. The 300,000 visitors each year who are attracted by the irresistible "creation myth" of baseball inject tens of millions of dollars into the economy of the picturesque village of 2,200. Author's collection.

was not responding to any invitation to share his early memories of baseball as part of some sort of grand inquiry or commission. His letter about his childhood memory of baseball in Beachville seems to have been spontaneous and unsolicited. He stood to gain nothing for his effort (which is what he received, at least during his lifetime).

Ford was 55 when he wrote about Beachville and was describing events he had seen the summer he turned seven, some 48 years earlier. For Graves, his story was tapped out on a typewriter when he was 71, or 66 years after the summer when he claimed to have witnessed the birth of a sport. Ford made no claim that the Beachville game was the first game of baseball played; Graves maintained that he was eyewitness to the invention of the game in Cooperstown. Other than that significant difference, both described with remarkable clarity how the game was played and provided the names of players. Both stories seemed plausible. It took subsequent research to determine the truth. And while Graves' tale failed the litmus test, there is no doubt that an early version of baseball was played in the area around the same time, as suggested by the writing of James Fenimore Cooper. Evidence also suggests that bat-and-ball

Merchants in Cooperstown have promoted baseball's creation myth to their financial advantage. "Birthplace of Baseball" appears on a wide range of souvenirs tourists take home each year. This retailer incorporates the myth into its name. Author's collection.

games were played throughout the wider area where both men spent their formative years, about 350 miles apart.[6]

To achieve recognition, Ford relied on politics in his early life, returning to it much later in Denver, where he said he delivered many speeches to political audiences. He was considered a fine raconteur, both orally and in written form. Accounts of his curling exploits were colorful and were so well received that he was repeatedly asked for more. Like Graves, Ford was an avid newspaper reader and was known to put pen to paper to share his thoughts with editors. Unlike Graves, his baseball story was told and then, for the most part, forgotten for nearly a century.

Ford's story about Beachville seems to ring true. Respected researcher and historian Robert Knight Barney, a New Englander with an American pedigree that dates to the Mayflower, is convinced of it. He and fellow researcher Nancy Bouchier were able to validate much of Ford's account. They resurrected a story that had been largely forgotten and their work proved persuasive in Canada. Their efforts saw the Canadian government issue a postage stamp in 1988, marking the 150th anniversary of the Beachville game. And the Canadian Baseball Hall of Fame and Museum found a permanent home near Beachville

The modest quarters of the Canadian Baseball Hall of Fame in St. Marys, Ontario. Because of space constraints in the former farmhouse, only one-third of its artifacts can be displayed. St. Marys, about 30 miles from Beachville, has been home of the hall since the early 1990s. Fundraising for a suitable new structure has been slow. Author's collection.

in St. Marys, the town to which Ford moved and from which he fled in disgrace after the poisoning case.

The game played in Beachville as described by Ford was not as evolved as the game played by the Knickerbockers seven or eight years later. Some historians believe that the elimination of "soaking" base runners with the ball marked the turning point that took town ball or other games into new territory. Indeed, it is likely that A.G. Mills eliminated that aspect of the game from Graves's account in order to show that it more closely resembled baseball as it was played in 1907. The Knickerbockers of 1845–46 dispensed with that aspect of the game and it has been argued that that innovation amounted to a watershed moment for baseball.[7] In Ford's game, "soaking" was still a feature, so it would be a tall order to make the case the 1838 game in Beachville was the first game of modern baseball. Neither Ford nor researchers Barney and Bouchier made such a claim.

The similarities between Abner Graves and Adam Ford are so uncanny that it's almost as if they were mirror images. Decades after the fact, they told

The bustling downtown of St. Marys, Ontario, known as "Stonetown" because of the extensive use of locally quarried limestone. The town, home of the Canadian Baseball Hall of Fame, is more than twice the size of Cooperstown and about seven hours west of it. Author's collection.

stories of baseball games played when they were boys. Those stories eventually led to celebrations, postage stamps and halls of fame in their respective countries. Graves and Ford had long connections to the sport and had moved to make fresh starts in life in a sport-obsessed city known for its saloon culture. The engineer and the doctor both liked alcohol and were rather extroverted types who welcomed the limelight. It is not hard to imagine them bragging about many things, among them baseball, while enjoying a beverage or two in a favorite downtown Denver watering hole.

Aside from their successes, they were no strangers to failure. Graves's business in Iowa floundered and the great potential predicted for his mine in Mexico was not realized. An apparently unhappy second marriage and the shooting of Minnie saw led to his death a mental hospital, a sad end to an otherwise productive life. For Ford, the poisoning case in St. Marys destroyed his reputation there and prompted his move west. His struggles with the addictions of his son Arthur, the unhappy experience with the Washington Sanitarium and the financial problems that kept him from sending much money back east to daughter Julia were among his other trials. Ford's death in modest quarters with overdue rent, his drug-addled son hovering nearby, marked a similarly sad end. Both Graves and Ford were involved in homicides in which poison, or talk of poison, was a factor. For Ford, poison caused the death of Robert Guest. And for his son, Arthur, it led to the death of a patient in his sanitarium and criminal charges. For Graves, it was his expressed fear of being poisoned by Minnie that prompted him to fire four shots into her body.

So, again, is the story told by Abner Graves a complete fabrication, an adaptation or a heist? We are left only with best guesses.

It would seem that the always opportunistic Abner Graves seized the day in Akron, Ohio, when he read Albert Spalding's article in the *Beacon Journal*. Caught up in the same zeal as the sporting goods magnate to prove baseball's origins were purely American, the fertile mind of Graves went to work. He may have taken some hazy memories of his playmates playing bat-and-ball games and decided that he could spin them into an engaging tale to help Spalding in his quest. He didn't need to look far for additional inspiration. For several years, Adam Ford, a fellow fan of the Denver Grizzlies and his business neighbor with mutual acquaintances, had been telling his own story about a baseball game he witnessed as a young boy. Ford's story helped Graves embellish his own recollections and these details, based in the reality of a game that most likely actually happened, increased the plausibility of Graves's tale. Graves likely borrowed not only the idea of telling a story about a game of ball from his youth, but certain aspects of the story itself. He wanted to draw attention to Cooperstown so he used elements of Ford's story as a basis to create his own. Like Ford, he described the practice of "soaking," which Graves called "plunking," and he named several of the players who took part in the game. He also described the location of the preferred playing field. Unlike Ford, however, he didn't attempt to provide distances between the bases, focusing more on how Abner Doubleday scratched out new rules and transformed town ball on the spot.

The similarity between the storytellers is as striking as parallels between the stories they told. Given everything they shared, it is hard to believe that their orbits didn't intersect at some point. No hard evidence has been unearthed to date that proves categorically that the two men met, but it is an irresistible conclusion based on a balance of probabilities. There are far too many points of potential contact to put their telling of stories down to sheer coincidence.

Abner Graves likely borrowed or, less charitably, stole the story about the first game of baseball, or at least parts of it. He created a story that could not have happened, taking inspiration from an event that actually occurred. The game as played in Beachville was brought into the colony by settlers who came either from Great Britain directly or after stopping first in New England, New York or Pennsylvania. Adam Ford's father, for instance, was born in a northern county of Ireland and lived for a time in Pennsylvania before moving north. Ford's father-in-law was born in Vermont before deciding his future lay a few hundred miles to the west. When newcomers came to build new lives in North

America, they brought along their customs and their values as well as their games. It can be no surprise that games resembling baseball were played in places like New England, New York City, Cooperstown and Beachville. Migration and evolution were key factors and muddy any quest to pinpoint when and where baseball came into being.[8]

Graves did not act alone. While his inspiration was likely drawn from Ford, his motivation unquestionably came from the appeal made by Albert Goodwill Spalding. Spalding was a man on a mission, goaded on by Henry Chadwick's bold 1903 assertion in Spalding's own baseball guide that there was "no doubt" that baseball was derived from rounders. Spalding, as we have seen, hand-picked a group of like-minded men to settle the paternity of baseball "for all time" and to prove its American origin. The chair for his committee, A.G. Mills, had declared years earlier at the Delmonico's banquet that "patriotism and research" had already established baseball's American pedigree. The fix was in and the die was cast—Spalding's kangaroo court stood by to do his bidding. A story that could meet the needs of Spalding and his cronies would be looked on favorably. All that was needed was some sort of evidence. Anything. And Graves delivered it. His tale had no independent corroboration, but there was no other story that fit the bill despite the three years during which Spalding and the Mills Commission sought one. The stage had been set for Abner Graves and he served up an account that was even better than Spalding could have imagined. No less than a Civil War figure, a lesser American icon, was the inventor of the game. Perfect. And for Mills it was a delightful revelation that his old friend Abner Doubleday was getting the credit. Never mind that despite their many conversations over the years, Doubleday never let on to Mills that he was the young genius who devised America's national pastime. Or that he failed to mention the achievement in his many speeches or books.

Having been delivered a story he liked, albeit one that he couldn't verify from other sources, Spalding felt that he finally had what he needed to trump his old friend Chadwick and to prove that baseball was not derived from a child's game in England that he had denounced as "an asinine pastime."[9] Baseball came from the inventive mind of a manly man, a national treasure, and on American soil. It couldn't get better—or more American—than that. And just as Spalding was determined to trump Chadwick, so too Graves may have been anxious to trump a talkative Canadian whose baseball story undermined the idea of a made-in-America sport.

While Spalding had originally been inclined to accept rounders as the father of the sport in which he excelled, his about-face in later years was dramatic and became an obsession. Chadwick, the promoter of rounders, seemed to laugh off the rounders-versus-baseball controversy, but for Spalding it became all-consuming. He had good reasons. The boy from small-town Illinois had lived the American dream by excelling at a game that became the national pastime, by moving on to become president of the Chicago White Stockings, then president of the National League. He was a hugely influential man in baseball and in business, a titan, the head of a highly successful sporting goods empire. Baseball—and America—had been very, very good to Albert Goodwill Spalding. He was a wealthy and influential man and had the means to get what he wanted. His way was the American way and he often ridiculed the English as too dim-witted and weak to play the game in which he starred. Cricket, he argued, was more suited to their physical and mental capabilities.[10] He was as determined, in his way, to sever the umbilical cord from Britain as the exasperated but determined men who signed the Declaration of Independence many decades earlier. Spalding, in his resolve to prove that there was no connection to England, was prepared to appropriate the game rooted in another country. He did so at a time when America was emerging as a world power and asserting itself on the world stage. Nothing could be more embarrassing for a man like Spalding than to concede that the national pastime of America was the offspring of a game played by English schoolchildren. He was prepared to go to extraordinary lengths to steal the game, if necessary. What other conclusion can be drawn from his comments on the subject, his appointment of like-minded men to prove his belief and then his acceptance, promotion and publication of the uncorroborated statements of Abner Graves? *America's National Game* was his celebration of pulling off a heist and creating history. It's hard to forget the over-the-top assertion Spalding made in its introductory pages, which captured his mindset:

> I claim that Base Ball owes its prestige as our National Game to the fact that as no other form of sport it is the exponent of American Courage, Confidence, Combativeness; American Dash, Discipline, Determination; American Energy, Eagerness, Enthusiasm; American Pluck, Persistency, Performance; American Spirit, Sagacity, Success; American Vim, Vigor, Virility.[11]

Spalding was a man on a mission and Abner Graves helped him to achieve that mission. If Abner Graves is guilty of adopting part, or all, of the story of a game from another storyteller, which seems likely, Albert Goodwill Spalding was an accomplice. Beyond that, Spalding's greater mission was to appropriate the game from the English and defeat the intransigent bulldog Chadwick. In that, Spalding succeeded. He found a nation ready and willing to believe the story that he promoted as fact. In 1939, Spalding was inducted into the Baseball Hall of Fame in the executive category, it being noted on his plaque that "he gained renown as the era's top promoter of baseball as the national game."

Graves, it would seem, lifted his story from his own "Chadwick" in the person of Adam Ford, a friendly rival and baseball lover born in a colony of Britain. Graves has been largely forgotten and often dismissed, unlike his partner in crime. Regardless, it can be argued that Spalding and his accomplice Graves pulled off a successful double steal for baseball.

# *Epilogue*

The story of Abner Doubleday's invention of baseball in Cooperstown in 1839 remains a dandelion in the field of baseball research. No matter how many historians have tried to kill it with facts, it persists.

The staying power of the tale is a testament to how much Americans wanted to believe it when it was told and how some Americans still want to believe it today (raise your hands, Bud Selig and Ron Keurajian). It's a wonderful story set in a picturesque real-life setting where a shrine to the myth has attracted fifteen million visitors and counting. So those who mess with Americana do so at their peril. But is the search for the true origins of baseball some sort of assault on America? Is it like the battle of science versus faith, pitting the Darwinists against the creationists? Author Steven Jay Gould suggested that trying to pinpoint the origins of a game that evolved is not unlike the ongoing argument between the pro-life and pro-choice factions about when life begins.[1] Opinions can be strong. Remember baseball card collector Keurajian, who insinuated that those who don't believe in Cooperstown are psychologically troubled? His words are worth recalling:

> These are the people with too much time on their hands and like to cause trouble ... I get so tired of those who have this uncontrollable need to distort facts in a weak attempt to change history.... Doubleday is the Father of the National pastime and will remain so for centuries to come. Sorry, that's just the way it is. To this small handful of baseball experts I suggest they concentrate of [sic] some other interest and stop trying to distort baseball history to satisfy some personal shortcomings."[2]

Keurajian's rage suggests that the myth will persist for a while yet, at least in some quarters. America has changed dramatically since it first embraced Doubleday and Cooperstown. Perhaps clinging to a story from so long ago is like the fundamental appeal of baseball itself, a reluctance to let go of an idealized, simple past. Will the love affair with Graves's story continue?

Timing was everything for baseball. At the beginning of the twentieth century, it caught the imagination of a country that was seeing major internal changes wrought by industrialization and a movement of large masses of people from farms to factories. Workers in the cities were beginning to find time for sport and baseball provided them a familiar pastoral game that recalled simpler times, simpler lives. Baseball teams gave them something with which to identify in their new surroundings. It had already attracted millions of fans when Graves sat down at his typewriter.

The game emerged as the country's favorite sport when America was coming of age and assuming a role on the international stage. Football, as we have seen, was still evolving and was plagued by a brutality that nearly saw it banned. America was developing extra-territorial ambitions with an expansionist-minded Teddy Roosevelt in the White House. Football has always been a game based on acquisition of territory. Clearly, football was more naturally aligned with an American mindset at the start of the twentieth century than baseball. However, baseball had the inside track because it was there first and had already become an ally for the military in missions abroad. Baseball wrapped itself in Old Glory at a pivotal time in U.S. history. And at the best possible time, along came a story that credited its invention to an army hero.

Abner Graves is the only person ever to link Abner Doubleday and Cooperstown to the birth of baseball. So he, as the creator, along with Spalding, the promoter, are responsible for misleading not only the Mills Commission, but a country. Graves wanted Spalding to know that he, too, believed that the game was American by birth and he couldn't stand the thought of the British laying claim to it. In his follow-up letter to Spalding, Graves wrote: "Just in my present mood I would rather have Uncle Sam declare war on England and clean her up than have one of her citizens beat us out of Base Ball."[3] Ego and recognition for Graves, along with promotion of his hometown, may also have been factors, the story of his life suggests. But where did he get a story that simply could not have been true? That question has never really been addressed. Did he invent it from whole cloth, embellish his own vague memories, or did he borrow it or adapt it from another source? The latter scenario seems most likely.

Researchers in recent times have dismissed Graves and his story because they are easy targets. Scorn has been heaped upon Graves because it is easy to do. Yet with little exception, no probe has been made into his life and times in an attempt to discover where he came up with his story that put a small village in central New York state on the world map. He was the only one to tell the tale that has become ingrained in the minds of many Americans. Graves, unlike another son of Cooperstown, James Fenimore Cooper, had no literary talent. Nonetheless, his story is as well known as Cooper's *The Last of the Mohicans* or *The Leatherstocking Tales*, likely more so. His tale overshadowed the man who told it and not even the Mills Commission saw fit to name Graves publicly when it accepted and promoted his story. An attempt to study Graves and seek a potential source for his so-popular tale has been long overdue.

While no incontrovertible proof exists that Abner Graves met storyteller Adam Ford, the conclusion is inescapable. The two men were close to each other geographically, psychologically, socio-economically and in their shared interests. Graves would have known the stories told by the talkative doctor.

The story recited by Graves was intended to prove that baseball's origin was American. But if borrowed or adapted from a story about a game played in a British colony, there is a fine irony. Spalding latched onto a story that had British colonial origins as he sought to sever any connection to England for the game. Henry Chadwick, the Father of Baseball, would smile.

The never-ending quest to find baseball's origins continues. In some respects, the task is like nailing jello to a wall. How does one pinpoint the birth of a game that evidence indicates gradually evolved over time? And why bother, for that matter? Would finding the Holy Grail of Baseball make the game any more or any less enjoyable to its fans and players? Does any other sport have this strange obsession with its origins? There is something intriguing about baseball, however, that prompts historians to continue searching for a game they can call the first. Books continue to be written, bloggers continue to blog and articles on the subject continue to be published. Millions upon millions of words have been written on the subject. No doubt, millions more will follow.

Major League Baseball commissioner Bud Selig, after his attachment to the story of Cooperstown and Doubleday became publicly known, announced an inquiry to "determine the facts of baseball's beginnings and its evolution."[4] If it wasn't Doubleday and Cooperstown, then, dammit, who invented it and where? Selig didn't handpick researchers to agree with him. There wouldn't have been any. But why is it so important to go over the same old ground? As the wise-beyond-his-words baseball icon Yogi Berra would say, it's like déjà vu all over again. John Thorn, the well-respected baseball historian, can be expected to do a thorough job, aided by an eleven-member blue-chip panel that includes documentary filmmaker and historian Ken Burns. A Mills Commission this is not.

If the latest inquiry can't establish the origins of the game, one hopes that the inquisitors will be wise enough to concede that. Expectations by Selig and within the baseball community must be modest and realistic. The pressure of an artificial deadline and an agenda cannot be allowed to become factors. Spalding and his Mills Commission can be considered a cautionary tale. As has been said so many times before, those who ignore the lessons of history are condemned to repeat them.

More knowledge about two very interesting men and their stories from more than a century ago won't help any baseball commission appointed, now or in the future, prove very much other than that there is a need to tread carefully. But the stories of two men from long ago help shed light on how an earlier commission got itself into a pickle and the legacy of that.

All kinds of stories have been told about baseball and many others will be told. Just as this effort marks the first telling of the stories of Abner Graves and Adam Ford in any great detail—and for the first time a case is made to link them—so too there will be more information, stories and theories about baseball to emerge in years to come. Unexpected finds of ancient baseball cards, vintage balls and bats and other memorabilia are not uncommon, so something somewhere is bound to be discovered in a dusty attic or elsewhere to shed even more light on the game. And even those who have written about it.

Such is the beauty of baseball.

# Appendix A

# *A. G. Spalding's Appeal for Information About Early Baseball (*Akron Beacon Journal, *April 1, 1905)*

[Note: Spelling and punctuation as they appeared in the original.]

"The Origin of the Game of Base Ball"
By A. G. Spalding

Nineteen hundred and five completes the 60th year of the life of base ball for it dates its birth from the organization of the original Knickerbocker Base Ball club of New York city, September 23, 1845, at which time the first playing rules of the game were formulated and published by that club.

There seems to be a conflict of opinion as to the origin of base ball. I think the game has arrived at an age and at a point in its development when this mooted question should be settled in some comprehensive and authoritative way and for all time.

Some authorities, notably Henry Chadwick, claim that base ball is of English origin and was a direct descendant of the old English juvenile pastime called "Rounders," while others claim that it was of entirely American origin and had nothing whatever to do with rounders or any other foreign game.

While I concede that Mr. Chadwick's rounder theory is entitled to much weight because of his long connection with base ball and the magnificent work he has done in the upbuilding of the game for upward of 50 years, yet I am unwilling longer to accept his rounder theory without something more convincing than his oft-repeated assertion that "base ball did originate from rounders."

For the purpose of settling this question I hereby challenge the Grand Old Man of Base Ball to produce his proofs and demonstrate in some tangible way, if he can, that our national game derived its origins from rounders.

Mr. Chadwick, who, by the way, is of English birth, and was probably rocked in a "rounders" cradle, says, in support of his theory, that "there is but one field game now in vogue on this continent which is strictly American in its origin, and that one is the old Indian game of lacrosse, now known as the Canadian national game. Base ball originated from the old English schoolboy game of rounders, as plainly shown by the fact that the basic principle of both games is the field use of a bat, a ball and bases."

I have been fed on this kind of "rounder pap" for upward of 40 years and I refuse to swallow any more of it without some substantial proof sauce with it.

In 1874 I visited England with the Boston and Philadelphia Athletic Base Ball clubs and while these clubs were playing exhibition games before English audiences it was not uncommon to hear expressions like this: "Why, it's nothing but our old game of rounders that we used to play with the gals when we were byes."

Again, during our base ball trip around the world in 1888-'89 we heard similar expressions in the English countries of New Zealand, Australia, India and in Great Britain. I made many inquiries of many people about this game of rounders, but never could get a very intelligent explanation of it and seldom could find any one that would admit that they had ever played the game.

After I had seen and played in a game of rounders I could quite understand why it had been so difficult to find anybody that would admit that they had ever played rounders and for a good deal of the same reason that a grownup man might be unwilling to admit that he had ever played "Drop the Handkerchief," "Copenhagen," "Ring Around the Rosy," or any other of rounders' sister pastimes.

It come about in this way: When our around-the-world base ball party arrived in England in 1889 we were again taunted with the similarity of our game to rounders, generally spoken in derision and intended to belittle base ball, and finally becoming desperate I issued a public challenge in behalf of our Chicago and All-American base ball teams to play a match game of Rounders with any rounder club in Great Britain if there really was such a club or such a game.

This challenge was accepted, and a game of rounders was arranged and played in Liverpool in March 1889, between the champion Rounder club of England and a picked team of our American "base ballers," as they called us. I was the "feeder" for our team of 11 men.

A one-inning rounder match (two innings constitute a full game), to be played under regular rounder rules, was arranged on condition that afterward we would play them a five-innings base ball match, under regular base ball rules.

Rounder rules permit (what we would call) the base runner to be put out by "soaking" him with the ball while running between the four boundary poles or posts, and this attractive feature was about the only rule of the game our players seemed to take any special interest in.

The game opened with the American eleven in the field, and as "feeder" I was handed a ball about the size of a golf ball covered with leather and comparatively soft, and the longed-for game of Rounders was ready to commence.

The first rounder batsman took his position with a sort of miniature cricket bat, or paddle—a cross between a potato masher and a pen holder. With his left hand behind his back and his right grasping this so-called bat, he struck a sort of John Hancock-signing-the-Declaration-of-Independence attitude, and the referee announced that the game was on. As a shoulder-high ball came over the plate he stuck out his flattened bat or paddle with about the same effort you would hand a friend a cigar, and the ball glanced off his bat over the catcher's head and out of the grounds. We insisted it was foul, but the referee said it was a good hit, and the batsman ran around the four boundary posts, which were about three feet high and the diameter of a broom handle, with a tiny blue flag on the top of each, and when he had completed the circuit the scorer announced that he had made four runs—a run being counted on each post was passed—and the audience applauded. The next batsman did the same thing, and the Englishmen had scored eight runs. I then had a conference with our catcher, and we decided that low balls close to the body might tend to make these dainty, but effective over-the-fence hits less frequent.

It worked well, for after that they only made three runs, and that was caused by one of our American players trying to "soak" a rounder base runner, but missed his target. Their eleven players were all put out, which closed their first innings. Then the Americans took their innings and tried to hit the ball out as we would in base ball, but as it was permissible to use only one hand it was found impossible to hit the ball any distance, but we finally succeeded in making eight runs before our eleven men were all put out. We were very desirous of playing a full game of two innings, for we were just getting the hang of it, but the Englishmen objected and insisted that the five-inning game of baseball be played as previously arranged.

The English rounder players were quite as green, if not more so, at our game than we had been at theirs, for they made no runs in the first inning of base ball; in fact, all their men struck out, and the Americans made 85 runs, with nobody out, and the match was called off on account of physical exhaustion all around, and the first inning of base ball was never finished.

Having read from boyhood, principally, the writings of Henry Chadwick that our American game of base ball originated from rounders, and having been taunted with this statement around the world, generally spoken in derision of our game, and having actually played in a game of rounders, I am now convinced that base ball did not originate from rounders any more than cricket originated from that asinine pastime. About the only tangible argument that

I ever heard advanced by Mr. Chadwick or another authority tending to prove that base ball did originate from rounders is the following:

In a recent letter to me Mr. Chadwick says: "You cannot go back on that base ball derived its origin from the old English game of rounders because the basic principle of both games is the field use of a bat, ball and bases."

Just imagine the argument you would get into and the touchiness an Englishman would show if you told him that his favorite game of cricket derived its origin from rounders; or the Scotchman's indescribable flow of words if you stated that his ancient game of golf originated from rounders; or the American Indian's grunt if it was explained to him that his game of lacrosse originated from rounders.

Now, boil down together the Englishman's indignation, the Scotchman's huff and the Indian's grunt into one composite mass and you have my feelings and that of every lover of base ball when a claim is made that our great American national game of base ball originated from rounders.

My investigation and research so far inclines me to the opinion that base ball did have its origin in the old colonial game of "One Old Cat." "One Old Cat" was played by three boys—a thrower, catcher and batsman. The latter, after striking the ball, ran to a goal about 30 feet distant, and by returning to the batsman's position without being put out, counted one run or "tally." "Two Old Cat" was played by four or more boys with two batsmen placed about 40 feet apart. "Three Old Cat" was played by six or more boys with three batsmen, the ground being laid out in shape of a triangle. "Four Old Cat" was played by eight or more boys with grounds laid out in shape of a square. "Four Old Cat" required four throwers, alternating as catchers, and four batsmen, the ball being passed from one corner to the next around the square field. Individual scores or tallies were credited to the batsmen making the hit and running from one corner to the next.

Some ingenious American lad naturally suggested that one thrower be placed in the center of the square, which brought nine players into the game, and which also made it possible to change the game into teams or sides, one side fielding and the other side batting. This was for many years known as the old game of "town ball," from which the present game of base ball may have had its origin.

One prominent baseball writer claims that he can prove that one of the founders of the old Knickerbocker club came onto the field one day in the early '40s with the original game of base ball worked out and described on a sheet of paper, and that this game was tried and liked so well that the game was adopted then and there, and the Knickerbocker club was organized to put it into effect.

If such ancestry can be established for base ball every American friend of the game will be delighted.

While "one old cat," or "town ball" may not rank much higher in the ancestral scale than "rounders," yet they strongly appeal to the lover of our national sport as distinctively American games.

In looking over the early history of base ball I find the names of 11 New York gentlemen who were the founders of the original Knickerbocker club, names that should be honored and remembered as the founders of our national game by the million base ball players of the present day. They are as follows: Colonel James Lee, Dr. Ransom, Abraham Tucker, James Fisher, W. Vail, Alexander J. Cartwright, William R. Wheaton, Duncan F. Curry, E. R. Dupignac, Jr., William H. Tucker and Daniel I. [sic] Adams.

Are not some of these gentlemen still living? Or possibly some of their heirs might throw some light on the early history and especially the origin of base ball.

In order to gather this information, I would suggest, and hereby respectfully request, that James E. Sullivan, president of the America Sports Publishing company, 15 Warren street, New York city, take the initiative in the work of collecting all possible facts, proofs, interviews, etc., calculated to throw light on this subject, and when collected submit same to a special board of base ball commissioners or judges, with the understanding that this board will impartially examine all the evidence of whatever nature and promulgate their decision as to the origin of base ball.

I would nominate for that board: Ex-Governor Morgan G. Buckley [sic], now United States senator from Connecticut, and the first president of the National league; Hon. Arthur P. Gorman, United States senator from Maryland, and old ball player and ex-president of the famous old National Base Ball club of Washington, D. C.; A. G. Mills of New York, an enthusiastic ball player before and during the Civil war and the third president of the National league; N. E. Young of Washington, D. C., a veteran ball player and the first secretary and afterward the fourth president of the National league; Alfred J. Reach of Philadelphia, and George Wright of Boston, both well known and two of the most famous ball players in their day, and such additional names as Mr. Sullivan or the above named board may deem it advisable to add. Mr. Sullivan to act as secretary of this commission.

As all of these gentlemen are interested in base ball I feel quite sure they will be willing to act in this capacity, and I am certain that their decision as to the origin of our national sport will be accepted by everyone as final and conclusive.

I would strongly urge that everyone interested in this subject tranmit [sic] as soon as possible to Mr. Sullivan, 19 Warren street, New York, any proof, data or information he may possess or can secure bearing on this matter, with the hope that before another year rolls around this vexed question as to the actual origin and early history of the great American national game of base ball may be settled for all time.

# Appendix B

## *Abner Graves's Response to Spalding (*Akron Beacon Journal, *April 4, 1905)*

[Note: Spelling and punctuation as they appeared in the original with a correction made to a line of type that was switched.]

ABNER DOUBLEDAY INVENTED BASE BALL
Abner Graves of Denver, Colorado, Tells How the Present National Game Had Its Origins

\* \* \*

Abner C. Graves, mining engineer of Denver, Col., claims to know all about the origin of the game of base ball. He is stopping at the Thuma hotel, and reading the article in Saturday's *Beacon Journal* from the pen of A. G. Spalding prepared the following article and submitted it to the *Beacon Journal* for publication:

"I notice in Saturday's *Beacon Journal* a question as to origin of base ball from the pen of A. G. Spalding, and requesting that data on the subject be sent to J. E. Sullivan, 15 Warren street, New York.

"The American game of base ball was invented by Abner Doubleday of Cooperstown, N. Y., either the spring prior or following the 'Log Cabin and Hard Cider' campaign of General Harrison for president, the said Abner Doubleday being then a boy pupil of Green's Select school in Cooperstown, and the same, who as General Doubleday won honor at the battle of Gettysburg in the Civil war. The pupils of Otesego academy and Green's Select school were then playing the old game of 'town ball' in the following manner:

"A 'tosser' stood beside the home 'goal' and tossed the ball straight upward about six feet for the batsman to strike at on its fall, the batter using a four-inch flat board bat, and all others who wanted to play being scattered all over the near and far field to catch the ball, the lucky catcher then taking his innings at the bat while the losing batsman retired to the field. Should the batsman

190

miss the ball on its fall and the tosser catch it on its first bounce he would take the bat and the losing batsman toss the ball.

"When the batsman struck the ball into the field he would run for an out goal about 50 feet and return, and if the ball was not caught on the fly, and he could return to home goal without getting 'plunked' with the ball thrown by any one, he retained his innings the same as in 'old cat.' There being generally from 20 to 50 boys in the field, collision often occurred in the attempt of several to catch the ball. Abner Doubleday then figured out and made a plan of improvement on town ball to limit the number of players and have equal sides, calling it 'base ball' because it had four bases, three being where the runner could rest free of being put out by keeping his foot on the flat stone base, while next one on his side took the bat, the first runner being entitled to run whenever he chose and if he could make the home base without being hit by the ball he tallied.

"There was a six-foot ring within which the pitcher had to stand and toss the ball to the batsman by swinging his hand below his hip. There were 11 players on a side, four outfielders, three basemen, pitcher, catcher, and two infielders, the two infielders being placed respectively a little back from the pitcher and between first and second base and second and third base and a short distance inside the base lines. The ball used had a rubber center overwound with yarn to a size some larger than the present regulation ball, then covered with leather or buckskin and having plenty of bouncing qualities, wonderful high flys often resulted. Any one getting the ball was entitled to throw it at a runner and put him out if he could hit him.

"This 'base ball' was crude compared with present day ball but it was undoubtedly the first starter of base ball and quickly superceded 'town ball' with the older boys, although we younger boys stuck to town ball and the 'old cats.' I well remember several of the best players of 60 years ago, such as Abner Doubleday, Elihu Phinney, John C. Graves, Nels. C. Brewer, Joseph Chaffee, John Starkweather, John Doubleday, Tom Bingham and others who used to play on the Otsego academy campus, although a favorite place was on the Phinney farm on the west shore of Otsego lake. "Base ball is undoubtedly a pure American game, and its birthplace Cooperstown, New York, and Abner Doubleday entitled to the first honor of its invention.

"ABNER GRAVES,
32 Bank Block, Denver, Col."

# Appendix C

## *Adam Ford's Letter*
## *(*Sporting Life, *May 5, 1886)*

[Note: Spelling and punctuation as they appeared in the original.]

### VERY LIKE BASE BALL

A Game of the Long-ago Which Closely Resembled Our Present National Game.

DENVER, Col., April 26.—Editor SPORTING LIFE—The 4th of June, 1838, was a holiday in Canada, for the Rebellion of 1837 had been closed by the victory of the Government over the rebels, and the birthday of His Majesty George the Fourth was set apart for general rejoicing. The chief event at the village of Beechville, in the county of Oxford, was a base ball match between the Beechville Club and the Zorras, a club hailing from the townships of Zorra and North Oxford.

The game was played in a nice, smooth pasture field just back of Enoch Burdick's shops. I well remember a company of Scotch volunteers from Zorra halting as they passed the grounds to take a look at the game. Of the Beechville team I remember seeing Geo. Burdick, Reuben Martin, Adam Karn, Wm. Hutchinson, I. Van Alstine, and, I think, Peter Karn and some others. I remember also that there were in the Zorras "Old Ned" Dolson, Nathaniel McNames, Abel and John Williams, Harry and Daniel Karn and, I think, Wm. Ford and William Dodge. Were it not for taking up too much of your valuable space I could give you the names of many others who were there and incidents to confirm the accuracy of the day and the game. The ball was made of double and twisted woolen yarn, a little smaller than the regulation ball of to day and covered with good, honest calf skin, sewed with waxed ends by Edward McNamee, a shoemaker.

The infield was a square, the base lines of which were twenty-one yards long, on which were placed five bags, thus: [drawing here]

The distance from the thrower to the catcher was eighteen yards; the catcher standing three yards behind the home bye. From the home bye, or "knocker's" stone, to the first bye was six yards. The club (we had bats in cricket but we never used bats in playing base ball) was generally made of the best cedar, blocked out with an ax and finished on a shaving horse with a drawing knife. A wagon spoke, or any nice straight stick would do.

We had fair and unfair balls. A fair ball was one thrown to the knocker at any height between the bend of his knee and the top of his head, near enough to him to be fairly within reach. All others were unfair. The strategic points for the thrower to aim at was to get it near his elbow or between his club and his ear. When a man struck at a ball it was a strike, and if a man struck at a ball three times and missed it he was out if the ball was caught every time either on the fly or on the first bound. If he struck at the ball and it was not so caught by the catcher that strike did not count. If a struck ball went anywhere within lines drawn between home and the first bye extended into the field the striker had to run. If it went outside of that he could not, and every man on the byes must stay where he was until the ball was in the thrower's hands. Instead of calling foul the call was "no hit."

There was no rule to compel a man to strike at a ball except the rule of honor, but a man would be despised and guyed unmercifully if he would not hit at a fair ball. If the knocker hit a ball anywhere he was out if the ball was caught either before it struck the ground or on the first bound. Every struck ball that went within the lines mentioned above was a fair hit; everyone outside of them no hit, and what you now call a foul tip was called a tick. A tick and a catch will always fetch was the rule given strikers out on foul tips. The same rule applies to forced runs that we have now. The bases were the lines between the byes and a base runner was out if hit by the ball when he was off of his bye. Three men out and the side out. And both sides out constituted a complete inning. The number of innings to be played was always a matter of agreement, but it was generally from 5 to 9 innings, 7 being most frequently played and when no number was agreed upon seven was supposed to be the number. The old plan which Silas Williams and Ned Dolson (these were gray-headed men then) said was the only right way to play ball, for it was the way they used to play when they were boys, was to play until one side made 18 or 21, and the one getting that number first won the game. A tally, of course, was a run. The tallies were always kept by cutting notches on the edge of a stick when the base runners came in. There was no set number of men to be played on each side, but the sides must be equal. The number of men on each side was a matter of agreement when the match was made. I have frequently seen games played with 7 men on each side and I never saw more than 12. They all fielded.

The object of having the first bye so near the home was to get runners on the base lines, so as to have the fun of putting them out or enjoying the mistakes of the fielders when some fleet-footed fellow would dodge the ball and come in home. When I got older I played myself, for the game never died out. I well remember when some fellows down at or near New York got up the game of base ball that had a "pitcher" and "fouls," etc., and was played with a ball hard as a stick. India rubber had come into use, and they put so much into the balls to make them lively that when the fellow tossed it to you like a girl playing "one o'd cat," you could knock it so far that the fielders would be chasing it yet, like dogs hunting sheep, after you had gone clear around and scored your tally. Neil McTaggart, Henry Cruttenden, Gordon Cook, Henry Taylor, James Piper, Almon Burch, Wm. Herrington and others told me of it when I came home from the University. We, with a "lot of good fellows more," went out and played it one day. The next day we felt as if we had been on an overland trip to the moon. I could give you pages of incidents, but space forbids. One word as to prowess in those early days. I heard Silas Williams tell Jonathan Thornton that old Ned Dolson could catch the ball right away from the front of the club if you didn't keep him back so far that he couldn't reach it. I have played from that day to this, and I don't intend to quit as long as there is another boy on the ground. Yours, DR. FORD.

# Chapter Notes

## Chapter One

1. Abner Graves letter to editor of *Akron Beacon Journal*, dated April 3, 1905, Abner Graves Papers, National Baseball Hall of Fame Library, Cooperstown, New York. Clearly it was typed by Graves himself. In 1921, in what he called his "Testimentary," a colorfully written will, many of the same spacing and punctuation problems appear. The document, shared with the author, is in the collection of Graves descendants, including his granddaughter Claire Graves Strashun.

2. Robert L. Tiemann and Pete Palmer, "Major League Attendance," in *Total Baseball: The Ultimate Encyclopedia of Baseball*, eds. John Thorn and Pete Palmer (New York: HarperCollins, 1993), 144.

3. A. G. Spalding, "The Origin of the Game of Baseball," *Akron Beacon Journal*, April 1, 1905, 6.

4. *Ibid.*

5. "Abner Doubleday Invented Base Ball," *Akron Beacon Journal*, April 4, 1905, 5.

6. Peter Levine, *A.G. Spalding and the Rise of Baseball* (New York: Oxford University Press, 1985), 3–21.

7. *Ibid.*, 76–79.

8. *Ibid.*, 112.

9. *Spalding's Official Base Ball Guide, 1878* (Chicago: A.G. Spalding and Brothers, 1878), 5.

10. Levine, *A. G. Spalding and the Rise of Baseball*, 112.

11. David Block, *Baseball Before We Knew It: A Search for the Roots of the Game* (Lincoln: University of Nebraska Press, 2005), 10.

12. *Spalding's Official Base Ball Guide, 1903* (New York: American Sports Publishing, 1903), 2.

13. *Ibid.*, 7.

14. Abner Doubleday Obituary, *Harper's Weekly*, January 26, 1893, quoted in Block, *Baseball Before We Knew It*, 35.

15. Letter from Spalding to Lowell, dated November 5, 1904, Jack Doyle Papers, Albert Spalding Scrapbooks, BA SCR 42, National Baseball Hall of Fame Library, Cooperstown, New York.

16. Block, *Baseball Before We Knew It*, 13–15.

17. "Report of the Special Base Ball Commission," written by A.G. Mills, quoted by Albert G. Spalding in *America's National Game* (New York: American Sports Publishing Company, 1911), 20.

18. The "Log Cabin and Hard Cider" campaign of General William Henry Harrison occurred in 1840. Political opponents of the old general from Ohio said he should have stayed in his old log cabin and enjoyed drinking cider instead of campaigning, a shot at his simple and rustic lifestyle to which he had retired. But those critics were considered Eastern and elitist and the young republic was growing westward and more Americans had a life in common with the old general than with his well-heeled opponents. Consequently, Harrison won the election in November of 1840. Graves wrote the game at Cooperstown was played "the spring prior or following" Harrison's campaign so it could just as easily have been in 1841. For more information about Harrison and his campaign, see Freeman Cleaves, *Old Tippecanoe* (Newtown, CT: American Political Biography Press, 1990).

19. Block, *Baseball Before We Knew It*, 16.

20. Thorn, *Baseball in the Garden of Eden: The Secret History of the Early Games* (New York: Simon & Schuster, 2011), 278.

21. Levine, *A.G. Spalding the Rise of Baseball*, 114.

22. Henry Chadwick to A.G. Mills, March 20, 1908, A.G. Mills Papers, BA MSS 13, National Baseball Hall of Fame Library, Cooperstown, New York.

23. Spalding, *America's National Game*, 3,4.

24. *Ibid.*, 6–7.

25. *Ibid.*, 11, 19.

26. *Ibid.*, 24–26.

27. Francis Richter to Albert Goodwill Spalding, December 26, 1911, in Spalding Scrapbook 7, New York Public Library, quoted in Levine, *A.G. Spalding and the Rise of Baseball*, 121.

28. Block, *Baseball Before We Knew It*, 16,17.

29. *Ibid.*, 17,18.

30. Spalding, *America's National Game*, 14.

31. Harold Peterson, *The Man Who Invented Baseball* (New York: Charles Scribner's Sons, 1969), 4.

32. *Ibid.*, 7.

33. Tim Arango, "The Myth of Baseball's Creation Endures with a Prominent Fan," *New York Times*, November 12, 2010, accessed January 5, 2012, http://www.nytimes.com/2010/11/3/sports/baseball/13doubleday.html.

34. "Bud Selig Thinks Abner Graves Invented Baseball. Of Course He Does," Deadspin, accessed December 30, 2011, http://deadspin.com/5684393/bud-selig-thinks-abner-doubleday-invented-baseball-of-course-he-does?skyline=true&s=i.

35. Arango, "The Myth of Baseball's Creation Endures with a Prominent Fan," *New York Times*.

36. "Breaking News," Hauls of Shame Blog, accessed January 5, 2012, http://haulsofshame.com/blog/?p=2250.

37. "Thorn to Lead Baseball Origins Committee," press release from Major League Baseball, March 15, 2011, accessed February 26, 2012, http://mlb.mlb.com/news/article.jsp?ymd=20110315&content_id=16957754&vkey=news_mlb&c_id=mlb.

38. Block, *Baseball Before We Knew It*, 50–57.

## Chapter Two

1. Thorn, *Baseball in the Garden of Eden*, 8, 275.

2. Claire Strashun, granddaughter of Abner Graves, in message to author, August 2011.

3. Block, *Baseball Before We Knew It*, 52–57.

4. Margalyn Hemphill, *A History of Abner Graves* (Bainbridge Island, WA: Preserving Heritage, 2008), 54.

5. Hugh MacDougall, "Abner Graves: The Man Who Brought Baseball to Cooperstown," unpublished dissertation, 2010, 2.

6. *Ibid.*, 3.

7. *Ibid.*, 4.

8. *Ibid.*, 35.

9. *Ibid.*, 37.

10. Roy L. Butterfield, "Gold Rush Days," *In Old Otsego: New York County Views its Past* (Cooperstown: Freeman's Journal, 1959), 37–41, quoted in MacDougall, "Abner Graves," 4.

11. MacDougall, "Abner Graves," 6–9.

12. Hemphill, *A History of Abner Graves*, 7.

13. "The Adams Express Company: 150 Years," accessed March 2, 2012, www.adamsexpress.com/files/u2/adams_history.pdf.

14. *Rocky Mountain News*, February 28, 1924, article facsimile contained in Hemphill, *A History of Abner Graves*, 16.

15. "History," Pony Express Museum, St. Joseph, Missouri, accessed March 4, 2012, www.ponyexpress.org/history.

16. *The Semi-Centennial History of the State of Colorado, Vol. II* (Chicago: The Lewis Publishing Co., 1913), 96.

17. "The Comstock Lode and the Mining Frontier," Closing the Western Frontier, Digital History, accessed March 4, 2012, http://www.digitalhistory.uh.edu/database/article_display.cfm?HHID=179.

18. Michael Franks, "Mark Twain and the Territorial Enterprise," accessed March 5, 2012, www.territorial-enterprise.com/tee.htm.

19. "Petrified Man," *Territorial Enterprise*, October 4, 1862, accessed March 5, 2012, http://twainquotes.com/18621004t.html.

20. "Local Column," *Territorial Enterprise*, December 30–31, 1862, accessed March 5, 2012, http://www.twainquotes.com/18621231t.html.

21. *Mark Twain in Virginia City Nevada* (excerpted chapters from *Roughing It*, published in 1872), (Las Vegas: Stanley Paher Nevada Publications, 1985), 113–114.

22. Mark Twain, "Local Column," *Territorial Enterprise*, January 6, 1863, accessed March 4, 2012, http://www. Twainquotes.com/18630106t.html.

23. Franks, "Mark Twain and the Territorial Enterprise."

24. *Ibid.*

25. MacDougall, "Abner Graves," 13.

26. *Ibid.*, 11.

27. *Ibid.*, quoting Biographic Sketch of Calvin Graves, in D. Hamilton Hurd, *History of Otsego County, New York* (Philadelphia: Everts and Fariss, 1878), 279–280. Text online at http://theusgenweb.org/ny/otsego/bios/280a.htm.

28. 1856 U.S. Census, Iowa, Linn County.

29. MacDougall, "Abner Graves," 13, citing *Wolfe's Cedar Rapids Directory*, January 1, 1876.

30. *Rocky Mountain News*, Denver, Colorado, February 27, 1924, quoted in Hemphill, *A History of Abner Graves*, 16.

31. MacDougall, "Abner Graves," 13, citing obituary of Caroline C. Boyce, *Cedar Rapids Evening Gazette*, April 21, 1913.

32. *Crawford County Marriages*, The Crawford County, Iowa, IAGenWeb Project, http://iagenweb.org/crawford/marriage/marriageregister16.html#b34

33. *1882 Dow City History, from History of Western Iowa* (Sioux City: Western Publishing Company, 1882), Sioux City, found at The Crawford County, Iowa, IAGenWeb Project, http://iagenweb.org/crawford/history/1882dowcityhistory.html.

34. *Ibid.*

35. *Early Dow City History from 1851*, The Crawford County, Iowa, IA GenWeb Project, http://iagenweb.org/crawford/history/dowhist.html.

36. "Denver Man Played First Baseball Game in History of Sport," *Denver Post*, May 9, 1912.

37. *The Cedar Rapids Times*, June 28, 1877, 2.

38. 1882 Dow City History.

39. "A Bright Letter from Dow City," *Denison Review*, March 12, 1890.

40. F.J. Meyers, *History of Crawford County, Iowa: A Record of Settlement, Progress and Achievement, Vol. 1* (Chicago: S.J. Clarke, 1911).

41. "Near to Death: The Peculiar Adventure of the President of the Dow City Bank," *Carroll City* (IA) *Herald*, March 30, 1880, 1.

42. *History of Monona County, Iowa* (Chicago: National Publishing Company, 1890), 195, quoted in MacDougall, "Abner Graves," 15.

43. Hemphill, *A History of Abner Graves*, 30.

44. Email correspondence to author from Claire Strashun, daughter of Nelson Dow Graves and granddaughter of Abner Graves, August 1, 2011.

45. *Iowa State Reporter*, May 23, 1883, cited in MacDougall, "Abner Graves," 17–18.

46. *The American Aberdeen-Angus Herd Book, Vol. 1* (Beecher, IL: American Aberdeen-Angus Breeders Association, 1886), 14.

47. *Report of the Board of Directors of the Iowa State Agricultural for the Year 1886* (Des Moines: State Printer, 1887), 315, cited in MacDougall, 16.

48. "Principles and Beliefs of Freemason," About Freemasons, accessed March 5, 2012, http://www.aboutfreemasons.com/Principles_and_Beliefs_of_Freemasons.

49. Copy of "Returns to the Grand Lodge of Iowa, May, 1 1883."

50. Hemphill, *A History of Abner Graves*, 48.

51. *1885 Iowa State Census, Dow City, Crawford County*, The Crawford County, Iowa, IAGenWeb Project.

52. *Denison Review*, February 12, 1886.

53. "Dow City news in the *Dennison Review*," 1870–1896, *Early Dow City History*, accessed March 5, 2102, http://iagenweb.org/crawford/history/dowhist.htm.

54. *History of Crawford County, Iowa, Vol. 1*, p. 197, cited in MacDougall, "Abner Graves," 17.

55. "For Heavy Damages: Irate Business Men Suing Bradstreet's Commercial Agency," *Omaha Daily Bee*, March 23, 1891, 3.

56. *Ibid.*

57. *Omaha Daily Bee*, July 15, 1899, 8.

58. *Bushnell's Des Moines City Directory, 1888–89*, quoted in MacDougall, "Abner Graves," 18.

59. *Des Moines and Polk County Directory*, 1892, 1893, 1894, quoted in MacDougall, "Abner Graves," 18.

60. "This is Mark Twain," University of California Press, accessed March 7, 2012, http://www.thisismarktwain.com/timeline/1894.html.

## Chapter Three

1. "Short History of Denver, Colorado," About Denver Colorado, accessed March 12, 2012, http://denvercolorado.org/history-places-of-interest/short-history-of-denver-colorado.

2. "History of the Mile High City," Visit Denver, accessed March 12, 2012, http://www.denver.org/metro/history.

3. *Ibid.*

4. Stephen J. Leonard and Thomas J. Noel, *Denver: Mining Camp to Metropolis* (Niwot: University Press of Colorado, 1990), 42.

5. "Leadville, Colorado, Cloud City, USA," *Legends of America*, accessed March 12, 2012, http://www.legendsofamerica.com/co-leadville.html.

6. *Ibid.*

7. *Ibid.*

8. "Spitting Lead in Leadville: Doc Holliday's Last Stand," History Net, accessed March 13, 2012, http://www.historynet.com/spitting-lead-in-leadville-doc-hollidays-last-stand.htm.

9. "Locations of Historical TB Sanatoriums in Colorado and Possible Relationships with the Current Distribution of Asthma Cases," Colorado Department of Public Health, Draft Report, September 2004, 3, accessed December 22, 2011, emaps.dphe.state.co.us./website/gis/documents/sanatoriums.doc.

10. *Health in Colorado: The First One Hundred Years,* (Denver: Colorado Department of Health, 1969), accessed December 29, 2011, www.coloradopublichealth.org/documents/HealthinColorado.pdf., 6, 8.

11. "A Letter From Adam E. Ford, M.D., LL.D," *Annual Report of the Ontario Curling Association, 1906,* 33.

12. Email, June 13, 2011, to author from Donna Bame, licensing supervisor, Colorado Department of Regulatory Agencies, Division of Registrations, Licensing and Support Section, Denver, Colorado.

13. Wakefield's letter is found in the Cruttenden/Ford/Clench collection at St. Marys Museum, St. Marys, Ontario.

14. "Lyster's Life," *Rocky Mountain News,* Denver, Colorado, January 27, 1882, 5.

15. "A Terrible Accident," *Rocky Mountain News,* Denver, Colorado, February 7, 1882, 5.

16. *Corbett and Ballenger's City Directories for Denver, 1882, 1883.*

17. "A Sad Accident," *Rocky Mountain News,* April 1, 1883.

18. "Frederick J. Bancroft, M.D. (1834–1903)," Colorado's Healthcare Heritage, accessed March 14, 2012, http://www.coloradohealthcareheritage.org/FrederickBancroft04.html.

19. *Ballenger and Richards' City Directory for Denver, 1885, 1886 and 1887.*

20. Confirmed by the registrars and keepers of records at the Colorado School of Mines, Boulder, Colorado; McGill University, Montreal, Quebec; and Queens University, Kingston, Ontario. Claims of his educational background appear on an undated brochure associated with a prospectus promoting Grass Valley Extension Mines of Grass Valley, California, and listing its directors. The brochure is believed to be from 1923 because of a letter accompanying it in the Adam Ford collection of papers in St. Marys Museum, St. Marys, Ontario.

21. "Advices from the Orient. The Tacoma Arrives from Yokohama and Hongkong," *Sacramento Record-Union,* September 15, 1897.

22. Letter, dated May 11, 1897, to Julia Ford from Leon Ford, indicated as being written in Kushima, Kagoshima, Japan. Original found in Cruttenden/Ford/Clench collection at St. Marys Museum, St. Marys, Ontario.

23. Several of Leon Ford's original handwritten letters to his sister Julia can be found in the Cruttenden/Ford/Clench collection at St. Marys Museum, St. Marys, Ontario.

24. The Law Society of Upper Canada confirmed by email to the author, April 25, 2011, that Arthur Ford attended the "Hilary" term in the first few months of 1878 only. He was listed as a lawyer on the U.S. Census return of 1910, enumeration of April 26 and 27, 1910. At the time he was a resident of the Insane Ward of the Denver County Hospital.

25. Confirmed by Manuscripts and Archives division of Yale University in emails to author, May 26 and June 24, 2011.

26. "A Letter From Adam E. Ford," *Ontario Curling Association Annual Report, 1906,* 33.

27. "Social Siftings: A Resume of the Week's Happenings in Good Society," *Rocky Mountain News,* Sunday, February 5, 1882, 2.

28. "A Foot Race," *Rocky Mountain News,* May 4, 1883, 4.

29. "Brief Notes and Comments," *Rocky Mountain News,* July 16, 1883, 2.

30. Letter to Adam Ford from Joseph Pope, personal secretary to Sir John A. Macdonald, Prime Minister of Canada, dated December 5, 1885, photocopy in Cruttenden/Ford/Clench collection at St. Marys Museum, St. Marys, Ontario.

31. "The Western League: The Organization Perfected and a Schedule Adopted," *Sporting Life,* April 7, 1886, 1.

32. "Sporting Notes," *St. Joseph Daily Gazette,* June 8, 1886, 6.

33. "A Sensation. Ball Players Charged With Selling Out. Cincinnati Players Accused—The Matter to be Thoroughly Investigated," *Sporting Life*, June 23, 1886, 1.

34. David Nemec, *The Beer and Whisky League: The Illustrated History of the American Association, Baseball's Renegade Major League* (New York, Lyons and Burford, 1994), 112.

35. *Denver Daily News*, July 3, 1886.

36. *Denver Daily News*, July 18, 1886.

37. *Denver Daily News*, July 19, 1886.

38. "The Tournament," *Aspen Weekly Times*, August 13, 1887, 4.

39. Amber Show, "The Impact of Francis Richter Upon the Development of Baseball," accessed March 18, 2012, http://www.uga.edu/juro/2003/shaw.htm.

40. "Toronto News," *Sporting Life*, February 3, 1886, 1.

41. "Then and Now. The Players of Ten Years Ago Compared With the Shining Lights of Today," "Reminscences of Tim Murnane," *Sporting Life*, March 24, 1886, 5.

42. "Very Like Base Ball. A Game of the Long-ago Which Closely Resembled Our Present National Game," *Sporting Life*, May 5, 1886, 3.

## Chapter Four

1. Death notice of Robert Ford, *St. Marys Argus*, September, 10, 1874, 2, and *1851 Census of Canada East, Canada West, New Brunswick, and Nova Scotia.*

2. *Argus* death notice.

3. Robert Knight Barney, "Whose National Pastime? Baseball in Canadian Popular Culture," *The Beaver Bites Back?: American Popular Culture in Canada*, eds. David H. Flaherty and Frank E. Manning (Montreal: McGill-Queen's University Press, 1993), 154.

4. Burnie McLay, "The Whole Truth And Nothing But: A Century of Actual Happenings in One Man's Family," unpublished manuscript, 1979, donated by Larry Pfaff, in the Cruttenden/Ford/Clench collection at St. Marys Museum, St. Marys, Ontario.

5. Larry Pfaff, *Historic St. Marys: A series of articles reprinted from the St. Marys Journal Argus*, (St. Marys: J.W. Eedy Publications, n.d.), 23.

6. *Ibid.*, 23, 120.

7. Kathryn Clarke, communications co-ordinator, College of Physicians and Surgeons of Ontario, in May 13, 2011, email to author. Victoria College, later federated with the University of Toronto, was then located east of the Lake Ontario city which two decades earlier had changed its name from York.

8. Mary Ainslie Smith, *Within These Portals: A History of the St. Marys Public Library* (St. Marys: St. Marys Museum, 2010), 9.

9. McLay, *The Whole Truth*, 21.

10. *Ibid.*, 24.

11. *Ibid.*, 21.

12. Smith, *Within These Portals*, 12. A copy of the newspaper advertisement with concert details is on page 13.

13. Nancy Bouchier and Robert Barney, "A Critical Examination of a Source on Early Ontario Baseball: The Reminiscence of Adam E. Ford," *Journal of Sport History* (Spring 1988), 78, citing annual reports of the Ontario Curling Association of 1903 to 1906 and 1975 and John A. Stevenson, *Curling in Ontario, 1846–1946* (Toronto: Ontario Curling Association, 1950). (Canada West was renamed Ontario in 1867, when Britain's North American colonies federated to become Canada.)

14. His own account was published in the *Annual Report of the Ontario Curling Association, 1905*, 7–9.

15. Barney, "Whose National Pastime?" 155.

16. *Railton's Directory for the City of London, Canada West 1856–57* (London, C.W.: George Railton, Notary Public, 1856), 25.

17. Bouchier and Barney, "A Critical Examination," 85–86.

18. Barney, "Whose National Pastime?" 155.

19. "Base Ball Meeting," *St. Marys Argus*, April 13, 1876, 2.

20. "Base Ball," *St. Marys Argus*, September 21, 1876, 2.

21. Stories about Ford being nominated, running and declining to run for local office can be found in the following issues of the *St. Marys Argus*: December 24, 1857, January 7, 1864, January 7, 1869, December 23, 1870, December 22, 1871, January 7, 1875, December 21, 1876, January 4, 1877, on page 2 in all editions.

22. McLay, 24.

23. St. Marys Town Council Minute Book, regular meeting of council, September 11, 1876, 153.

24. *St. Marys Argus*, December 21, 1876, 2.

25. St. Marys Town Council Minute Book of February 9, 1877, 183. Ford and two others were to "make arrangements with GTRR authorities as towards removing the station." Minute book in St. Marys Museum, St. Marys, Ontario.

26. St. Marys Town Council Minute Book, June 11, 1877, meeting, 207, St. Marys Museum, St. Marys, Ontario.

27. "Charge of Assault in St. Marys," *St. Marys Argus*, June 28, 1877, 2.

28. *Ibid.*

29. St. Marys Town Council Minutes, July 3, 1877, 209.

30. *Ibid.*, December 10, 1877, 240.

31. "Public Meeting," *St. Marys Argus*, January 3, 1878, 2.

32. *Ibid.*, 2.

33. "The Rine Movement," *St. Marys Argus*, January 31, 1878, 2.

34. *St. Marys Argus*, February 7, 1878, 2.

35. *St. Marys Argus*, February 14, 1878, 2.

36. Email correspondence from Paul Leatherdale, Archivist, Law Society of Upper Canada, Toronto, to author, April 21, 2011. Ford either failed or never completed his studies, but was never called to the bar of Ontario.

37. "The Rine Case," *St. Marys Argus*, May 2, 1878 2.

38. This section is gleaned from multiple newspaper accounts from the *London Advertiser* and *London Free Press*, beginning June 7, 1878, the *St. Marys Argus*, from June 13, and from the *Stratford Beacon* of June 23.

39. "St. Marys Poisoning Case," *London Free Press*, June 7, 1878, 4.

40. "The St. Marys Tragedy," *London Advertiser*, June 8, 1878, 2.

41. *Ibid.*, 2.

42. "The Poisoning Case," *St. Marys Argus*, June 13, 1878, 2.

43. "The St. Marys Poisoning Case," *London Free Press*, June 21, 1878, 2.

44. "The Death of Mr. Guest," *Stratford Beacon*, June 23, 1878.

45. "The Poisoning Case," *London Free Press*, June 22, 1878, 1.

46. *St. Marys Argus*, June 20, 1878, 2.

47. "The Poisoning Case," *London Free Press*, June 24, 1878, 1.

48. "St. Marys Poisoning Case," *London Free Press*, July 1, 1878, 1.

49. "The Poisoning Case," *St. Marys Argus*, June 27, 1878, 2.

50. "The Guest-Ford Case," *St. Marys Argus*, March 13, 1879, 3.

# Chapter Five

1. David O. Whitten, "The Depression of 1893," *Economic History Services Encyclopedia*, accessed December 5, 2011, http://www.eh.net/encyclopedia/article/whitten.panic.1893.

2. *Ibid.*

3. *Ibid.*

4. Bob Adelman, "The Panic of 1893: Boosting Bankers' Money and Power," accessed December 6, 2011, http://www.thenewamerican.com/6989-the-panic-of-1893-boosting-bankers-money-and-power.

5. Walter Coffey, "The Panic of 1893," *Suite 101.com*, accessed December 5, 2011, http://www.waltercoffey.suite101.com/the-panic-of-1893-a227824.

6. Adelman, "The Panic of 1893."

7. Coffey, "The Panic of 1893."

8. *Ibid.*

9. Jeremy Miller, "History Ghost Story," *5280 Magazine*, Denver, July 2010, accessed April 29, 2011, http://www.5280.com/magazine/2010/07/history-ghost-story. The first entry in the Denver city directory for Graves at that address does not appear until 1901.

10. *Ballenger and Richards' 26th Annual Denver City Directory for 1920* (Denver, 1920), 1148.

11. Stephen J. Leonard and Thomas J. Noel, *Denver: Mining Camp to Metropolis* (Niwot: University Press of Colorado, 1984), 103.

12. *Ibid.*

13. Phil Goodstein, *The Ghosts of Denver: Capitol Hill* (Denver: New Social Publications, 1996), 19.

14. *Ibid.*, 104.

15. *Ibid.*, 110.

16. "Southern California News," *Los Angeles Times*, May 16, 1895, 13, quoted in Thorn, *Baseball in the Garden of Eden*, 279.

17. *Los Angeles Times*, August 26, 1895, 6, quoted in Thorn, *Baseball in the Garden of Eden*, 279.

18. *The Semi-Centennial History of the State of Colorado, Vol. 2* (Chicago: The Lewis Publishing Company, 1913), 97.

19. *Ibid.*, 97.

20. *Ballenger and Richards' City Directory for Denver, 1898*, 31.

21. "History of Mineral Palace Car," City of Pueblo, Colorado, accessed December 6, 2011, http://www.co-pueblo.civicplus.com/DocumentView.aspx?DID=675.

22. "The Colorado Train: It Will Contain Living Pictures of Life in That State—Latest Scheme to Attract Capital," *New York Times*, September 28, 1902.

23. *New York Times*, June 30, 1898.

24. "The Mining Congress: Next Meeting Will Be Held in Milwaukee," *Fairplay (CO) Flume*, July 15, 1898, 1.

25. *Salt Lake City Tribune*, July 10, 1898, quoted in MacDougall, "Abner Graves," 20.

26. *Omaha Daily Bee*, July 15, 1899, 8.

27. Hemphill, *A History of Abner Graves*, 30–31.

28. Letter to author from Claire Graves Strashun, August 1, 2011.

29. Hemphill, *A History of Abner Graves*, 32.

30. *Ibid.*, 32.

31. *Denver Times*, as quoted in *Des Moines Daily Leader*, February 23, 1902, quoted in MacDougall, "Abner Graves," 20.

32. *Ibid.*

33. *Ibid.*, 21.

34. Claire Graves Strashun, daughter of Nelson Graves, letter of reminiscences to her daughter Barbara and her husband Tom Hemphill, September 1, 1976, copy in the possession of author.

35. Goodstein, *The Ghosts of Denver*, 94.

36. "Denver Man Played First Baseball Game In History of Sport," *Denver Post*, May 9, 1912.

37. *Phoenix Weekly Arizona Republican*, June, 11, 1903, cited in MacDougall.

38. Hemphill, *A History of Albert Graves*, 1, 38.

39. *Ballenger and Richards' City Directory for Denver, 1902.*

40. Thomas J. Noel, *The City and the Saloon: Denver, 1858–1916* (Boulder: University Press of Colorado, 1996), 116.

41. Ibid.

42. Noel, *The City and the Saloon*, 75.

43. Claire Strashun, letter of reminiscences to children, September 1, 1976.

44. Noel, *The City and the Saloon*, 100.

45. *Ibid.*, 35.

46. *Ibid.*, 104.

47. *Ibid.*, 91.

48. Email from Denver baseball historian Jay Sanford to author, September 12, 2011.

49. *Ibid.*

50. Jay Sanford, *The Denver Post Tournament*, a project of the Rocky Mountain Chapter of the Society for American Baseball Research and the Denver Post (Denver: SABR/Denver Post, 2003), 1.

51. *Ibid.*, 1.

52. Phil Goodstein, *Denver in Our Time: A People's History of the Modern Mile High City* (Denver: New Social Publications, 1999), 171.

53. *Ibid.*

54. *Ballenger and Richards' City Directory for Denver, 1900.*

55. Portrait and Biographical Record—Denver and Vicinity, 1898, accessed December 16, 2011, http://www.memoriallibrary.com/CO/1898DenverPB/pages/pbrd0404.htm#dnstradley.

56. Share certificate, Washington Sanitarium, Inc., January date in 1901 indecipherable, in the Cruttenden/Ford/Clench family papers collection of Burnie McLay at St. Marys Museum, St. Marys, Ontario, Canada.

57. Untitled and undated newspaper clipping from the Cruttenden/Ford/Clench family papers, St. Marys Museum, St. Marys, Ontario, Canada.

58. "Poisoned. Coroner's Jury Finds that Maggie Hunsucker Did Not Commit Suicide," *The Seattle Star*, February 27, 1901, 1.

59. Unknown drug. Perhaps it was pilocarfine, a drug used to combat dry mouth. "Medline Plus: Trusted Health Information For You," U.S. National Library of Medicine, accessed December 17, 2011, http://www.nlm.nih.gov/medlineplus/druginfo/meds/a608039.html.

60. *The Seattle Star*, February 27, 1901, 1.

61. "Manslaughter. Charged by Coroner's Jury For Death of Maggie Hunsucker," *The Seattle Star*, February 28, 1901, 2.

62. "The Hunsucker Poisoning Case," *The Seattle Star*, April 9, 1901.

63. *Wet Mountain Tribune* (Westcliffe, Custer County, Colorado), September 13, 1902, 2.

64. *Wet Mountain Tribune*, June 14, 1902, 3.

65. Ibid.

66. *Wet Mountain Tribune*, April 5, 1902.

67. *Rifle Reveille* (Garfield County, Colorado), September 12, 1902, 3, and *Golden (CO) Daily Transcript*, September 17, 1902, 7.

68. "Sudden Call. Francis I. Meston Dead," *Wet Mountain Tribune*, September 13, 1902, 2.

69. *Ballenger and Richards' City Directories for Denver, 1902–1905.*

70. Letter to Julia Ford from Adam Ford, dated June 15, 1904, in the Cruttenden/Ford/Clench family papers, St. Marys Museum, St. Marys, Ontario, Canada.

71. *Annual Reports of the Ontario Curling Association, 1905–06,* excerpt photocopies in the Cruttenden/Ford/Clench collection at the St. Marys Museum, St. Marys, Ontario, Canada.

72. *Annual Report of the Ontario Curling Association, 1905,* 7.

73. "A Letter from Adam E. Ford: Ontario Curling Years Ago," *Ontario Curling Association Annual Report, 1906,* 33, (italics were used by Ford).

74. *Ibid.,* 35.

75. Email from Jay Sanford to author, September 12, 2011.

76. Greg Stewart, "What is Freemasonry: An E-Book on the Ancient and Honorable Fraternity," accessed December 9, 2011, http://www.freemasoninformation.com.

77. Noel, *The City and the Saloon,* map five, 77.

78. Letter from Claire Strashun to author, August 1, 2011.

## Chapter Six

1. Mary Ainslie Smith, *Within These Portals: A History of the St. Marys Public Library* (St. Marys: St. Marys Museum: 2010), 28. Nearby Stratford was granted $15,000 and because of the persistence of William Ford, St. Marys council applied for and received a Carnegie grant of $10,000 in 1904 for construction of a library that still serves the community to this day.

2. A sketch of William Ford's life was related upon his death in the *St. Marys Argus,* May 19, 1910.

3. *Annual Report of the Ontario Curling Association 1903–1904,* 5, excerpt photocopies in the Cruttenden/Ford/Clench collection at St. Marys Museum, St. Marys, Ontario, Canada.

4. "Further Reminiscences from Dr. Ford," *Ontario Curling Association Annual Report, 1905,* 8, excerpt photocopies in the Cruttenden/Ford/Clench collection at St. Marys Museum, St. Marys, Ontario, Canada.

5. *Ibid.,* 9.

6. "The Marquess of Dufferin and Ava," Government of Canada Governor General Archives, accessed December 14, 2011, http://www.archive.gg.ca/gg/fgg/bios/01/dufferin_e.asp

7. *Ibid.*

8. Presumably from the Ontario Curling Association Annual Report of 1907, as quoted in Burnie McLay, "The Whole Truth And Nothing But: A Century of Actual Happenings in One Man's Family," 1979, 25, unpublished manuscript donated by Larry Pfaff, in the Cruttenden/Ford/Clench collection at St. Marys Museum, St. Marys, Ontario, Canada.

9. "The Thistle and Terpsicore," *Rocky Mountain News,* March 31, 1885.

10. "Denver Cricketers Defy The Whole World," *Denver Times,* March 8, 1900.

11. Certificate of Life Membership in the Denver Curling Club, dated November 9, 1904, photocopy in the Cruttenden/Ford/Clench collection at St. Marys Museum, St. Marys, Ontario, Canada.

12. McLay, "The Whole Truth and Nothing But," 35.

13. Letter from Adam Ford to Julia Ford, dated May 3, 1906 from Denver, Colorado, copy contained in the Cruttenden/Ford/Clench collection at St. Marys Museum, St. Marys, Ontario, Canada.

14. Eric Niederost, "The Great 1906 San Francisco Earthquake and Fire," *American History Magazine,* April 2006, accessed April 7, 2012, www.historynet.com/the-great-1906-san-francisco-earthquake-and-fire.

15. McLay, 43–44 and document "Emma A. Versus Emma M.," 2–3, as well as photocopies of correspondence to and from Alice Stoddart, including from Archie Stoddart, all in the Ford/Cruttenden/Clench collection at St. Marys Museum, St. Marys, Ontario, Canada.

16. McLay, 44, and obituary of Alice Stoddart, *St. Marys Journal-Argus,* February 25, 1937, 4.

17. McLay, "More Past (Ford) History," 1. Located in Cruttenden/Ford/Clench collection at St. Marys Museum, St. Marys, Ontario, Canada.

18. "Once Wealthy, Dr. Ford Dies Alone In Want," *Denver Post,* May 18, 1906, 1.

19. State of Colorado death certificate for Adam Ford, dated May 19, 1906, document number SL562307. Certified copy in possession of author.

20. Letter from Arthur Ford to Julia and Jane Ford, postmarked May 19, 1906, in Denver, Colorado. Located in the Cruttenden/Ford/Clench collection at St. Marys Museum, St. Marys, Ontario, Canada.

21. Letter from Leon Ford to Julia and Jane Ford, dated May 21, 1906, in Denver, Colorado. Located in the Cruttenden/

Ford/Clench collection at St. Marys Museum, St. Marys, Ontario, Canada.

22. Letter from Harold Ford to Julia and Jane Ford, dated May 20, 1906, in Denver, Colorado. Located in the Cruttenden/ Ford/Clench collection at St. Marys Museum, St. Marys, Ontario, Canada.

23. Copies of arrest warrant, complaint for inquisition of lunacy, finding of a jury, citation for lunacy and release order in collection of the author.

24. "Here Goes Wreck Words of Suicide," *Denver Post*, August 13, 1917.

25. "Shoots Himself in Denver," *Spokesman Review* (Spokane), August 18, 1917.

26. Prospectus for Grass Valley Extension Mines Co., San Francisco, California, located in the Cruttenden/Ford/Clench collection at St. Marys Museum, St. Marys, Ontario, Canada.

27. McLay, 35.

# Chapter Seven

1. Thorn, *Baseball in the Garden of Eden*, 154.

2. *Spalding's Official Baseball Guide, 1878* (Chicago: A. G. Spalding and Brothers, 1878), 5.

3. Levine, *A. G. Spalding and the Rise of Baseball*, 99.

4. *Ibid.*, 100.

5. *Ibid.*, 106.

6. Robert Elias, *The Empire Strikes Out: How Baseball Sold U.S. Foreign Policy and Promoted the American Way Abroad* (New York: The New Press, 2010), 25.

7. *Ibid.*, 26.

8. Levine, 109.

9. Thorn, *Baseball in the Garden of Eden*, 6.

10. Block, *Baseball Before We Knew It*, 43.

11. Correspondence between Spalding and Sullivan, August 13, 1905, James Doyle Papers, Albert Spalding scrapbooks, BA SCR 42, National Baseball Hall of Fame Library, Cooperstown, New York.

12. Letter from Spalding to Abner Graves, November 10, 1905, James Doyle Papers. Albert Spalding scrapbooks, BA SCR 42, National Baseball Hall of Fame Library, Cooperstown, New York.

13. Graves letter to Spalding, James Doyle Papers, Albert Spalding scrapbooks, BA SCR 42, Hall of Fame Library, Cooperstown, New York.

14. Thorn, *Baseball in the Garden of Eden*, 281.

15. MacDougall, "Abner Graves," 28.

16. Ralph Birdsall, *The Story of Cooperstown* (New York: Charles Scribner's Sons, 1917), 254–255, accessed May 6, 2012, http://www.gutenberg.org/files/18621/18621-h/18621-h.htm.

17. A. G. Spalding, "Mr. A.G. Spalding Contends that Base Ball is of American Origin," July 27, 1907, in *Spalding's Official Baseball Guide , 1908*, 41–42, ed. Henry Chadwick (New York: American Sports, 1908), 41–42.

18. Letter from James E. Sullivan to A. G. Mills, October 12, 1907, A. G. Mills Papers, BA MSS 13, National Baseball Hall of Fame Library, Cooperstown, New York.

19. "Learn About the Progressive Era," Digital History, accessed April 29, 2012, www.digitalhistory.uh.edu/modules/progressivism/index.cfm.

20. G. Edward White, *Creating the National Pastime: Baseball Transforms Itself, 1903–1953* (Princeton, NJ: Princeton University Press, 1996), 7.

21. Edmund Morris, *Theodore Rex* (New York: Random House, 2001), 20.

22. *Ibid.*, 21.

23. Elias, *The Empire Strikes Out*, 48.

24. *Ibid.*, 47.

25. Spalding, *America's National Game*, 7.

26. Henry Chadwick, *How to Play Base Ball* (New York: A. G. Spalding, 1889), quoted in Elias, *The Empire Strikes Out*, 34.

27. *Ibid.*, 35.

28. Elias, *The Empire Strikes Out*, 51.

29. C. H. Claudy, *The Battle of Base-Ball* (Jefferson, NC: McFarland, 2005), 9, 14.

30. George Carlin, *Brain Droppings* (New York: Hyperion, 1997), 51.

31. John S. Watterson, "The Gridiron Crisis of 1905: Was it Really a Crisis?" *Journal of Sport History* Volume 27, Number 2, (Summer 2000), 294, accessed April 25, 2012, www.la84foundation.org/SportsLibrary/JSH/JSH2000/JSH2702f.pdf.

32. John J. Miller, *The Big Scrum: How Teddy Roosevelt Saved Football* (New York: HarperCollins, 2011), 1–10.

33. Theodore Roosevelt, "The Value of an Athletic Training," *Harper's Weekly*, December 23, 1993, 1236, quoted in Miller, *The Big Scrum*, 133.

34. Charles W. Eliot, "The Evils of Football," *Harvard Graduates Magazine*, March 1905, 383–387, quoted in Miller, *The Big Scrum*, 181, 182.

35. About the NCAA, History, accessed April 23, 2012, http://ncaa.org/wps/wcm/connect/public/NCAA/About+the+NCAA+history.

36. Miller, *The Big Scrum*, 180.

37. Watterson, "The Gridiron Crisis of 1905: Was it Really a Crisis?" citing figures from the *New York Times* and *Chicago Tribune*, 294.

38. Harrington Crissey, "Abner Doubleday Would Have Been Proud," *Baseball Research Journal* (1976), 33–36, quoted in Elias, *The Empire Strikes Out*, 50.

39. Elias, *The Empire Strikes Out*, 283.

## Chapter Eight

1. *The Encyclopedia Americana: A Universal Reference Library* (New York: Scientific American Compiling Department, 1905).

2. Letter from A. G. Mills to James E. Sullivan, secretary, Special Base Ball Commission, New York, December 30, 1907, A.G. Mills Papers, BA MSS 13, National Baseball Hall of Fame Library, Cooperstown, New York.

3. Spalding, *America's National Game*, 20.

4. *Ibid.*, 21.

5. Richard J. Tofel, "The Innocuous Conspiracy of Baseball's Birth," *Wall Street Journal*, July 19, 2001, quoted in Thorn, *Baseball in the Garden of Eden*, 290.

6. Chadwick letter to Mills, March 20, 1908, A. G. Mills Papers, BA MSS 13, National Baseball Hall of Fame Library, Cooperstown, New York.

7. Alfred H. Spink, *The National Game*, 2d ed., (St. Louis: The National Game, 1911), 54, quoted in Block, *Baseball Before We Knew It*, 17.

8. "Home of Baseball," *Freeman's Journal*, March 26, 1908, 1, quoted in Rowan D. Spraker, *Doubleday Field: Home of Baseball* (Cooperstown: Freeman's Journal, 1965), 24.

9. *Ibid.*, 1.

10. "Baseball Originated Here," *Freeman's Journal*, May 22, 1912, 4, quoted in Spraker, *Doubleday Field*, 25–26.

11. Daniel Ginsburg, "John Tener," a BioProject of the Society for American Baseball Research, accessed May 9, 2012, http://sabr.org/bioproj/person/c90d4ea9.

12. "Play First Game Here, Cooperstown Boys Baseball Originators," *Freeman's Journal*, June 28, 1916, 1, quoted in Spraker, *Doubleday Field*, 26.

13. "Would Return Here for Ball Game in 1919," *Freeman's Journal*, December 18, 1916, 1, quoted in Block, *Baseball Before We Knew It*, 55.

14. Spraker, *Doubleday Field*, 2

15. *Ibid.*, 2–4.

16. "John Heydler, NL President 1909, 1918–1934," National League Presidents, accessed May 7, 2012, http://sportsecyclopedia.com/mlb/nl/heydler.html.

17. Spraker, *Doubleday Field*, 32.

18. *Ibid.*, 34.

19. "Cooperstown is to Have a Ball Park," *Freeman's Journal*, June 4, 1919, 1, quoted in Spraker, *Doubleday Field*, 27.

## Chapter Nine

1. MacDougall, "Abner Graves," 22.

2. Noel, *The City and the Saloon*, 91.

3. *Ibid.*, 111.

4. "Enthusiastically Impressed with Rico," *Daily Journal* (Telluride, San Miguel County, Colorado), August 1, 1907.

5. Hemphill, *A History of Abner Graves*, 43.

6. *Ibid.*, 63.

7. Goldstein, *The Ghosts of Denver*, 26.

8. Hemphill, *A History of Abner Graves*, 49.

9. The *Ballenger and Richards' Denver City Directory 1908*, shows Abner and Nelson Graves living at 1535 Logan, presumably from information gathered during 1907 or early 1908, but Abner Graves did not marry Minnie Latham until late February 1909. Because the first reference to Graves Investment Company also appears in 1909, Graves may have felt there was some benefit in transferring the Logan property into Minnie's name. Or she may simply have demanded it and he agreed. We may never know.

10. *Ballenger and Richards' Denver City Directory, 1909*, quoted in MacDougall, "Abner Doubleday," footnote, 22.

11. *Dow City Enterprise*, March 19, 1909.

12. Hemphill, *A History of Abner Graves*, 62.

13. *Ballenger and Richards' Denver City Directory 1911*.

14. "Denver Man Played First Baseball Game in History of Sport," *Denver Post*, May 9, 1912, 3.

15. MacDougall, "Abner Graves," 32–34.

16. Spalding, *America's National Game*, 21.

17. *The Semi-Centennial History of the*

*State of Colorado, Vol. 2* (Chicago: The Lewis Publishing Company, 1913), 95,96.

18. Hemphill, *A History of Abner Graves*, 51.

19. "Colorado State News," *Fairplay Flume* (Fairplay, Park County, Colorado), November 12, 1915, 2.

20. "Would Return Here for Ball Game in 1919," *Freeman's Journal*, December 18, 1916, 1, quoted in Block, *Baseball Before We Knew It*, 55.

21. "Cooperstown Is to Have a Ball Park," *Freeman's Journal*, June 4, 1919, 1, quoted in Spraker, *Doubleday Field*, 27.

22. Hemphill, *A History of Abner Graves*, 60.

23. "Noble Grandpa of Shrine Was Here in 1849," photocopy of clipping from unknown San Francisco newspaper, June 1922, from the collection of documents of Barbara Hemphill and Claire Strashun, shared with author.

24. "Denver Man, 90, Celebrating Birthday Smokes Five Cigars for Health's Sake," *Rocky Mountain News*, February 28, 1924, 16.

25. "Denver Invalid, 90, Shoots Wife," *Denver Post*, June 17, 1924, 1.

26. "Denver Man, 90, Shoots Wife After Quarrel," *Rocky Mountain News*, June 17, 1924, 1.

27. "Denver Man, 90. Shoots Wife, 48, Woman Is Dying," *Denver Express*, June 17, 1924, 1.

28. "Graves Is Cut Off in Will of Wife, Made on Deathbed," *Rocky Mountain News*, June 20, 1924.

29. Sam Jackson, "Abner Graves, 90, Killer of Wife May Not Hang," *Denver Express*, June 18, 1924, 1.

30. "Fight for Life of Wife Killer, 90, Is Begun," *Denver Express*, June 25, 1924.

31. State of Colorado, Certificate of Death Number 9782, filed October 5, 1926.

32. "Abner Graves, Who Killed Wife, Left Estate of $10,000," *Denver Post*, February 17, 1927.

33. Hemphill, *A History of Abner Graves*, 69.

## Chapter Ten

1. *History of Cooperstown* (Cooperstown: New York State Historical Association, 1976), 210, accessed May 20, 2012, www.library.nysha.org/online/historyofcooperstown/.

2. *Ibid.*, 240.

3. Steve Wulf, "The Stuff of Legend," accessed May 20, 2102, http://sportsillustrated.cnn.com/vault/article/magazine/MAG1068492/index.htm.

4. "Singer Presidents," in *Singer Memories*, accessed May 19, 2012, http://singermemories.com/cast-characters-singer-presidents.

5. *Ibid.*

6. "Stephen C. Clark, Art Patron, Dead," *New York Times*, September 18, 1960, 86.

7. James A. Vlasich, *A Legend for the Legendary: The Origins of the Baseball Hall of Fame* (Bowling Green, OH: Bowling Green State University Popular Press, 1990), 28.

8. *History of Cooperstown*, 243.

9. Spraker, *Doubleday Field*, 6.

10. Wulf, "The Stuff of Legend."

11. Spraker, *Doubleday Field*, 6.

12. *Ibid.*, 7.

13. Vlasich, 37, 38; *History of Cooperstown*, 247.

14. *Ostego Farmer*, August 30, 1970, quoted in Vlasich, *A Legend for the Legendary*, 39.

15. Vlasich, 37.

16. *History of Cooperstown*, 251.

17. Vlasich, 54.

18. *New York Sun*, February 3, 1939; *New York Times*, February 3, 1939, quoted in Vlasich, *A Legend for the Legendary*, 156.

19. Monica Nucciarone, *Alexander Cartwright: The Life Behind the Baseball Legend* (Lincoln: University of Nebraska Press, 2009), 213, 214.

20. Letter from John Hamilton to Alexander Cleland, May 27, 1938, Cleland Files, National Baseball Hall of Fame Library, Cooperstown New York.

21. Letter from Alexander Cleland to John Hamilton, June 23, 1938, Cleland Files, National Baseball Hall of Fame Library, Cooperstown, New York.

22. Nucciarone, *Alexander Cartwright*, 221.

23. *Ibid.*, 22.

24. Frank G. Menke, *Encyclopedia of Sports* (New York: A. S. Barnes; 1939), 34.

25. *Sporting News*, February 23, 1939, quoted in Vlasich, *A Legend for the Legendary*, 173.

26. John Kieran, "A Challenge of History," Sports of the Times column, *New York Times*, April 15, 1939, 13, quoted in Block, *Baseball Before We Knew It*, 19.

27. *The Otsego Farmer*, February 10, 1939,

quoted in Vlasich, *A Legend for the Legendary*, 173.

28. *The Otsego Farmer*, April 28, 1939, quoted in Vlasich, *A Legend for the Legendary*, 175.

29. Letter of Alexander Cleland to Walter Littell, Alexander Cleland Collection, Don Cleland, Las Vegas, Nevada, and the *Otsego Farmer*, March 25, 1938, quoted in Vlasich, *A Legend for the Legendary*, 139.

30. Vlasich, 185–186.

31. "Hall of Fame Welcomes 15 Millionth Visitor," accessed June 2, 2012, http://baseballhall.org/news/museum-news/hall-fame-welcomes-15-millionth-visitor.

32. Harry Paxton, "The Myths of Cooperstown," *Saturday Evening Post*, January 30, 1960, 64, quoted in Vlasich, *A Legend for the Legendary*, 225.

33. *Otsego Herald*, June 6, 1816.

34. James Fenimore Cooper, *Home as Found*, 1838 (reprint Rockville MD: Wildside Press, 2008) beginning at paragraph 32, Chapter XI, accessed July 11, 2012, http://www.gutenberg.org/files/10149/10149-h/10149-h.htm.

35. James Fenimore Cooper Society Website; http://external.oneonta.edu/cooper/cooperstown/baseball.html.

36. "The Doubleday Myth is Cooperstown's Gain," http://baseballhall.org/museum/experience/history.

37. Steven Jay Gould, "The Creation Myths of Cooperstown: Or Why the Cardiff Giants are an Unbeatable and Appropriately Named Team," *Natural History Magazine*, November 1989 accessed August 6, 2012 http://www.naturalhistorymag.com/editors_pick1989_11_pick.html?p.

38. Vlasich, *A Legend for the Legendary*, 231.

## Chapter Eleven

1. Additional history of Claire Graves and family provided by her daughter, Barb Hemphill, in an email to author May 28, 2012. Barb consulted with her mother, aged 91 and still sharp, to confirm details.

2. Hemphill, *A History of Abner Graves*, 54.

3. Letter from Barb Hemphill to author, April 1, 2011, in response to ten questions posed to her mother, Claire Strashun, only grandchild of Abner Graves. Barb transcribed her mother's answers.

4. Email message from Barb Hemphill to author, August 27, 2011.

5. Letter from Claire Strashun to Barb and Tom Hemphill, dated September 1, 1976. Provided to author by Barb Hemphill.

6. Email message from Barb Hemphill to author, August 27, 2011.

7. MacDougall, "Abner Graves," 42.

8. Email letter from Larry Pfaff to author, May 22, 2012, outlining the background and work of Burnie Lancaster McLay, his collaborator on research into the Cruttenden, Clench and Ford families of St. Marys, and also Pfaff's efforts to preserve and research information relating to them.

9. Burnie McLay, "The Poor Fords," in "The Whole Truth and Nothing But: A Century of Actual Happenings in One Man's Family," 35.

10. *Ibid.*, 41.

11. *Ibid.*, 42.

12. Email message from Larry Pfaff to author, June 6, 2012.

## Chapter Twelve

1. Obituary for Blanche Barney, ObitsforLife, accessed June 11, 2012, http:www.obitsforlife.com/obituary/397448/Barney-Blanche.php.

2. "Whose National Pastime? Baseball in Canadian Popular Culture," *The Beaver Bites Back? American Popular Culture in Canada*, eds. David H. Flaherty and Frank E. Manning (Montreal: McGill-Queen's University Press; 1993), 152.

3. Brief curriculum vitae for Robert Knight Barney, Ph.D.

4. William Humber, *Cheering for the Home Team* (Erin, Ontario: Boston Mills Press, 1983), 12.

5. Robert Knight Barney, "Hallowed Halls and Baseball History: The Evolution of the Canadian and American Baseball Halls of Fame," *NINE: A Journal of Baseball History and Social Policy Perspectives*, Volume 4, Number 1 (Fall 1995), 19.

6. An excellent recitation about the influx of Americans into Upper Canada can be found in Alan Taylor, *The Civil War of 1812: American Citizens, British Subjects, Irish Rebels, and Indian Allies* (New York: Alfred A. Knopf, 2011), 50–57.

7. Marjorie E. Cropp, *Beachville: The Birthplace of Oxford*, 2d ed. (Beachville: Beachville Centennial Committee, 1973),

originally published in "Western Ontario History Nugget," Number 14 (London, Ontario: University of Western Ontario, n.d.), 18.

8. Taylor, *The Civil War of 1812*, 454–457.

9. Barney, "Hallowed Halls and Baseball History," 19.

10. Nancy Bouchier and Robert Knight Barney, "A Critical Examination of a Source on Early Ontario Baseball: The Reminiscence of Adam E. Ford." *Journal of Sport History*, Volume 15, Number 1 (Spring 1988), 76.

11. *Annual of the Ontario Curling Association for 1906–1907*, Volume 32, 29–30, quoted in Bouchier and Barney, "A Critical Examination," 78n.

12. Bouchier and Barney, "A Critical Examination," 81.

13. *Ibid.*, 82.

14. Melvin L. Adelman, *A Sporting Time: New York City and the Rise of Modern Athletics, 1820–1870* (Urbana: University of Illinois Press, 1985), 3–11, quoted in Bouchier and Barney, "A Critical Examination," 84.

15. *Sporting Life*, May 5, 1886, 5.

16. Bouchier and Barney, "A Critical Examination," 85.

17. *New York Clipper*, August, 18, 1860, quoted in Bouchier and Barney, "A Critical Examination," 86.

18. *Ibid.*, June 22, 1861, quoted in Bouchier and Barney, "A Critical Examination," 86.

19. Bouchier and Barney, "A Critical Examination," 87.

20. *Ibid.*, 78n.

21. Barney, "Hallowed Halls and Baseball History," 19.

22. "In the Beginning," *150 Years of Baseball in Canada, 1838–1988* (Toronto: Canadian Baseball Hall of Fame and Museum, 1988), 15.

23. Block, *Baseball Before We Knew It*, 65.

24. "Canadian Baseball 'Hall' Established," *London Free Press*, October 27, 1982, and "Quick, What's Beachville Famous For?" *London Free Press*, June 9, 1984, A1.

25. Hank Daniszewski, "Hall of Fame, But at What Cost?" *London Free Press*, December 24, 1994, C1.

26. Barney, "Hallowed Halls of Baseball History," 27.

27. Stephen Brunt, "St. Marys Vies to be Cooperstown for 'Our Game,'" *Globe and Mail*, September 16, 1995, A20.

## Chapter Thirteen

1. MacDougall, "Abner Graves," 36–37.

2. For example, "Enthusiastically Impressed with Rico," *Daily Journal* (Telluride, San Miguel County, Colorado), August 1, 1907.

3. "Denver Man Played First Baseball Game in History of Sport," *Denver Post*, May 9, 1912, 3.

4. MacDougall, "Abner Graves," 21.

5. Block, *Baseball Before We Knew It*, 50–57.

6. Various sources including as far back as the *Encyclopedia Americana*, 1905.

7. Block, *Baseball Before We Knew It*, 59.

8. Barney, "Whose National Pastime? Baseball in Canadian Popular Culture," 154.

9. Spalding, "The Origin of the Game of Base Ball," *Akron Beacon Journal*, April 1, 1905, 6.

10. Spalding, *America's National Game*, 5.

11. *Ibid.*, 4.

## Epilogue

1. Steven Jay Gould, "The Creation Myths of Cooperstown: Or Why the Cardiff Giants are an Unbeatable and Appropriately Named Team," *Natural History Magazine*, November 1989, accessed August 6, 2012, http://www.naturalhistorymag.com/editors _pick1989_11_pick.html?p.

2. "Breaking News," Hauls of Shame Blog, accessed January 5, 2012, http.://hauls ofshame.com/blog/?p=2250.

3. Graves letter to Spalding, James Doyle Papers, Spalding scrapbooks, BA SCR 42, National Baseball Hall of Fame Library, Cooperstown, New York.

4. "Thorn to Lead Baseball Origins Committee," accessed July 18, 2012, http:// mlb.mlb.com/news/press_releases/press_release.jsp?ymd=20110315&content_id=169570 38&vkey=pr_mlb&fext=.jsp&c_id=mlb.

# Bibliography

## Books

Block, David. *Baseball Before We Knew It: A Search for the Roots of the Game.* Lincoln: University of Nebraska Press, 2005.

Carlin, George. *Brain Droppings.* New York: Hyperion, 1997.

Claudy, C.H. *The Battle of Base-Ball.* Reprint edition ed. Gary Mitchem and Mark Durr. Jefferson, NC: McFarland, 2005.

Cleaves, Freeman. *Old Tippecanoe: William Henry Harrison and His Time.* Reprint Newtown, CT: American Political Biography Press, 1990.

Cropp, Marjorie E. *Beachville: The Birthplace of Oxford,* 2d ed. Beachville: Beachville Centennial Committee, 1973.

*Denver Athletic Club 1884–1984.* Denver: Denver Athletic Club, 1983.

Elias, Robert. *The Empire Strikes Out: How Baseball Sold U.S. Foreign Policy and Promoted the American Way Abroad.* New York: The New Press, 2010.

*Encyclopedia Americana, 1905.* New York: Scientific American, 1905.

Goodstein, Phil. *Denver in Our Time: A People's History of the Mile High City. Volume One: Big Money in the Big City.* Denver: New Social Publications, 1999.

_____. *The Ghosts of Denver: Capitol Hill.* Denver: New Social Publications, 1996.

*Health in Colorado: The First One Hundred Years.* Denver: Colorado Department of Health, 1969.

Hemphill, Margalyn. *A History of Abner Graves.* Bainbridge Island, WA: Preserving Heritage, 2008.

Leonard, Stephen J., and Thomas J. Noel. *Denver: Mining Camp to Metropolis.* Niwot: University Press of Colorado, 1990.

Levine, Peter. *A. G. Spalding and the Rise of Baseball.* New York: Oxford University Press, 1985.

Menke, Frank G. *Encyclopedia of Sports.* New York: A. S. Barnes, 1939.

Miller, John J. *The Big Scrum: How Teddy Roosevelt Saved Football.* New York: HarperCollins, 2011.

Morris, Edmund. *Theodore Rex.* New York: Random House Trade Paperbacks, 2002.

Nucciarone, Monica. *Alexander Cartwright: The Life Behind the Baseball Legend.* Lincoln: University of Nebraska Press, 2009.

Nemec, David. *The Beer and Whisky League: The Illustrated History of the American Association—Baseball's Renegade Major League.* New York: Lyons and Burford, 1994.

Noel, Thomas J. *The City and the Saloon: Denver, 1858–1916.* Boulder: University Press of Colorado, 1996.

Peterson, Harold. *The Man Who Invented Baseball.* New York: Charles Scribner's Sons, 1969.

Pfaff, Larry. *Historic St. Marys.* St. Marys, Ontario: J. W. Eedy Publications, n.d.

*The Semi-Centennial History of the State of Colorado, Vol 2.* Chicago: The Lewis Publishing Co., 1913.

Smith, Mary Ainslie. *Within These Portals: A History of St. Marys Public Library.* St. Marys, Ontario: Thames Label and Litho, 2010.

Spalding, A.G. *America's National Game.* New York: American Sports Publishing, 1911.

*Spalding's Base Ball Guide, 1878.* Chicago: A. G. Spalding and Brothers, 1878.

*Spalding's Base Ball Guide, 1903.* New York: American Sports Publishing, 1903. Reprint edition St. Louis, Horton, 1990.

Spraker, Rowan D. *The Story of Doubleday Field.* Cooperstown, NY: Freeman's Journal Co., 1965.

Taylor, Alan. *The Civil War of 1812: American Citizens, British Subjects, Irish Rebels and Indian Allies.* New York: Alfred A. Knopf, 2011.

Thorn, John. *Baseball in the Garden of Eden: The Secret History of the Early Game.* New York: Simon & Schuster, 2011.

Twain, Mark. *Mark Twain in Virginia City Nevada.* Las Vegas: Stanley Paher Nevada Publications, 1985.

Vlasich, James A. *A Legend for the Legendary: The Origin of the Baseball Hall of Fame.* Bowling Green, OH: Bowling Green State University Popular Press, 1990.

White, G. Edward. *Creating the National Pastime: Baseball Transforms Itself 1903–1953.* Princeton: Princeton University Press, 1996.

## Articles

Barney, Robert Knight. "Hallowed Halls and Baseball History: The Evolution of the Canadian and American Baseball Halls of Fame." *NINE: A Journal of Baseball History and Social Policy Perspectives,* Volume 4, Number 1, Fall 1995.

_____. "Whose National Pastime? Baseball in Canadian Popular Culture." *The Beaver Bites Back?* Ed. David H. Flaherty and Frank E. Manning. Montreal: McGill-Queen's University Press, 1993.

Bouchier, Nancy B., and Robert Knight Barney. "A Critical Examination of a Source on Early Ontario Baseball: The Reminiscence of Adam E. Ford." *Journal of Sport History,* Volume 15, Number 1, Spring 1988.

MacDougall, Hugh. "Abner Graves: The Man Who Brought Baseball to Cooperstown." Paper delivered by Official Cooperstown Village historian MacDougall to the Center for Continuing Adult Learning, Oneonta, New York, 2010.

Miller, Jeremy. "History Ghost Story." *5280 Magazine,* Denver, July 2010.

## Newspapers and Other Publications

A.G. Mills Papers, 1877–1929, BA MSS 13, National Baseball Hall of Fame Library, Cooperstown, NY.

*Akron Beacon Journal*

*Annual Report Ontario Curling Association.* Toronto: Ontario Curling Association, 1905, 1906.

*Denver Post*

*Denver Times*

John Doyle Papers (Spalding Scrapbooks), BA SCR 42, National Baseball Hall of Fame Library, Cooperstown, NY.

*London Advertiser*

*London Free Press*

*Rocky Mountain News*

*St. Marys Argus*

*Sporting Life*

Various Iowa and Colorado weekly newspapers

# Index

Page numbers in *bold italics* indicate illustrations.